MW00615675

ACTS OF
GOD AND MAN

MICHAEL R. POWERS

ACTS
of
GOD
and
MAN

*Ruminations
on Risk
and
Insurance*

⧩ **Columbia Business School**
Publishing

Columbia University Press
Publishers Since 1893
New York   Chichester, West Sussex
cup.columbia.edu
Copyright © 2012 Michael R. Powers

Library of Congress Cataloging-in-Publication Data

Powers, Michael R.
Acts of god and man : ruminations on risk and insurance / Michael R. Powers
p. cm.
Includes bibliographical references and index.
ISBN 978-0-231-15366-9 (cloth : alk. paper)—ISBN 978-0-231-52705-7
1. Risk (Insurance)   2. Risk management.   I. Title.

HG8054.5.P69   2012
368—dc23   2011038071

Columbia University Press books are printed on permanent and durable
acid-free paper.
This book is printed on paper with recycled content.
Printed in the United States of America

c 10 9 8 7 6 5 4 3 2 1

To the memory of my father,
John Nolan Powers

CONTENTS

FOREWORD

It is a pleasure to write a foreword for this book of both scholarship and humor. It factors in the various concepts of risk, but provides both theory and practical guidance on those "aloof risks" suitable for insurance. The author manages to create a text for students of insurance while raising the deep philosophical problems in the formulation and application of probability theory.

The division of the opus into three segments on "Living with Risk," "The Realm of Insurance," and "Scientific Challenges" is most appropriate to providing context and width of view, yet motivating an appreciation for the institution of insurance as it is together with its many operational problems in a dynamic, evolving world. The book uses simple yet basic models to open the eyes of those who wish to appreciate the many subtle paradoxes of probability together with the many applied problems of how one goes about insuring risk. At the end of each chapter an imaginative and often humorous dialogue is presented that helps to drive home a central point of the chapter. For those who read with care an estimate of the author's intended lifespan can be obtained.

Uncertainty surrounds us. Many humans cycle through obliviousness to risk when immersed in the habitual routines of everyday life, until a non-routine event shatters those routines. Complacency can easily be displaced by formless fear and even panic. The appreciation of both exogenous risk and strategic risk is manifested here. Thus, the author covers the intersection of insurance with not only probability and statistics, but also phenomena arising from games of strategy.

Insurance theory, economic theory, accounting, and finance have in many ways grown further apart as disciplines specialize more and more and the sub-disciplines insulate themselves from their companions, trading in breadth for depth. Unfortunately we need both. A great insurance expert, finance or accounting specialist, or economist needs not merely to have a deep understanding of technique and theory but an appreciation of how his or her expertise links with others; and above all a sense of context.

There is an old canard in some circles that comes in the form of a riddle:

Q. Why did Joe become a statistician?

A. Because he did not have the charisma to become an accountant!

Fortunately this is a libel by those who understand neither the basic roles of probability and statistics, nor the critical role of trying to keep the books consistent in any form of dynamics that is always present in the economics of everyday life.

The book ahead of the reader is a monument to the proposition that wit, humor, and scholarship can be combined to provide insight and promote interest in a domain where the accusation of drabness or dullness of the topics covered is usually a self-accusation by the claimant. In spite of the great advances on the philosophical underpinnings of probability since Hume, many of the questions of the last sixty years are still open questions. The third section rightly is labeled "Scientific Challenges."

The book at one point raises the question as to how one measures happiness. I cannot guarantee that happiness and fun have similar measures, but in keeping with thought on science and measurement I am happy to state that reading this book is fun and the mixture of wit, scholarship, and nonconventional practicality provides a deep service to the topics covered.

Martin Shubik
Branford, CT
April 2011

PREFACE

> Daisy and Gatsby danced.... Then they sauntered over to my house and sat on the step for half an hour, while at her request I remained watchfully in the garden. "In case there's a fire or flood," she explained, "or any act of God."
>
> —NICK CARRAWAY (NARRATOR OF F. SCOTT FITZGERALD'S
> *THE GREAT GATSBY*, 1925)

The present volume offers a journey into the world of *risk* and the ways in which this concept, and our perceptions of it, affect various aspects of human life. Before embarking on this adventure, there are a few things that need to be mentioned.

First, I want to state clearly that the book's primary focus is those risks traditionally viewed as "insurance" perils: earthquakes, storms, fires, injuries, illnesses, thefts, assaults, and various types of liability. Described as "aloof" or "quasi-aloof" risks, these sources of uncertainty can influence other financial risks over time, but are themselves largely immune from the effects of such "non-aloof" risks as stocks, bonds, commodities, loans, and other financial instruments.

Admittedly, the decision to focus on insurance risks is somewhat a matter of personal taste. However, I believe this preference is well founded in the experiences—and especially exigencies—of human existence. After all, art *does* imitate life; and when Daisy Buchanan's tragic automobile accident seals Jay Gatsby's fate, there is nothing the bond trader Nick Carraway can do about it.

Second, I would note that the word *risk*, taken as a noun, possesses numerous meanings, even when confined to its technical uses within the fields of risk management and insurance. For example, the term can refer to:

- a source of uncertainty ("the risk from driving at high speeds is unacceptable");
- something exposed to uncertainty ("that automobile insurance company underwrites more than 10,000 risks");
- the probability of a given uncertain outcome ("the risk of a traffic fatality is greater on the highway");
- the anticipated magnitude of a given uncertain outcome ("the financial risk of an automobile liability claim is great"); and
- the variability of the magnitude of a given uncertain outcome ("if the members agreed to pool their collision losses, then each could reduce his or her individual risk").

Although each of the above meanings is perfectly acceptable in the appropriate context, it is clear that the word *risk* is highly overworked. Therefore, in the interest of clarity, I will generally restrict its use to the first meaning—that is, a source of uncertainty—which often will be taken to be approximately synonymous with *peril* or *hazard*. For the other meanings, alternative terms, such as *exposure, probability, chance, average, expected value, dispersion, standard deviation, variability,* etc. will be employed.

Finally, I wish to emphasize that the book's objectives are both to challenge and to inform—and ideally, to achieve the latter by way of the former. Although the topics addressed are broad ranging, they are more eclectic than exhaustive, and their treatment more speculative than conventional. At times, the ruminations are highly personal, brazenly citing the author's writings to the exclusion of competing views. Also, certain discussions are not only U.S.-centric, but also *Pennsylvania-* (and even *Philadelphia-*) centric, in deference to the author's affiliations with the Pennsylvania Insurance Department and Temple University.

In substance, the book is intended to provide a bemusing starting point for the consideration of an insurance-oriented science of risk that possesses as much in common with physics, engineering, environmental science, and medicine as it does with finance. Part 1, "Living with Risk," provides an overview of how risk impacts our lives, health, and possessions, and then introduces the statistical concepts and methods necessary to analyze uncertainty. Part 2, "The Realm of Insurance," explores the experience of risk from the perspectives of both policyholders and insurance companies, as well as the role of government as both market regulator and potential "insurer of last resort." Part 3, "Scientific Challenges," offers an interdisciplinary investigation into the nature of uncertainty, employing ideas from physics, philosophy, and game theory to assess the fundamental difficulties of a science of risk.

Naturally, I would hope that some course instructors—at least the more iconoclastic—will find the work a useful supplement to standard risk and insurance materials at both the undergraduate and the graduate level. To all readers of the volume, regardless of background or predilection, I promise nothing short of the giddiness experienced by Gatsby's other accident-prone guest upon examining the books in his host's library: "[They're a]bsolutely real—have pages and everything. . . . It's a triumph. What thoroughness! What realism!"

ACKNOWLEDGMENTS

The publication of *Acts of God and Man* would not have been possible without the inspiration, guidance, and support of many friends and colleagues. In this regard, I am particularly indebted to Verna Dreisbach of Dreisbach Literary Management and Myles Thompson and Bridget Flannery-McCoy of Columbia Business School Publishing. I also would like to take this opportunity to thank my mentors in the professional and academic realms of risk, who have been unwavering in their generosity: Lena Chang, Constance Foster, Moshe Porat, John Pratt, Martin Shubik, and Kai Yu.

In writing the book, I have incorporated materials from certain prior publications. These include a number of collaborative articles and book chapters, for which I am deeply grateful to my distinguished coauthors: Zaneta Chapman, R. B. Drennan, Piyawadee Khovidhunkit, Edward Lascher, Moshe Porat, Thomas Powers, David Schizer, Zhan Shen, and Martin Shubik. In addition, several discussions are based upon a series of editorials composed for the *Journal of Risk Finance* over the past few years, and I would like to thank my colleagues at Emerald Group Publishing— Kelly Dutton, Stephanie Grosz, Simon Linacre, Adam Smith, Sarah Roughley, and Anna Torrance—for the opportunity to experiment with these ideas.

To facilitate the citation of the above works as they appear throughout the book, I have arranged them into a list, titled "Author's Editorials and Other Writings," immediately following the main text. Each item of this list is presented by date of publication and assigned a number (i.e., [1], [2], [3], etc.) for citation purposes. All other references are provided in the Bibliography.

Finally, I would like to thank my wife, Imelda Powers, for her reinsurance expertise and comments on the final manuscript, as well as my colleagues Bonnie Averbach, Norman Baglini, and Siwei Gao for their comments on an earlier draft. Naturally, all errors in the text are attributable to chance alone.

ACTS OF
GOD AND MAN

1

Living with Risk

1

The Alpha and the Omega of Risk
The Significance of Mortality

At bottom no one believes in his own death, . . . in the unconscious every one of us is convinced of his own immortality.

—SIGMUND FREUD (*REFLECTIONS ON WAR AND DEATH*, 1915)[1]

The relationship between human beings and the risks of their world is both ancient and complex.[2] It is the stuff of myth and literature as well as philosophy and science. Wars, plagues, famines, floods, and earthquakes mark many of the turning points of the Hebrew Bible, and Greek mythology provides a generous reservoir of risk-related metaphors: Achilles' heel, the Sword of Damocles, Pandora's box, the Lernean Hydra, etc. In modern times, epic disasters—such as the *Titanic*, Pearl Harbor, *Apollo 13*, and Chernobyl—have assumed their own roles in our collective psychology.

Today, problems of risk form the basis for insurance and other financial services industries and are studied rigorously by scholarly researchers. But regardless of how these problems are formulated and analyzed, I would argue that they all flow from the same source: *the specter of mortality*. Like a serpent coiled around the trunk and branches of the Tree of Life, the risk of death squeezes at every aspect of human existence.

Downside Risk Versus Upside Risk

In recent decades, we have come to believe that the course of biological evolution on Earth was changed dramatically by chance encounters between our planet and approaching asteroids or comets. Instructively, these cataclysmic impacts—leading, among other things, to the extinction of the dinosaurs and the ascendancy of the mammals—point up one important aspect of *risk*: although the word generally has negative connotations because of its association with destruction, it also can suggest positive, albeit uncertain, developments. Like the Hindu god Shiva, whose destructive nature paves the way for creation and growth, risks have their positive side.

The asymmetry between the positive and negative aspects of risk arises because random change is more likely to damage than to enhance the carefully wrought equilibrium of the status quo, especially in the short run. This is nowhere clearer than in evolutionary biology, where for every salutary genetic mutation there are countless lethal deviations. Nevertheless, whether we see risk as primarily negative or as a balance between negative and positive potentials is largely a matter of perspective. If I assume that a human being's life on Earth should be unending, then clearly I will see any degree of mortality risk as negative. However, if I view each human being as entitled to only the expected lifetime given by the actuary's mortality table, then I will acknowledge a reasonable balance between negative outcomes (early deaths) and positive outcomes (late deaths).

When embedded in the financial products of modern economic markets, risks naturally assume a degree of symmetry by way of the pricing mechanism. Although an office building, taken as an isolated entity, is exposed primarily to the *pure* (i.e., entirely negative) risks of fire, wind, etc., the *purchase* of an office building at market price is subject to *speculative* (i.e., both positive and negative) risks, including an increasing demand for office space, as well as a decreasing supply of space (which, for example, could be caused by fire or wind damage to competing buildings). Likewise, stocks, bonds, and various financial indexes and derivatives generally trade at prices that recognize the potential for both increases and decreases in value.

In today's business world, professional risk managers often construct extensive lists of pure and speculative risks, including every imaginable type of uncertainty to which individuals and firms are exposed. Among pure risks, one finds traditional "insurance" perils such as fire, wind, theft, disease, and professional negligence, along with more complex hazards such as substandard construction, inadequate security, technological obsolescence, and political instability.[3] Speculative risks include real estate, common financial securities (stocks, bonds, commodities, etc.), and interest- and currency-derivative products, as well as market-specific changes in

the prices of raw materials, human capital, and end-of-line goods and services. In Chapter 6, I will propose an alternative to the conventional pure/
speculative risk dichotomy that distinguishes between the "aloof" and
"quasi-aloof" risks of insurance and the "non-aloof" risks of other financial markets.

Fundamental Exposures

Fortunately, a remarkable simplicity underlies these myriad risks. Despite
the great number of individual *sources* of risk, there are only a very few
exposures subject to risk. These fundamental exposures are life, health,
and possessions. Table 1.1 shows (in rough terms) how this short list of exposures can be applied at the levels of individuals, corporations, and society at large.

To simplify things further, one could collapse the two rightmost columns
into one composite column representing quality of life. Probing this new
category, one then might ask: Why should we be concerned about the quality
of life? I would argue that the following two principles provide the answer:

- **The Morbidity Principle.** An individual/corporation/society
  whose quality of life is damaged will have a greater chance of im-
  minent death.
- **The Lost-Gratification Principle.** An individual/corporation/
  society whose quality of life is damaged may not have the opportunity to enjoy recovery of health or restitution of possessions before

Table 1.1
Life, Health, and Possessions: The Fundamental Exposures

		Quality of Life	
	Life	Health	Possessions
Individual	Personal Survival	Personal Health	Personal Possessions
Corporation	Firm Survival	Firm Revenue, Market Share, etc.	Firm Profitability, Net Worth, etc.
Society	Collective Survival	Aggregate (Average) Quality of Health	Aggregate (Average) Standard of Living

death occurs (i.e., "a good quality of life today is worth more than a good quality of life tomorrow").

In short, the life exposure underlies all other types of exposures.

For individuals and societies, the morbidity principle would have been particularly evident in the Old Stone Age, when human beings had developed useful tools, but were still primarily hunter-gatherers. At that time, quality-of-life exposures, although they existed, could not be separated easily from the life exposure because the loss of health (through injury or illness) or possessions (clothing, shelter, or hunting implements) would increase significantly the chance of death in the near future. Hence, in many cases loss of quality of life would be tantamount to loss of life.

The morbidity principle continues to apply to individuals and societies today, but not as dramatically. Despite the various "safety nets" that modern governments provide for their more vulnerable citizens, it is still an empirical fact that the injured and ill, as well as the economically poor, die at faster rates than others. This is also true for societies at large, as can be seen in the declines of certain populations in Eastern Europe since the dissolution of the Soviet Union. With regard to corporations, reductions in revenue, market share, and/or profitability are in many cases harbingers of bankruptcy.

Although a cursory review of today's financial products might give the impression that quality-of-life exposures actually overshadow the life exposure—after all, the only financial product that specifically addresses mortality is life insurance—the lost-gratification principle belies such a conclusion. If anything, the role of mortality is difficult to discern because it is so prevalent that we tend to overlook it.

The life exposure underlies all traditional insurance policies, whether held by individuals or commercial enterprises. This is because the policies are designed to provide reasonably quick medical attention or restitution of property, presumably before the policyholder's life terminates. In addition, the life exposure is fundamental to all financial transaction risks. Lenders, whether they be individuals, corporations, or government bodies, must be compensated for the possibility that they will cease to exist before their loans are repaid; and the early death of a borrower can transform this possibility into a certainty. In other words, mortality is the essential reason, even in an economy with no expected change in either income or prices, "a dollar today is worth more than a dollar tomorrow," and thus the reason the nominal risk-free rate of return (often taken to be the nominal return on a U.S. Treasury bill) must be strictly greater than 0.

Reading from the Book of the Dead

For corporations and societies, mortality risk is difficult to measure because times of "death" are often ambiguous.[4] Moribund firms may merge with or be acquired by healthier firms, and analogous fates await societies in decline. For individuals, however, mortality is a well-defined and extensively studied phenomenon.

The first comprehensive mortality table was published in 1693 by British mathematician and astronomer Edmond Halley. Based upon historical age-at-death records from the Polish-German city of Breslau, Halley's table permitted the British government to sell the world's first actuarially based life annuity products.[5] Given the age-old association of human mortality with concepts of fate and destiny, it seems rather felicitous that the man who made the first scientific prediction of a comet's appearance—long considered a portent of good or bad fortune—should also offer the first scientific analysis of the human life span.

There are numerous ways to depict the risk of mortality graphically. One is to provide a theoretical histogram of the time of death for a newborn baby selected at random from a human population. This would look something like Figure 1.1, which is based upon the 2001 Commissioners Standard Ordinary (CSO) tables approved by the National Association of Insurance Commissioners.[6] Since death can occur at any time of the year and at any time of the day, it is most realistic to treat the time of death as a continuous variable. In practice, however, insurance and annuity companies often make the simplifying (albeit disquieting) assumption that an individual's death will occur on his or her birthday.

Figure 1.1 suggests that the great majority of people born today will die in the age-band from 50 to 100, with the most likely single time of death (mode) at about 83 for men and 88 for women. In addition, there is a much smaller, but noticeable, group of individuals that will die within the first couple years of life, primarily because of life-threatening congenital defects and disease vulnerabilities associated with infancy.

Although a simple histogram answers the question "What is the likelihood that a newborn will die at age x?" it fails to address another fundamental question of interest: What is the likelihood that an individual at age x will die within the next year? Using Figure 1.1 to compare the probability of death of a man at age 45 to that of a man at age 100, one might be tempted to conclude that they are approximately the same—after all, the height of the histogram is about the same at both ages. However, such an

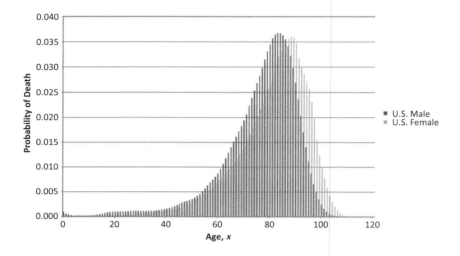

Figure 1.1
Histogram of Age at Death for One Individual (Selected Randomly at Birth) Source:
Commissioners Standard Ordinary (CSO) Mortality Tables (2001).

analysis fails to account for the fact that as x increases, there are progressively fewer people subject to the risk of death. In other words, although the histogram readings at 45 and 100 are approximately the same, one must adjust for the fact that there are many fewer individuals still alive at age 100 than at age 45.

Since the 100-year-olds who die are members of a smaller and more elite club (i.e., those who were lucky enough to survive to age 100), one naturally can conclude that the likelihood that a 100-year-old will die is greater than the corresponding likelihood for a 45-year-old. To show this result graphically, it is necessary to transform the histogram to adjust for the number of individuals alive at each age x. This is accomplished by dividing the value of the histogram at each point x by the proportion of individuals that survive to at least x, to obtain the one-year probability of death, or one-year *mortality hazard rate*, shown in Figure 1.2.[7]

From this figure, it can be seen quite clearly that the probability of death for a 100-year-old is vastly (approximately 135 times) greater than that for a 45-year-old. The mortality hazard rate makes such comparisons rather easy. Overall, the hazard rate decreases from age 0 to age 5 and then appears to increase (at least monotonically) after that, assuming an exponential-like growth beginning at about age 6. This general form tends to agree with intu-

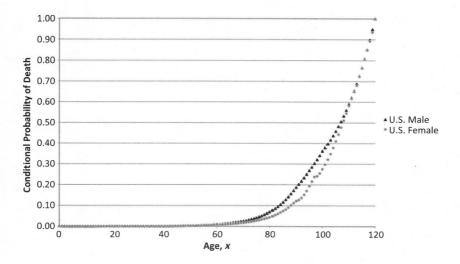

Figure 1.2
One-Year Mortality Hazard Rate Source: Commissioners Standard Ordinary (CSO)
Mortality Tables (2001).

ition: the higher risk of infant mortality decreases as the child grows out of infancy, and then mortality risk increases thereafter as a result of the human aging process (i.e., senescence). However, there is no guarantee that such a straightforward hazard curve applies to every human population. For example, in Figure 1.2 the U.S. male population's hazard rate actually decreases over the short range from 28 to 31 as the dramatic difference between male and female mortality risk—which begins in the early teenage years and is attributable to higher accident and homicide rates among males—begins to subside. (See Figure 1.3.)

The smoothly increasing nature of the hazard curve from a certain age (32 for males, 6 for females) onward has led many demographers and actuaries to posit that human mortality follows a simple mathematical formula. Perhaps the most successful of these rules is the Gompertz-Makeham law, which states that the mortality hazard rate at age x can be written as the linear combination of a constant term and an exponentially increasing function of x.[8] Although such a simplification of a complex process like human mortality is esthetically attractive, one must be careful not to imagine the presence of an underlying "scientific" principle where none exists. (I will say more about this in Chapter 12.)

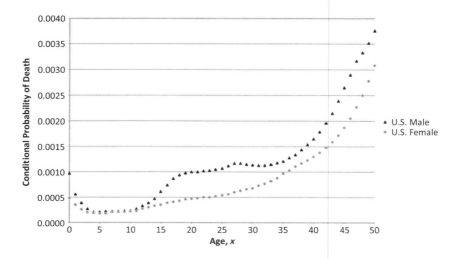

Figure 1.3
One-Year Mortality Hazard Rate (Ages 0 to 50) Source: Commissioners Standard Ordinary (CSO) Mortality Tables (2001).

Of course, rarely does an individual of age x have precisely the mortality hazard rate shown by Figure 1.2 for age x. Just by virtue of ordinary genetic and lifestyle variations among individuals, some will tend to have a higher hazard rate than others. Furthermore, each time an individual is sick, his or her hazard rate rises a bit, and the more serious the illness, the higher it goes. A man diagnosed with testicular cancer at age 27, for example, might find his hazard rate higher than that of an ordinary 72-year-old. However, if he is fortunate enough to survive the disease (and treatments), then his hazard rate will drop back to about where it should have been in the first place. If the cured individual adopts a healthier lifestyle, with improved diet and exercise, then he even may achieve a hazard rate that is lower than the average for his age.

In short, there is considerable heterogeneity among the true mortality hazard rates associated with individuals of age x, and so actuaries recognize that the hazard rates presented in Figure 1.2 are simply averages across the insured U.S. population. In addition to dividing the population by gender, CSO data include separate tables for nonsmokers and smokers—two segments of the population with markedly different hazard curves. Although it is not feasible to assemble data for every possible subpopulation of interest (such as men diagnosed with testicular cancer) simply because the data would be too sparse for the smaller subpopulations, it is possible to account for the substantial heterogeneity that arises from one particularly salient (and controversial) factor: race.

The use of race as an insurance risk classification has been banned in the United States since the 1970s. Consequently, no separate CSO tables are published for this variable. However, the Centers for Disease Control and Prevention do collect an extensive amount of mortality-related information on the basis of race and ethnicity, which offers a number of sobering insights into contemporary American society. Figure 1.4 provides a simple summary of the relationship between the hazard curves of black and white Americans by plotting, for males and females separately, the ratios (black to white) of one-year mortality hazard rates for various ages. This figure shows that with the exception of ages 16 and 17 for young women, it is substantially more dangerous to be African American than European American for people of all ages from birth to the late 80s.

Although general health differences—resulting from a combination of economic, educational, cultural, and genetic factors—account for most of the discrepancy at age 35 and above, the most striking disparity involves the underlying causes of death for individuals aged 10 through 34. As can be seen in Table 1.2, black males are more than 3.5 times more likely to be

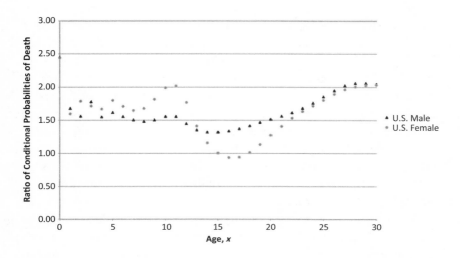

Figure 1.4
Mortality-Hazard-Rate Ratios (U.S. Blacks to U.S. Whites) Source: National Vital Statistics Reports, Centers for Disease Control and Prevention (2007).

Table 1.2
One-Year Mortality Hazard Rates for Most Significant Causes of Death (by Age, Gender, and Race)

	W. Male 10–14 Yrs.	B. Male 10–14 Yrs.	W. Male 15–19 Yrs.	B. Male 15–19 Yrs.	W. Male 20–24 Yrs.	B. Male 20–24 Yrs.	W. Male 25–34 Yrs.	B. Male 25–34 Yrs.
Accident	7.2	8.0	45.9	33.1	75.5	46.2	58.6	55.2
Homicide	1.1	4.1	8.7	66.3	12.6	112.2	9.3	86.2
Suicide	1.4	1.7	12.3	7.0	21.9	14.5	21.1	15.5
Heart Disease	0.8	1.5	1.9	3.7	4.0	7.2	9.4	24.4
Cancer	2.4	2.4	3.9	3.7	5.5	5.4	8.6	10.0

	W. Female 10–14 Yrs.	B. Female 10–14 Yrs.	W. Female 15–19 Yrs.	B. Female 15–19 Yrs.	W. Female 20–24 Yrs.	B. Female 20–24 Yrs.	W. Female 25–34 Yrs.	B. Female 25–34 Yrs.
Accident	4.5	4.6	21.0	10.1	21.4	15.6	18.9	14.7
Homicide	0.6	1.7	1.9	7.9	2.9	11.3	2.5	11.1
Suicide	0.6	*	3.0	1.3	3.7	2.3	5.3	1.8
Heart Disease	0.6	1.2	0.9	2.7	1.9	5.0	3.9	12.6
Cancer	2.0	1.8	2.5	2.4	3.6	4.4	9.1	12.5

Notes: Mortality hazard rates are expressed in deaths per 100,000 individuals. Asterisk indicates category with insufficient data to provide a meaningful estimate.
Source: National Vital Statistics Reports, Centers for Disease Control and Prevention (2007).

murdered than white males by ages 10 through 14, and this increases to more than 9.0 times more likely by the ages of 25 through 34. Similarly, black females are more than 2.5 times more likely to be murdered than white females by ages 10 through 14, and this exceeds 4.0 times by ages 25 through 34.

Just as data from deceased black youths tell the story of one scandal, data from deceased white youths recount a second one. As is apparent from even a casual look at Figure 1.4, there are conspicuous "dips" in the ratios of black-to-white mortality hazard rates between ages 15 and 24. (The dip in the plot for females is especially dramatic.) What accounts for these dips, which appear—quite counterintuitively—just at the time black youths begin to be murdered in large numbers, is that white youths begin to die of accidents at a disproportionately high rate (as documented in Table 1.2). Of course, these "accidental" deaths are largely associated with automobile collisions, which—like homicides—could be reduced through improved social policies. It seems rather remarkable that U.S. policymakers find such high death rates among the nation's youth a tolerable "cost of do-ing business."

The Death of Mortality?

Will we ever be able to protect the life exposure from all mortality risks?

Looking to the distant future, it seems reasonable to believe that scientists and engineers will not only take control of the human aging process, but also develop techniques to preserve an individual's consciousness and memory indefinitely in organic or inorganic media. As we approach that privileged time, the notion of risk inevitably will undergo dramatic change and perhaps even disappear from the human vocabulary.

Along these lines, one might ask: How will the mortality hazard curve change as modern health care technology continues to improve human longevity? Naturally, the value of the curve at each age x should diminish, but will this happen uniformly across all ages or will certain age groups benefit more than others?

In the last century, modern medical advances, while reducing the hazard curve for all ages, have achieved certain particularly marked effects at the extremes—both high and low—of the human life span. In other words, modern medicine has done more to help a newborn survive to age 1 and a 60-year-old survive to age 61 than a 30-year-old survive to age 31. Such a result is not surprising, since ages with lower mortality risk have less room to gain. Additionally, it might be observed that modern science tends to do more to treat the life-threatening illnesses associated with infant mortality and old age than to improve wellness generally.

Let us suppose that this general pattern continues into the future, and the net result is that the entire human mortality hazard curve—from age 0 onward—tends to flatten out toward its overall minimum value of about 0.0002, currently achieved around age 5. What would such a flat hazard curve imply?

Certainly, decreases in the mortality hazard rate anywhere (without corresponding increases elsewhere) imply an increase in life expectancy. However, a flattening of the curve would introduce an additional property. A flat hazard curve means that aging, or senescence, has little or no impact. People continue to die because of accidents and disease, but the rate of death is independent of age. No matter how long one already has lived, this fact becomes irrelevant in assessing how long he or she ultimately will live.

At first blush, the idea of a constant (or decreasing) mortality hazard rate seems counterintuitive—not just for human beings, but for any life form or other perishable entity. After all, how can the rate at which something expires not be affected by how long it already has existed? Does not existence, in and of itself, cause an entity to "wear out" by a natural aging process?

A Role Model, the Hydra

Interestingly, there is at least one life form that appears to possess a constant mortality hazard rate. The lowly hydra (*Hydra vulgaris*), favorite specimen for microscopic viewing in introductory biology courses, seems to have exactly this property; that is, regardless of how long a hydra has lived, its probability of dying in the next instant remains unchanged.

How can this work? What is the physiological or metabolic explanation of the hydra's chance of dying being unaffected by age? Clearly, one cannot ignore the concept of wearing out (aging) over time. Hydras, like all other living organisms, are subject to wear from various types of body damage, including nonfatal accidents and illnesses. Therefore, if the hydra's death rate is constant, then there must be some other factor—some other force—that counters the effect of wear; in fact, not only must this latent factor offset the effect of wear, but it must counter it *exactly*.

To understand just how special this type of phenomenon is, consider a metaphor from the physical sciences: the story of how Galileo challenged the accepted Aristotelian wisdom of his time that two stones of different weights would fall toward Earth at different speeds, with the heavier stone falling faster. In fact, Aristotle's intuition was not that unreasonable. Even with the benefit of Newton's Law of Gravity, it is known that the physical force between Earth and the heavier stone is actually greater than the corresponding force between Earth and the lighter stone. So why does the heavier stone *not* fall faster?

The answer to this question is comparable to the explanation of the hydra puzzle. Just as there must exist a latent factor or force that exactly counters the hydra's wear over time, there must be a physical factor or force that exactly offsets the greater force between the heavier stone and Earth. In the case of gravity, the latent factor is the inertia of the heavier stone's greater mass. In other words, just as Earth pulls harder on the heavier stone (i.e., the force of gravity is greater), the heavier stone offers greater resistance to Earth's pull.

In the case of the hydra's survival, the latent factor could be either (or a combination) of two things: (1) a physiological mechanism within the organism that rapidly repairs the damages of wear as they occur; or (2) the selection process that occurs as time passes and each particular organism lives or dies. The former possibility essentially means that the hydra suffers no natural senescence. The latter possibility is subtler and arises from the observation—made in conjunction with our discussion of the histogram in Figure 1.1—that a life form that survives longer becomes a member of a smaller, more selective club. Although a randomly selected hydra of age x_2 has experienced more wear than a randomly selected hydra of age x_1 (such that x_1 is less than x_2), the older organism also is a member of a more elite group: those whose track record demonstrates a greater ability to endure the natural wear of living.

Given that the hydra's latent factor exactly offsets the effect of wear (aging), the first explanation seems more plausible (and appears to be supported by scientific research).[9] This is because a physiological mechanism that repairs damage quickly and dependably easily explains the precise offsetting of wear; that is, the mechanism essentially erases the effect of wear as it appears, thereby making it irrelevant to the mortality hazard rate. This is comparable to the way in which the inertial force is proportional to the stone's mass in the falling-body metaphor, thereby exactly offsetting the force of gravity, which also is proportional to the stone's mass.

The second effect (selection), on the other hand, might easily overcompensate or undercompensate for the increased risk caused by greater wear. After all, the selection factor could be weaker than the wear factor, as it is for human beings above the age of 5, or stronger than the wear factor, as it is for human beings below the age of 5. (Essentially, human beings below the age of 5 manifest a decreasing mortality hazard rate because the selection effect—that is, the demonstration of greater hardiness that accompanies survival—more than offsets the small effect of aging in this group.)

The Hydra-ization of Humanity

Note that a constant mortality hazard rate provides no guarantee of long life. As the human hazard curve flattens from improved health care, the reason that the human life span increases is that the flattening occurs by reducing the curve's higher portions, rather than raising its lower portions. Nevertheless, a constant hazard rate does provide one clearly positive effect: that an individual would never sense the approach of death as he or she grew older. Death would remain a significant and inevitable part of life, but people would never experience a feeling of "running out of time."

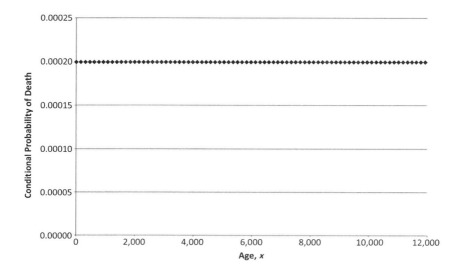

Figure 1.5
Constant One-Year Mortality Hazard Rate

Although a constant mortality hazard rate is not equivalent to immortality, it does allow for the possibility of arbitrarily long—but not
infinite—life. In other words, if the hazard curve truly flattened to the
constant 0.0002 mentioned earlier (as shown in Figure 1.5), then one would
expect to see individuals surviving to ages beyond 200, 500, 1,000, 5,000,
10,000, etc., but with exponentially decreasing frequency (as shown in the
age-at-death histogram of Figure 1.6). Note that the unboundedness of the
age at death is a critical aspect of not knowing when death will occur. If
human life were bounded—even at 100,000 years—then as people drew
closer to the terminal age, they would know that their chance of dying was
increasing.[10]

One wonders about perceptions of death in such a futuristic society. If
life expectancy were 5,000 years—as would be the case with a one-year
mortality hazard rate of 0.0002—then would death be seen as *more* terrible (because the amount of life lost is more significant) or as *less* terrible
(because the increased supply of life makes it seem less valuable)? When
the mortality hazard rate is constant over all ages and everyone, regardless
of age, has the same expected remaining lifetime, will the death of an
older person seem just as terrible as the death of a younger person (because the expected amount of life lost is the same)?

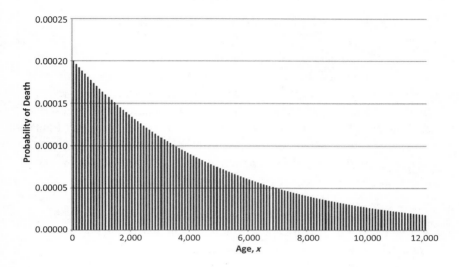

Figure 1.6
Histogram of Age at Death for One Individual (Subject to Constant Mortality Hazard Rate)

Ungrateful Mortals

While a young child (but old enough to be troubled by the knowledge that everyone eventually dies), I took a measure of comfort from a table of futuristic predictions made by British writer Arthur C. Clarke. Published as an appendix to his 1962 book, *Profiles of the Future*, Clarke's table indicated that human immortality would be achieved sometime in the last decade of the twenty-first century.[11]

Doing the necessary arithmetic, I initially was discouraged by the fact that I would have to live beyond 130 years to survive until the desired time period. However, upon closer inspection, I noticed that Clarke also predicted a process of suspended animation by 2050—suggesting that I need survive only to about age 90, at which point I could be frozen promptly, and then thawed and immortalized in forty or so additional years.[12]

Apart from specific futuristic predictions, some would argue that human beings can take comfort in the *anthropic principle*—the idea that the universe must be conducive to our form of life for the simple reason that we exist to observe it. Stronger forms of the anthropic principle suggest that life can get only better and longer for intelligent beings because consciousness will continue to exist only in those realities that permit it to exist.

If hydras possessed the intelligence and consciousness necessary to ponder such things, they might conclude from their constant mortality hazard rate that their universe has been constructed according to a strong "hydra-opic" principle that not only ensures their ability to exist and observe the universe, but also ensures that mortality risk is constant from the moment of birth to that of death. Certainly, it would seem somewhat special to the intellectual hydra to be gifted with complete uncertainty as to when death is likely to occur, since growing older does not increase the rate of death.

In his novel *Fiasco*, Polish writer Stanislaw Lem offers a deep insight into the nature of human beings (as well as putative extraterrestrial intelligences) that directly challenges these anthropic ideas:[13]

> Whatever had called them into existence gave them only one sure thing: their mortality. Indeed, they owed their very existence to mortality, for without it the billion-year alternations of emerging and dying species never would have taken place. They were spawned by the pit, by the deaths of the Archeozoic, the Paleozoic, the successive geological periods, and along with their Intelligence received the guarantee of their own demise.

Thus, according to Lem, mortality is the logically necessary price of intelligence—a scientific metaphor for the biblical idea that eating the fruit of the Tree of Knowledge led to banishment from paradise and the mortal nature of man. Extrapolating this reasoning into the future, one might conclude that, in a world in which human beings have developed the technological means of avoiding death, human intelligence and progress will stagnate as biological evolution reaches its terminus. So perhaps the much-feared mortality risk is actually a *good* thing.

ACT 1, SCENE 1

[A psychiatrist's office. Doctor sits in chair; patient sits on couch.]

DOCTOR: Tell me, Mrs. Morton, what's on your mind?
PATIENT: I hate to admit it, Doctor, but I think I'm suffering from hydraphobia.

DOCTOR: I see. That's a fairly common problem, usually caused by a near-drowning or some other traumatic encounter with water in early childhood.

PATIENT: No, Doctor—that's not what I mean.

DOCTOR: Of course, another common cause of hydrophobia is rabies; but the fear of water generally appears only in the later stages—and you don't appear to be foaming at the mouth. You haven't been bitten by any wild animals lately, have you? [Laughs.]

PATIENT: No, you've misunderstood. I said "hydraphobia," not "hydrophobia." I know it's irrational, but I'm terrified of hydras.

DOCTOR: Hydras?

PATIENT: Yes. You know, those unpleasant little creatures with tentacles that one can see under the microscope.

DOCTOR: Oh, of course—hydras. And what's the problem with hydras? They live in the water, don't they? Are you sure it's not the water you're afraid of?

PATIENT: I'm quite sure it's not the water. I'm simply afraid of being stung by hydras.

DOCTOR: I see—a fear of being stung by hydras. And what exactly is it that concerns you about being stung by hydras?

PATIENT: Well, first of all, I'm afraid it would hurt. But more importantly, I'm afraid of being poisoned.

DOCTOR: Ah—a fear of poisoning, eh? And what is it about being poisoned that bothers you?

PATIENT: Well, naturally, I'm afraid of dying.

DOCTOR: *Dying*, you say? I think we finally may be getting to the bottom of this. What is it about dying that frightens you?

PATIENT: I'd think that's obvious, isn't it? It would mean the end—the end of me, of my entire existence!

DOCTOR: Yes, of course, of course. But is that so bad? After all, it would mean the end of your hydrophobia as well, wouldn't it?

PATIENT: That's hydraphobia, Doctor.

DOCTOR: Yes, quite right—hydraphobia. Now, where were we?

2

Into the Unknown
Modeling Uncertainty

Though there be no such thing as *chance* in the world; our ignorance of the real cause of any event has the same influence on the understanding, and begets a like species of belief or opinion.

—DAVID HUME ("OF PROBABILITY," *AN ENQUIRY CONCERNING HUMAN UNDERSTANDING*, 1748)[1]

Every manifestation of risk is associated with one or more unknown quantities. In the case of the inevitable death of an individual, it is primarily the time of death that is unknown. In the case of damage to a building, automobile, or other piece of property, it is a combination of the incidence of damage (i.e., whether or not it occurs), along with both the timing and the amount of damage. And in the case of a financial investment, it is the sequence of future prices of the instrument involved.

In all of the above examples, the principal reason the quantity is unknown is that it is displaced in time (specifically, it is associated with a future event). However, there are other reasons a quantity may be unknown. Even an event that already has occurred may involve quantities that remain unknown because they were never recorded, for any of a number of reasons: impossibility of measurement, high cost of observation, or simple lack of interest at the time of occurrence.

Random Variables

Statisticians and other scientists typically model an unknown quantity using something called a *random variable*. While deferring a close examination of the concept of randomness until much later (Chapter 11), for the moment I will speak of a random variable simply as a mathematical quantity, denoted by a symbol such as X, whose behavior is completely described by two items:

1. a *sample space*, which is the set of all distinct possible values (x) that the random variable can assume;[2] and
2. a *probability function*, $p(x)$, which identifies the relative likelihood (frequency) with which the random variable takes on each of the distinct values x in the sample space. (By convention, the "sum" of all such values must "add up" to 1.)[3]

To illustrate these properties, let X be the outcome of tossing one standard (six-faced) die. Then the sample space for the random variable is

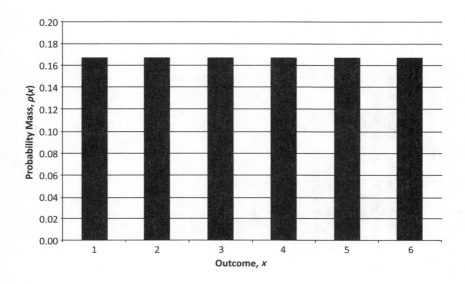

Figure 2.1
PMF of One Die Roll (i.e., Discrete Uniform Random Variable Defined on $\{1, 2, 3, 4, 5, 6\}$)

simply the set of integers from 1 through 6, and the probability function is given by the frequency 1/6 for all values in the sample space, as shown in the histogram of Figure 2.1. This random variable possesses several special properties worth noting: Its sample space is *discrete*, consisting of a set of elements, *x*, that can be indexed by the positive integers (in this case, the numbers from 1 through 6); its sample space is *finite*, comprising only six elements; and its probability function, *p(x)*, is *uniform* (i.e., constant) over all the elements in the sample space.

As a matter of terminology, any random variable whose sample space is discrete is, quite naturally, said to be a *discrete random variable*. At first glance, one might suspect that all such random variables have finite sample spaces, but that is not true. Consider, for example, a different random variable *X* whose sample space is the infinite set of all *positive integers*, {1, 2, 3, . . . }, and whose probability function begins with a *p*(1) of 1/6, and then decreases by a factor of 5/6 each time *x* increases by one unit. This particular probability distribution, called the *geometric* distribution with parameter 1/6, is captured by the histogram in Figure 2.2 and is very similar to the age-at-death probability distribution presented in Figure 1.6.[4]

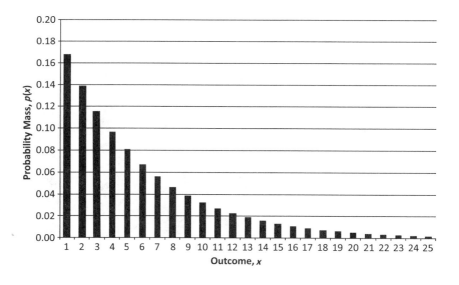

Figure 2.2
PMF of Geometric Random Variable with Parameter 1/6 (Defined on Positive Integers)

For the geometric random variable, the sample space is both discrete and infinite. Nevertheless, there is a price to pay for extending the sample space to the infinite set of positive integers: namely, having to use a more complicated probability function to make sure that the individual probabilities, $p(x)$, add up to 1. In fact, to construct a random variable whose sample space is both discrete and infinite, one must give up any hope of having a uniform probability function. Another way of saying this is that it is impossible to select a positive integer at random in such a way that each integer is equally likely to be chosen.[5]

Although accepted with little thought by statisticians, this last observation is quite interesting, perhaps even profound. Essentially, what it means is that we, as "acquaintances" of the integers, can never be truly egalitarian in our associations; inevitably, we must favor an incredibly small subset in some finite neighborhood $\{1, 2, \ldots, n\}$, where the magnitude of n—whether recorded in thousands, millions, or googols[6]—is dwarfed by an infinitely greater set of completely unfamiliar larger integers.

Paradoxically, despite the foregoing discussion, there does remain a way to construct a random variable that possesses both an infinite sample space and a uniform probability function. To accomplish this, however, one must relinquish the property of discreteness.

The Continuum

As noted above, a discrete sample space consists of a set of elements, x, that can be indexed by the positive integers. In other words, the total number of elements in such a set can be no larger than the total number of elements in the set of positive integers—that is, no larger than *infinity*. This seems like an easy condition to satisfy and, in fact, an impossible one to contradict. So how can a sample space *not* be discrete? To find such spaces, one first must find a number that is, in some sense, "larger" than infinity itself!

One approach to breaking through the "infinity barrier" might be to attempt to double the size of the set of positive integers by adding the equally large set of negative integers to it. More precisely, letting $\{1, 2, 3, \ldots\}$ be the set of positive integers and $\{\ldots, -3, -2, -1\}$ be the set of negative integers, one could consider the conjoined set, $\{\ldots, -3, -2, -1, 1, 2, 3, \ldots\}$. If N denotes the (infinite) number of elements in either $\{1, 2, 3, \ldots\}$ or $\{\ldots, -3, -2, -1\}$, then the number of elements in $\{\ldots, -3, -2, -1, 1, 2, 3, \ldots\}$ must be $2 \times N$. However, as will be seen, $2 \times N$ is actually no larger than N.

To compare the sizes of two different infinite sets, one must attempt a one-to-one matching between their respective elements. If each element in one set can be associated with a unique element in a second set, without any elements being left over in either set, then the two sets are said to have the same *cardinality* (size). If, however, there are some elements left over in either of the two sets after the matching takes place, then the set with the extraneous elements is said to have a larger cardinality.

Now consider what happens if one attempts to match the elements of $\{\ldots, -3, -2, -1, 1, 2, 3, \ldots\}$ with those of $\{1, 2, 3, \ldots\}$. Suppose one writes the elements of the former set as $\{1, -1, 2, -2, 3, -3, \ldots\}$, and then matches the first, third, fifth, etc. members of this list with the positive integers 1, 3, 5, etc. while matching the second, fourth, sixth, etc. members of the list with the positive integers 2, 4, 6, etc. A careful examination of this pairing reveals that it is indeed one-to-one, with no elements left over in either set. Consequently, the cardinalities of the two sets must be the same, and so $2 \times N$ equals N. More generally, if m is any finite positive integer, then $m \times N$ equals N. Rather remarkably, even multiplying N by itself a finite number of times does not increase its cardinality, and so neither the addition nor multiplication of Ns is sufficient to obtain a number larger than N.

The German logician Georg Cantor was the first to overcome the infinity barrier, and he did so by using exponentiation.[7] Specifically, he was able to prove that the number $m \times m \times \ldots \times m$ [N times], where m is any finite positive integer greater than 1, is larger than N. Interestingly, this new number, called C, denotes the cardinality of the set of *real numbers* in the interval from 0 to 1. Any set of this cardinality is called a *continuum*.

To see why the number of points in the interval [0,1) is given by C, first note that any real number between 0 and 1 can be represented as an infinite decimal expansion $0.d_1d_2d_3\ldots$, where each of the digits $d_1, d_2, d_3, \ldots$ equals one of the ten distinct digits $0, 1, 2, \ldots, 9$. Then, to count how many such expansions exist, simply observe that there are ten possible values for d_1, ten possible values for d_2, ten possible values for d_3, etc. It immediately follows that the total number of expansions must be $10 \times 10 \times \ldots \times 10$ [N times], which equals C (since m may be taken to equal 10).

Let us now consider how to select a number at random from the infinite set—or continuum—of real numbers in [0,1) in such a way that each real number has the same chance of being chosen. Intuitively, this could be accomplished by using an infinitely thin knife to slice the interval into two pieces, with each point in [0,1) equally likely to serve as the cutting point. But to express this idea formally, I need to introduce the concept of a *continuous random variable*—that is, a random variable whose sample space is a continuum.

Let Y denote a random variable whose sample space consists of all the real numbers in the interval [0,1). Since I now am dealing with a continuum, I cannot simply break up the sample space into a collection of discrete points, y, for which a probability function can be stated. Rather, I must partition it into a large number (n) of small intervals, each of equal length, $1/n$. I then can write the probability for the ith interval—denoted by $p(y_i)$—as $f(y_i) \times (1/n)$, where $f(y_i)$ is the relative likelihood (frequency) with which Y takes on a value in that particular interval (compared with the other intervals of equal length).

If Y is a *uniform* random variable, then I know that $f(y_i)$ must equal some constant value, k, for each interval. Given that the sum of the probabilities $p(y_i)$ must equal 1, it follows that k equals 1 and thus $p(y_i)$ equals $1/n$, as shown in the histogram of Figure 2.3.

Now consider what happens as n becomes infinitely large, so that each interval shrinks toward a single point in the [0,1) continuum. Clearly, this will cause the probabilities functions, $p(y_i)$, to shrink to 0, and so the probability associated with any given point in the continuum must be exactly

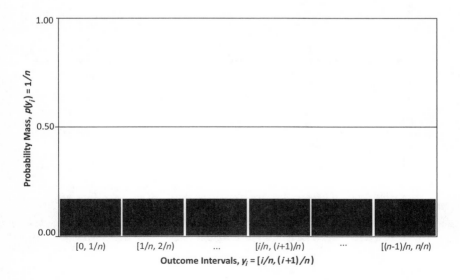

Figure 2.3
Forming a Continuous Uniform Random Variable (Defined on Interval [0, 1))

o. Note, however, that at the same time the value of each probability decreases to o, the number of these probabilities increases to infinity (actually, to C). Thus, by the magic of the calculus, the "sum" of the probabilities can still equal 1.

Here, then, is a bit of a puzzle: If I can "sum up" an infinite number of o-valued probabilities in the continuum to obtain 1, then why am I unable to do the same thing with the positive integers? In other words, what prevents me from selecting an element from the set of positive integers with uniform probability simply by setting $p(x)$ equal to o for each integer x, and then "adding up" all the os to get 1?

The resolution of this paradox rests on the fact that probabilities are defined quite differently for continuous and discrete sample spaces.[8] In the former case, $p(y_i)$ equals $f(y_i) \times (1/n)$, where $f(y_i)$ indicates a *probability density* spread out over the ith small interval (of length $1/n$). In the latter case, $p(x)$ denotes a *probability mass* associated with the individual point x. It thus follows that probabilities of o can be assigned to all individual points in a continuous space while still preserving positive densities over various small intervals. Assigning probabilities of o to all points x in a discrete space, however, leaves no masses to be accumulated.[9]

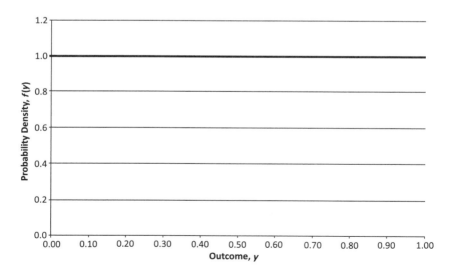

Figure 2.4
PDF of Continuous Uniform Random Variable (Defined on Interval [o, 1))

An important consequence of this difference is that when working with discrete random variables, one can use the probability function, $p(x)$—which henceforth will be called the *probability mass function* (PMF)—as plotted in Figures 2.1 and 2.2; however, when working with continuous random variables, one finds that $p(y)$, which always equals 0, is useless, and so one must employ $f(y)$—the *probability density function* (PDF)—as plotted for the uniform distribution on [0,1) in Figure 2.4.

Just as the uniform random variable on [0,1) constitutes a continuous analogue of the discrete uniform random variable, the *exponential* random variable, whose PDF is presented in Figure 2.5 (for the parameter value 1/6), forms a continuous analogue of the geometric random variable. The exponential distribution shares with the geometric distribution the notable property of having a constant hazard rate (which naturally must be defined in continuous time, rather than discrete time). It also provides an example of a continuous distribution whose sample space goes from 0 to infinity and is therefore unbounded. Intriguingly, the cardinality of the unbounded continuum is exactly the same as the cardinality of any bounded continuum, that is, C. In other words, the real number line from 0 to infinity contains no greater number of points than does the interval from 0 to 1!

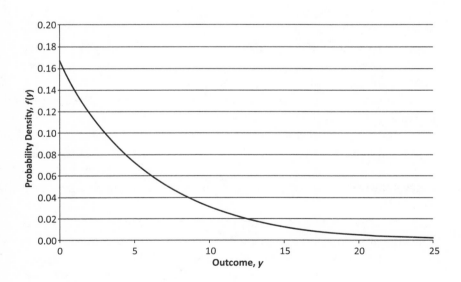

Figure 2.5
PDF of Exponential Random Variable with Parameter 1/6 (Defined on Positive Real Numbers)

Whence Probabilities?

As already mentioned, a random variable is intended to represent an unknown quantity. However, the use of a PMF, $p(x)$, or PDF, $f(y)$, clearly suggests that *something* is known about the variable. This observation raises an issue of deep philosophical (and practical) importance: How is information about the probabilities obtained?

To make the problem more concrete, let us return to a random variable discussed in Chapter 1—the ultimate age at death of a newborn baby—and focus on the histogram presented in Figure 1.1. Since a histogram is simply the plot of a discrete random variable's PMF against the values in its sample space, it is easy to read from this figure the respective probabilities, $p_{\text{Male}}(x)$ or $p_{\text{Female}}(x)$, that a newborn male or female baby will die at a given age, x. So where do these numbers come from?

The Frequency/Classical Paradigm

In the case of human mortality data, actuaries typically obtain the various probabilities of death by computing death rates from large samples of an actual human population. For example, $p_{\text{Male}}(45) = 0.0025$ might result from observing that in a selected group of 10,000 U.S. males born in the same year, exactly 25 died at age 45. Essentially, this is the *classical approach* to estimating (approximating) probabilities, and it presupposes a *frequency interpretation* of the probabilities themselves.

By frequency interpretation, I mean that each probability $p(x)$ is viewed as the long-run rate with which the outcome x—often called a "success" (even when a death is involved)—occurs among a sequence of repeated independent observations of the random variable. Thus, assuming that the life spans of individual males are unrelated to one another, the quantity $p_{\text{Male}}(45)$ denotes the overall proportion of males to die at age 45 among all males in the selected group.

Given the view of a probability as a long-run rate or proportion over a large, possibly infinite, population, it is natural to approximate the probability by considering a randomly chosen subset of the total population—called a *sample*—and using the observed ratio of the number of successes to the corresponding number of trials within that subset. This is the classical approach to estimation. Thus, the quantities $p_{\text{Male}}(x)$ or $p_{\text{Female}}(x)$ in Figure 1.1 are *not* in fact the true probabilities associated with the age-at-death random variable, but only approximations of those probabilities and so are more properly written as $\hat{p}_{\text{Male}}(x)$ or $\hat{p}_{\text{Female}}(x)$.[10] From the law of large numbers (to be discussed further in Chapter 4), it is known that these approximations tend to become increasingly more accurate as the sizes of the associated random samples increase.

Life would be much simpler if the frequency interpretation of probability and the classical approach to estimation were appropriate for all random variables. However, as consequences of their very definitions, both paradigms run into obstacles in certain contexts. For the frequency interpretation, the principal difficulty is that many random variables are unique, rendering the concept of a sequence of repeated observations meaningless. Since the classical approach rests upon the frequency interpretation—otherwise, there is no basis for using a random sample to approximate $p(x)$—it follows that classical estimation also is inapplicable in the case of unique random variables. A further problem with the classical approach is that even if the frequency interpretation is in force, the law of large numbers has little effect when one is working with only a few repetitions in a sequence of observations.

In short, settings with unique random variables and/or few repetitions are problematic for the frequency/classical paradigm. Although such settings tend to arise at the extremes of human experience, they are still reasonably common in real life. Examples include: property perils associated with landmark buildings, historic monuments, and celebrated artwork; potential liabilities associated with large "one-time" sporting and music events; and perhaps most amusingly, accident/disability hazards associated with the specific talents of prominent entertainers and athletes (a dancer's legs, a pianist's hands, a tennis player's elbow, etc.).

These types of risks are often termed "unique and unusual" in the insurance world, and special policies are written for them. Naturally, a major challenge for insurance companies is to obtain the probabilities $p(x)$ associated with such random losses so that appropriate premiums can be charged. To see how this is accomplished, let us consider a hypothetical example.

Loaning Mona (The Subjective/Judgmental Paradigm)

Suppose that an insurance company underwriter has been asked by officials at the Philadelphia Museum of Art to provide property coverage for the Leonardo da Vinci masterpiece *Mona Lisa* while the painting is on a special thirty-day loan from the Louvre. Clearly, the subject work of art is unique, not just in the mundane sense that every fine painting is a unique expression of its creator, but more significantly, because it is the most widely recognizable—and perhaps the most valuable—Old Master painting in the world. Also, the exhibition is unique in that the painting has never traveled to Philadelphia previously and is unlikely to do so again in the foreseeable future.

For simplicity, the underwriter assumes that during its thirty-day visit, the *Mona Lisa* will be exposed to a limited number of perils—theft, fire, vandalism, terrorist attack, and natural disaster (including storm, flood, earthquake, volcano, etc.)—and that any loss would be *total* (i.e., there is no such thing as reparable partial damage). Although the painting is clearly priceless in the sense that it is truly irreplaceable, it does enjoy an assessable market value (i.e., the estimated amount that it would fetch at auction) that the underwriter assumes to be the equivalent of $1 billion.

Given these assumptions, the random variable of interest, X, has a sample space with just two points: $x = 0$ or $x = 1$ (in $billions). Analyzing things further, one can express $p(1)$ as the sum

Probability of Theft + Probability of Fire + Probability of Vandalism + Probability of Terrorist Attack + Probability of Natural Disaster,

and $p(0)$ as $1 - p(1)$.

Now the question is: Given the uniqueness of the *Mona Lisa*'s sojourn in Philadelphia, what does it mean to speak of quantities such as probability of theft, probability of fire, etc.? Clearly, the frequency interpretation cannot apply, because there is no sense in which the thirty-day visit can be viewed as one observation from a sequence of repeated trials. Therefore, what is meant by a probability in this case is a purely cognitive metaphor or degree of belief—that is, something that the human brain apprehends as being equivalent to a frequency while not being a frequency per se. This is the *subjective interpretation* of probability.

Without the frequency interpretation, the underwriter naturally cannot use the classical approach to estimation. Just as the notion of probability itself is a cognitive metaphor under the subjective interpretation, so must be any estimation technique employed in conjunction with it. Consequently, the subjective interpretation restricts the underwriter to *judgmental estimation* methods. Such approaches come in various degrees of sophistication:

- **Naïve Judgment.** The simplest thing that an underwriter can do is to use his or her personal experience to estimate the value of a quantity such as probability of theft, without any formal method of aggregating this experience or rationalizing the final estimate. For example, when considering probability of theft, the underwriter may obtain the estimate 1/10,000 seemingly out of thin air, simply because this number appears to be appropriately small.
- **Collective Judgment.** Naturally, the highly personal nature of naïve judgment may make an underwriter feel somewhat insecure. After all, how would the underwriter explain his or her estimated probability if someone were to challenge it (which invariably would happen if the *Mona Lisa* were stolen)? To mitigate this problem, the most obvious thing to do is to seek safety in numbers by asking several additional professionals (e.g., fellow underwriters and/or actuaries) to provide independent estimates of probability of theft, and then to average these guesses to obtain a final estimate. For example, the underwriter might consult three professional colleagues and receive separate estimates of 1/1,000, 1/5,000, and 1/50,000. Averaging all these values with his or her own estimate of 1/10,000 then yields a final estimate of 33/100,000. Not only does this method provide the appearance of greater due diligence, but it also takes advantage of the frequency/classical paradigm (applied to judgmental estimates, rather than loss events) to reduce the variability of the final estimate.
- **Educated Judgment.** The principal problem with the above two approaches is that they do not employ any formal—or possibly even conscious—method of incorporating the estimators' personal experiences into their estimates. To overcome this shortcoming, an underwriter may attempt to identify which particular items in his or her experience are most relevant to the estimation problem at hand, and then research, evaluate, and integrate these items in an intelligent way. For example, the underwriter may recall, following some reflection, that he or she once read an actuarial report summarizing art museum theft data. From an extensive Internet search, the underwriter then may locate the desired document and discover that it indicates an overall annual theft rate of 1/1,000—equivalent to a thirty-day probability of about 1/12,000—based upon several decades of loss experience from museums throughout the United States. Although this estimate is proffered under the frequency/classical paradigm, it is not directly applicable to the problem at hand because it is based upon: (1) old data; (2) paintings insured as part of a museum's permanent collection; and (3) a cross-section of all paintings, rather than just the most valuable artwork. Nevertheless, the probability of 1/12,000 may serve as an upper bound on probability of theft if it is reasonable to assume that security measures: (1) have improved over time; (2) are better for visiting

artwork than for permanent collections; and (3) are better for the most promi-nent artwork on display. While researching, the underwriter also may uncover the fact that the *Mona Lisa* itself was once stolen from the Louvre (in 1911). Di-viding this one event by the roughly 200 years that the painting has been on display at the Louvre, he or she would obtain an annual theft rate of about 1/200—equivalent to a thirty-day probability of about 1/2,400. Again, although this estimate rests on the frequency/classical paradigm, it is not directly ap-plicable to the current problem because it is based upon old data as well as the *Mona Lisa*'s history as part of the Louvre's permanent collection. However, as before, the probability of 1/2,400 may serve as another upper bound on pro-bability of theft. Given these analyses, the underwriter may conclude that 1/2,400 is a reasonably conservative (that is, high) estimate of the desired probability.

- **Rational Judgment.** Perhaps the most attractive type of judgmental estimate is one that can be supported by a logical or physical argument, with-out the need for individual guessing or empirical verification. For example, suppose that the underwriter has discussed matters with a game theorist who constructed a formal mathematical model of art theft based upon the oppos-ing strategies of art thieves and museum security teams. Suppose further that under this game-theoretic model, the thirty-day probability of a painting's being stolen is given by the expression $\sqrt{V}/100,000,000$, where $\sqrt{V}$ denotes the *square root* of the painting's value (in U.S. dollars).[11] Plugging the *Mona Lisa*'s assessed value of \$1 billion into this formula then yields an estimated probability of approximately 31,623/100,000,000.

Of course, a decision maker need not adhere exclusively to any one of the above estimation methods, and hybrid approaches—for example, averag-ing educated guesses with naïve guesses—are quite common.

To summarize, there are two principal pairings of probability inter-pretations and estimation methods: (1) the frequency/classical approach, often called *frequentism*, which requires both the possibility of repeated trials and a large number of actual repeated trials; and (2) the subjective/judgmental approach, often called *Bayesianism*,[12] which works for unique trials and any number of repeated trials. Of these two, the latter approach is clearly more flexible.

Alternative Perspectives

The study of risk, like all mathematical disciplines, ultimately rests upon a foundation of intuition and metaphor.[13] In formal expositions, this foundation is provided by a collection of assumptions called *axioms* (or *postulates*). Although mathematical purists might deny that such fundamental statements need be intuitively plausible—arguing that they are simply convenient starting points from which theory can be derived—any theory arising from a set of axioms without a strong metaphorical connection to basic human intuitions is difficult to peddle in the marketplace of ideas.

In introducing the various concepts of this chapter, I have focused on those ideas and methods that I believe appeal most strongly to human intuition; and that is the approach I will pursue throughout the remainder of the book. The price to be paid for such an emphasis is that many less-intuitive paradigms will be afforded scant attention or even completely ignored.

One significant mathematical theory possessing a nonintuitive foundation is *possibility theory*, a "fuzzy" alternative to traditional probability theory based upon the denial of Aristotle's *law of the excluded middle* (LEM).[14] A cornerstone of formal logic, the LEM states that "either a proposition is true, or its opposite is true—there is no third alternative." Although few assumptions would seem more unassuming and self-evident than the LEM, a variety of interesting and provocative techniques have grown out of its negation.

Methods denying the LEM have been found to be particularly useful in contexts in which it is difficult to draw clear lines of demarcation between categories of entities, as in the detection of insurance fraud, where one cannot separate claims easily into two mutually exclusive and jointly exhaustive categories—"fraudulent" and "legitimate"—because of various intermediary cases: moral hazard, opportunistic fraud, litigiousness, etc.[15] Nevertheless, these approaches have not gained great traction among scholars, at least partly because they negate the highly intuitive LEM.

Two decades ago, British statistician Dennis Lindley staked out the (somewhat extreme) anti-fuzzy position as follows:[16]

> Probability is the only sensible description of uncertainty and is adequate for all problems involving uncertainty. All other methods are inadequate. . . . Anything that can be done with fuzzy logic, belief functions, upper and lower probabilities, or any other alternative to probability can better be done with probability.

Whether or not Lindley's claim that "probability is the only sensible description of uncertainty" will be judged legitimate or fraudulent by history remains an open question. But as a purely philosophical matter, I would observe that a proposition that denies its opposite (i.e., is consistent with the LEM) seems more cogent than one admitting of self-contradiction.

ACT 1, SCENE 2

[A police interrogation room. Suspect sits at table; two police officers stand.]

GOOD COP: Hello, Ms. Cutter. I understand that you've waived your right to legal counsel; is that correct?

SUSPECT: Well, not really.

GOOD COP: Not really?

SUSPECT: No. You see, I'm an attorney myself, and so I can't avoid having legal counsel present.

GOOD COP: Oh, well, that's fine, of course. What I meant to say is, you've waived your right to *additional* legal counsel, is that correct?

SUSPECT: Yes, Officer; that is quite correct.

GOOD COP: Now, Ms. Cutter, I must be perfectly frank—the evidence against you is rather overwhelming. During the past year, the bodies of twelve separate murder victims have been found across the Commonwealth of Pennsylvania. In each case, the victim was killed in the same manner: While he or she slept, the killer sliced through the victim's jugular vein—cleanly and deeply—with a crisp new $1,000 bill.

SUSPECT: A rather unusual weapon, don't you think?

GOOD COP: Yes, it certainly is. And I think you'll be interested to know that we found *your* fingerprints—yours and yours *alone*—on each of these "unusual weapons." Can you explain that?

SUSPECT: No, I'm afraid I can't. Not only can I not explain it, but I can't understand it.

BAD COP: Look, lady, I don't know what kind of word games you think you're playing. What my partner is telling you in his polite, but somewhat roundabout way is that this is an open-and-shut case; we already have all the evidence needed to put you on death row. So if you want to do yourself a favor, then answer the questions; and maybe the judge will be in a better mood when he sentences you.

SUSPECT: I assure you it has been my intention all along to cooperate. I simply said that I don't believe your partner's assertion that no one else's fingerprints were on the $1,000 bills. You see, when I picked them up at the bank, the bank teller must have handled at least some of them.

[Pause.]

BAD COP: Let me get this straight. You admit that the murder weapons belonged to you?

SUSPECT: Well, now it's *you* who are playing word games. You call them "murder weapons," but I'm afraid I can't agree with that characterization.

GOOD COP: We're talking about the crisp new $1,000 bills found at the twelve murder scenes. In all cases, they had blood on them—blood that matched the blood of the respective murder victims. And we have pathologists' reports stating unequivocally that the bills were used to slit the victims' throats.

SUSPECT: I agree. That is exactly how I killed them. But I insist that I did not "murder" them.

BAD COP: So what are you saying? That you killed a dozen people in their sleep, but it wasn't murder? What was it: *self-defense?*

SUSPECT: No, it was an experiment.

BAD COP: What?

SUSPECT: It was an experiment—to test the "letter of the law." Officers, do you happen to know how many citizens there are in the state of Pennsylvania?

GOOD COP: About twelve million, I believe.

SUSPECT: Yes, almost twelve and one-half million, in fact. And how many people did I kill?

GOOD COP: Well, we believe you killed twelve. That's what our questions are about.

SUSPECT: Yes, I killed twelve; twelve out of twelve and one-half million. Do you know what proportion of the state population that is?

BAD COP: What does that matter?

GOOD COP: Twelve divided by twelve and one-half million gives something less than 1/1,000,000.

SUSPECT: Yes, less than 1/1,000,000.

BAD COP: Again, so what? We're talking about murder here. Your batting average doesn't matter.

SUSPECT: Oh, but it does, Officer. Do either of you know what the term *negligible risk* means?

BAD COP: I've had about enough of—

GOOD COP: Let her talk. Go on, what about negligible risk?

SUSPECT: You see, the government, at both the state and federal levels, considers a death rate of less than 1/1,000,000 to be a negligible risk. That is, anything—be it pesticides, exhaust fumes, or whatever—that kills fewer than 1/1,000,000th of the population is considered so unimportant as to be ignored.

GOOD COP: Well—I thought I had heard every excuse in the book; but that one is new to me.

SUSPECT: Yes, I do believe it's a true innovation. So I take it you'll be releasing me?

3

The Shapes of Things to Come
Probabilities and Parameters

It has been often recognized that any probability statement, being a rigorous statement involving uncertainty,
has less factual content than an assertion of certain fact
would have, and at the same time has more factual content than a statement of complete ignorance.
—RONALD A. FISHER (*STATISTICAL METHODS AND SCIENTIFIC
INFERENCE*, 1956)[1]

In the first two chapters, we encountered a few simple probability distributions. Now, we will examine more complex distributions whose shapes
make them appropriate for characterizing insurance and other financial
risks. In particular, two important families of distributions will be introduced: the Pareto family and the symmetric Lévy-stable family, both of
which are frequently used to model particularly "risky" random variables
with heavy tails (i.e., with large amounts of weight spread over the more
extreme values of the random variable).

To describe the measurement of risk, I will begin by defining the statistical moments of a distribution, and then show how these quantities are
used to compute the expected value (mean), standard deviation, and other
helpful parameters. Although many moments are quite informative, none
of them—not even the mean—exist for *all* distributions. Interestingly, it is
easy to show that "pathological" distributions without means, standard
deviations, etc. can be generated by very simple and natural random processes and thus cannot be overlooked.

Probability Distributions and Risk

So far, we have seen graphical illustrations associated with four probability distributions: specifically, the PMFs of the discrete uniform and geometric distributions and the PDFs of the continuous uniform and exponential distributions. Although these distributions arise in a number of important contexts, they are not particularly useful for describing insurance loss amounts or the returns on investment portfolios. For the former case, I will focus on continuous random variables defined on the positive real numbers (since individual loss amounts generally are viewed as positive real numbers that are rounded to the nearest cent for convenience), and for the latter case, I will consider continuous random variables defined on the entire real number line (since investment returns generally are computed as natural logarithms of ratios of "after" to "before" prices, which can be either negative or positive).

Insurance Losses

Although the exponential distribution (whose PDF is shown in Figure 2.5) is defined on the positive real numbers, it is not commonly used to model insurance loss amounts because it cannot accommodate a very wide range of distributional shapes. This limitation arises from the fact that it is a *one-parameter* family; that is, the PDF contains only *one* mathematical quantity that can be varied to obtain the different members of the family. All members of the exponential family possess PDFs that look exactly like the one in Figure 2.5, except that their curves may be stretched or compressed horizontally. (In Figure 2.5, the value of the parameter happens to equal 1/6.)

A richer, two-parameter family that is commonly used to model insurance losses is the Pareto family,[2] for which several PDFs are plotted on the same pair of axes in Figure 3.1.[3] From this figure, one can see that as the positive parameter *a* grows smaller, the tail of the PDF becomes heavier (thicker), so that more weight is spread over very large values in the sample space. Naturally, the heaviness of the PDF's tails is crucial in determining how variable the associated random loss is.

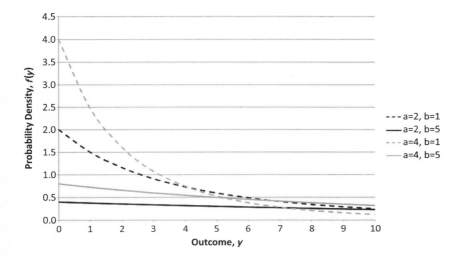

Figure 3.1
PDFs of Pareto Random Variables with Various Parameters (Defined on Positive
Real Numbers)

Asset Returns

In Chapter 6, I will offer an explanation of the fundamental qualitative differences between traditional insurance-loss risks and those, such as asset returns, arising in other financial contexts. For the moment, however, I simply observe that these two types of risks are quantitatively different in terms of the probability distributions commonly used to model them. As noted above, whereas insurance losses are generally taken to be positive real numbers, asset returns may take on any real values, negative or positive. Since asset prices tend to be set so that they have an approximately equal chance of going up or down, one also finds that asset-return distributions are fairly symmetrical.

The most commonly used family of probability distributions for modeling asset returns is the two-parameter *Gaussian* (or *normal*) family,[4] for which several PDFs are plotted on the same pair of axes in Figure 3.2. In fact, much of financial *portfolio theory* is often derived by explicitly assuming that asset returns are Gaussian. However, since the seminal work of French mathematician Benoît Mandelbrot, it has become increasingly clear that the tails of the Gaussian PDF are too light (thin) to account for rare, but persistently observed large and small values of asset returns.[5] Fortu-

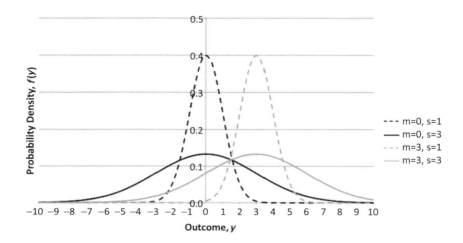

Figure 3.2
PDFs of Gaussian Random Variables with Various Parameters (Defined on All
Real Numbers)

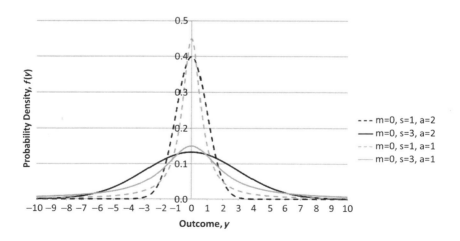

Figure 3.3
PDFs of Symmetric Lévy-Stable Random Variables with Various Parameters
(Defined on All Real Numbers)

nately, it is quite straightforward to generalize the Gaussian distribution to the three-parameter *symmetric Lévy-stable* family[6] by adding a parameter a that is analogous to the a parameter in the Pareto family (for values of a in the interval (0,2], where a equals 2 for the Gaussian case). As is shown in Figure 3.3, the tails of the symmetric Lévy-stable PDF become heavier as a becomes smaller. Here again, the heaviness of the PDF's tails is crucial in determining how variable the associated random asset return is.

Moments to Remember

The above observations regarding the a parameter of the Pareto and symmetric Lévy-stable families introduce a very simple, yet remarkably powerful idea: that a single numerical quantity, by itself, can provide a useful measure of the total amount of variability embodied in a given random variable. Such a parameter is called a *risk measure*, and researchers have given much attention to the selection of quantities appropriate for this purpose.

Some, but not all, commonly used risk measures are based upon one or more of a random variable's *moments*. To define a moment, one first needs to define the *expected value* or *mean* of a random variable. This quantity represents the weighted average of all values in the random variable's sample space, which is found by multiplying each value by its corresponding probability, and then "adding up" the resulting products.

For the discrete uniform random variable X representing the outcome of a single die roll, it is known that the sample space consists of the integers $\{1, 2, \ldots, 6\}$ and that $p(x)$ equals 1/6 for all possible values of x. Thus, in this case, the expected value—denoted by $E[X]$—is given by the simple sum

$$1 \times (1/6) + 2 \times (1/6) + 3 \times (1/6) + 4 \times (1/6) + 5 \times (1/6) + 6 \times (1/6),$$

which equals 3.5. Analogously, for the continuous uniform random variable Y defined on the interval [0,1), we saw that the sample space may be partitioned into a large number (n) of small intervals, each of equal length, $1/n$. Since $p(y_i)$ equals $1/n$ for each interval i, it follows that the expected value, $E[Y]$, is given by the sum

$$(1/n) \times (1/n) + (2/n) \times (1/n) + \ldots + (n/n) \times (1/n),$$

as n becomes infinitely large, which equals 0.5.

Once one knows how to compute the expected value of a given random variable, X, it is rather straightforward to define the expected value of any function of the original random variable, such as X^2 (i.e., X *squared*, or $X \times X$), in an analogous way. For example, if X represents the outcome of a single die roll, then the expected value of X^2—denoted by $E[X^2]$—is given by the sum

$$1^2 \times (1/6) + 2^2 \times (1/6) + 3^2 \times (1/6) + 4^2 \times (1/6) + 5^2 \times (1/6) + 6^2 \times (1/6),$$

which equals approximately 15.2.

In general, the kth *moment* of a random variable X is simply the expected value of X^k (i.e., X *to the power k*, or $X \times X \times \ldots \times X$ [k times]). Among other things, this means that the expected value of X, $E[X]$, is the same thing as the *first moment* of X. This quantity is often used as an indicator of the *central tendency* (location) of the random variable, or more precisely, a forecast of what the random variable is likely to be (made before it is actually observed).

To capture the *dispersion* (spread) of the random variable X around its mean, one turns to the *second moment*, $E[X^2]$, and defines the difference $E[X^2] - (E[X])^2$ to be the *variance* of X, denoted by $Var[X]$. This is, in a sense, the most primitive measure of risk that is commonly calculated. However, it is often more useful to work with the square root of the variance, known as the *standard deviation* and denoted by $SD[X]$, because the latter quantity possesses the same units as the original random variable.[7] Hence, the standard deviation is actually the most broadly used risk measure.[8] The next two higher moments, $E[X^3]$ and $E[X^4]$, are often employed in computing quantities to capture the random variable's *skewness* (asymmetry) and *kurtosis* (peakedness), respectively.

In the insurance world, both standard deviations and variances are frequently used in the pricing of products. In particular, policyholder premiums are sometimes calculated explicitly as the expected value of losses plus a profit loading proportional to one of these two risk measures. Although this may be reasonable when an insurance company has a large loss portfolio (thereby justifying the Gaussian approximation, as will be discussed in Chapter 4), it is clearly inappropriate when dealing with large loss amounts from single events (such as large liability awards or catastrophe losses). Such loss distributions not only are highly asymmetric, but also can possess heavy tails that are inconsistent with the Gaussian approximation.

In financial portfolio theory, the standard deviation often is used to capture the risk dimension in a *risk-versus-return* analysis. Specifically,

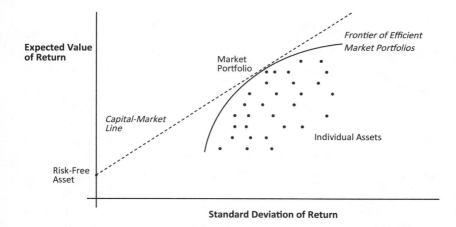

Figure 3.4
Risk vs. Return in Financial Portfolio Theory

the expected value of a portfolio's return is plotted against the standard deviation of the return, and the set of optimal portfolios is determined by the *capital-market line* (see Figure 3.4) formed by all possible weighted combinations of the risk-free asset (often taken to be a U.S. Treasury bill) and the average market portfolio.

The use of the standard deviation in financial portfolio theory is often justified mathematically by either (or both) of two assumptions: (1) that asset returns have a Gaussian distribution (so that the standard deviation captures all characteristics of the distribution not reflected in its expected value); or (2) that the investor's utility function (a concept to be introduced in Chapter 5) is quadratic (so that the first and second moments of the investment-return distribution capture everything of importance in the investor's decision making). Unfortunately, neither of these assumptions is particularly reasonable in practice.

Heavy Tails

Returning to Figures 3.1 and 3.2, one can see how the means and standard deviations are affected by distinct parameter values in the Pareto and Gaussian families. In the Pareto case, both the mean and standard deviation decrease as the *a* parameter increases (consistent with the tail's becoming lighter), whereas both the mean and standard deviation increase as the *b* parameter increases. In the Gaussian case, the m and s parameters actually denote the mean and standard deviation, respectively, and so the relationships between the two parameters and these latter quantities are evident.

One intriguing aspect of the Pareto distribution is that the mean and standard deviation are not finite for all values of the a parameter. Whereas a can take any positive real value, the mean is finite if and only if a is greater than 1, and the standard deviation is finite if and only if a is greater than 2.[9] This property is rather disturbing, for both theoretical and practical reasons. On the theoretical side, it seems rather counterintuitive that finite measures of location and spread do not exist in some cases. In particular, the fact that a well-defined random variable may not have a finite mean, or average, seems somewhat bizarre. On the practical side, the absence of these measures of location and spread makes it substantially more difficult to summarize the shape of the underlying distribution with one or two numerical quantities and certainly makes it impossible to compare the affected distributions with other distributions simply by comparing their respective means and standard deviations.

The underlying cause of the missing means and standard deviations is fairly easy to apprehend, even if the effect seems unnatural. As the a parameter becomes smaller, the tail of the Pareto distribution becomes heavier, and so there is increasingly more weight spread out over very large values in the sample space. Given that the sample space is unbounded above, one can imagine that at a certain value of a there is so much weight placed in the tail that when one multiplies each X in the sample space by its corresponding probability and then "adds up" the resulting products, one obtains an infinite value of $E[X]$. This occurs when a equals 1. Since X^2 is much greater than X when X is large, it follows that this phenomenon should occur even sooner (i.e., at a larger value of a) for X^2; and indeed, $E[X^2]$ (and therefore $SD[X]$ as well) becomes infinite when a equals 2.

Although the Gaussian distribution does not possess sufficiently heavy tails to preclude the existence of any moments, the symmetric Lévy-stable generalization does have this property for values of its a parameter that are less than 2. As with the Pareto distribution, the second moment (and therefore the standard deviation) is infinite for all values of a less than 2, and the mean is not well defined for all values of a less than or equal to 1. What is even stranger in the symmetric Lévy-stable case, however, is that the mean is not *infinite* when a is less than or equal to 1, but rather *indeterminate*, revealing that it is not arbitrarily large (in either the positive or negative direction), but truly *meaningless!*

The Humble Origins of Heavy Tails

One reason that infinite or indeterminate means and infinite standard deviations defy intuition is that such phenomena are rarely encountered in practice and so tend to be viewed as somewhat "pathological."[10] Of course, this sentiment could be as much an effect as a cause; that is, the reason one fails to see these "pathologies" very often may be simply that one shies away from them because they are difficult to work with, sort of like the man who dropped his keys on the sidewalk at night but refused to look for them outside the area illuminated by a single streetlight. In the present section, I will argue that heavy-tailed insurance losses and asset returns are actually quite easy to generate from simple random processes and that the area outside the reach of the streetlight is therefore much too large to be ignored.

Heavy-Tailed Insurance Losses

Most commonly, insurance loss processes are modeled either as sums of random components or as *waiting* or *first-passage* times to a certain sum in an accumulation of random components. In particular, one can consider two basic models of accidental damage involving an abstract "box" containing a vulnerable "cargo item" and a large number of homogeneous "protective components" that are subject to destruction, one after the other, by the force of the accident.

In the first case, the accident lasts a fixed amount of real time, and a constant amount of damage is done to the cargo item for each protective component that is overcome (randomly) in sequence during that time period. If the components fail as *independent* random variables,[11] each with the same small failure probability p_{Failure}, then this model is appropriate for *claim frequencies* (i.e., numbers of individual loss events). In the second case, the accident lasts until a fixed number of the protective components are overcome (randomly), and a constant amount of damage is done to the cargo item for each unit of real time that passes before this event. If the components again fail as independent and identical random variables with small p_{Failure}, then this model is appropriate for *loss severities* (i.e., sizes of individual losses).

It is the latter type of model—for loss severities—that creates the potential for heavy tails. Taking the simplest possible version of the model, in which the accident lasts until *exactly one* protective component is overcome (randomly), the resulting random variable will have the exponential distribution, which was discussed previously. Although this particular distribution is not heavy-tailed, it can easily become so through a simple transformation. Specifically, if the random variable L has an exponential distribution with parameter ℓ, where ℓ is itself an exponential random variable with parameter b, then the unconditional distribution of L is Pareto with parameters $a = 1$ and b, for which both $SD[L]$ and $E[L]$ are infinite.

Given the ease with which such infinite-mean losses can be generated from a simple model, it is not surprising that insurance companies have developed a rather peremptory technique for handling them: namely, the *policy limit* (cap), which cuts off the insurer's coverage responsibility for a loss's tail. Under a conventional policy limit, the raw loss amount, L, is capped at a fixed dollar amount, c, and the policyholder retains responsibility for that portion of the loss exceeding c. Naturally, such truncated losses have the lightest possible tails (i.e., *no* tails), and so all issues of infinite means and standard deviations should, in principle, vanish.

Unfortunately, there is one rather unsettling problem with the policy limit: like any contract provision, it is subject to litigation and so can be overturned by the whim of a civil court. Rather remarkably, this possibility, regardless of how slight, completely vitiates the policy limit as a protection against infinite means.

Suppose, for example, that a manufacturing company has accumulated a pool of toxic waste on its property and that the pool begins to leak into a nearby housing development, causing serious health problems as well as lowering property values. When the victims of the seepage seek financial recovery for their damages, the manufacturer's insurance company will, under normal circumstances, set aside reserves and pay claims according to the provisions of the relevant pollution liability policy. However, if the total amount that the insurance company is required to pay under the contract is capped by a finite limit—say, $10 million—then the insurer will stop paying claims as soon as that amount is reached, leaving uncompensated claims as the sole responsibility of the manufacturer.

Now suppose further that: (1) when confronted with these unpaid claims, the manufacturer realizes that the only way to avoid bankruptcy is to challenge successfully the $10 million limit in civil court (based upon some novel reading of contract law proposed by a talented attorney); and (2) a court will overturn the policy limit with some small positive probability, p_{Overturn}. Assuming that the raw total of pollution-related damage caused by the manufacturer is given by a Pareto random variable, L, with parameters $a = 1$ and b (so that $E[L]$ is infinite) and that the amount the insurance company originally agreed to pay under its contract, capped by the $10 million limit, is denoted by L^* (where $E[L^*]$ must be finite), it then follows that the insurance company's actual mean loss is given by

$$(1 - p_{\text{Overturn}}) \times E[L^*] + p_{\text{Overturn}} \times E[L],$$

which is infinite. In other words, no matter how small the positive probability p_{Overturn}, the insurer's actual mean loss is truly infinite in a world with both infinite-mean raw losses and active civil courts.

Given the serious potential for overcoming policy limits in the highly litigious United States, it is rather strange that infinite-mean losses are not more frequently discussed. The subject is rarely identified as a significant solvency issue by insurance practitioners and regulators, although it is occasionally broached by academic researchers.[12] Part of the reason for this omission is, of course, that the concept of an infinite mean is rather counterintuitive (as discussed above). However, I suspect that the principal explanation for the reluctance to discuss infinite-mean losses is something far more prosaic, as suggested by certain historical events.

Instructively, at the nadir of the U.S. asbestos/pollution liability "crisis" in the mid-1990s to late 1990s, it was not uncommon for insurance actuaries and executives to speak of "inestimable" incurred losses, characterized by infinite means.[13] At the time, the concern was that such losses, upon entering the books of any member of an insurance group, could spread throughout the entire group and beyond. (This is because any proportional share of an infinite-mean liability, no matter how small the proportion, is yet another infinite-mean liability.) To defend against such statistical contagion, Lloyd's of London formed the legally separate Equitas companies in 1996 to isolate its accrued asbestos/pollution liabilities and thereby protect the solvency of Lloyd's as a whole. In the same year, Pennsylvania's CIGNA Corporation worked out a similar scheme with state regulators to cast off its asbestos/pollution liabilities via the legally separate Brandywine Holdings—a controversial move that received final court approval only in 1999.

These dramatic developments suggest that the political fear of confronting the most pernicious aspect of infinite-mean losses—that is, their potential to spread like a dread disease from one corporate entity to another—may well offer the best explanation of their absence from common discourse. For if infinite-mean losses are observed and identified and cannot be effectively quarantined or amputated, then their ultimate financial course will be fatal. And in such circumstances, many patients simply prefer to remain undiagnosed.

Heavy-Tailed Asset Returns

When it comes to asset returns, I would offer a different, but equally simple model to show how heavy-tailed distributions can arise in the context of market prices for exchange-traded assets. In the spirit of Mandelbrot (1963), let P_t denote the market price of one pound of exchange-traded cotton at (discrete) time t, and consider the observed return given by the natural logarithm of the ratio P_t/P_{t-1} (i.e., $\ln(P_t/P_{t-1})$). I will begin by positing a simple descriptive model of cotton price formation—in other words, a characterization of how P_t (the "after" price) is formed from P_{t-1} (the "before" price).

Assume that there are a fixed number of traders in the cotton market and that each trader can be in either of two states at any given time: (1) holding one pound; or (2) holding no pounds.[14] Let us propose that P_t is given by the ratio

$$\frac{\text{Total Dollars Bid to Buy One Pound at Time } (t-1)}{\text{Total Number of Pounds Offered for Sale at Time } (t-1)},$$

which in turn is equal to

$$\frac{\text{Total Number of Traders Wanting to Buy One Pound at Time } (t-1)}{\text{Total Number of Traders Wanting to Sell One Pound at Time } (t-1)}$$

and therefore

$$\frac{\text{Proportion of No-Pound Traders Wanting to Buy at Time } (t-1)}{\text{Proportion of One-Pound Traders Wanting to Sell at Time } (t-1)}$$
$$\times \frac{\text{Number of No-Pound Traders at Time } (t-1)}{\text{Number of One-Pound Traders at Time } (t-1)}.$$

If one assumes that an individual trader's decision to buy or sell at time $t-1$ is governed by a random process reflecting his or her private information, then it is straightforward to show that the cotton-return random variable can be expressed as the natural logarithm of the ratio of two random proportions plus a constant; that is, $\ln(P_t/P_{t-1})$ may be written as $\ln(\hat{p}_{\text{Buy}}/\hat{p}_{\text{Sell}}) + \text{constant}$, where

$\hat{p}_{Buy}$ = Proportion of No-Pound Traders Wanting to Buy at Time $(t-1)$

and

$\hat{p}_{Sell}$ = Proportion of One-Pound Traders Wanting to Sell at Time $(t-1)$.

A close analysis of the random variable $\ln(\hat{p}_{Buy}/\hat{p}_{Sell})$ shows further that under a variety of reasonable assumptions, this random variable has tails that are comparable with those of the exponential distribution, possibly with time-dependent parameters, ℓ_{t-1}.[15]

This finding is rather striking because exponential tails fall distinctly and conspicuously between the light-tailed Gaussian assumption so commonly (but unrealistically) employed in theoretical discussions of asset returns and the heavy-tailed symmetric Lévy-stable model (for values of a less than 2) borne out by many empirical studies.[16] The observation yields two further implications of remarkable significance given the parsimony of the simple price-formation model employed:

- The Gaussian assumption provides a poor starting point for asset-pricing models (leaving one rather puzzled by its historical popularity).[17]
- Empirically observed heavy-tailed behavior is quite possibly the result of time-dependent components in the exponential tail parameters.[18]

Alternative Risk Measures

In the contexts of heavy-tailed insurance losses or asset returns, practitioners cannot use the standard deviation as a risk measure and therefore typically employ one or more "tail-sensitive" risk measures, with names such as: (1) *value at risk* (VaR); (2) *tail value at risk*; (3) *excess tail value at risk*; (4) *expected deficit*; and (5) *default value*.[19] Unfortunately, none of risk measures (2) through (5) is well defined if the underlying loss or return random variable X has an infinite or indeterminate mean. Consequently, the only commonly used risk measure that works in the case of a badly behaved mean is the VaR, which, for a preselected small tail probability, α_{Tail}, is defined as the $100 \times (1 - \alpha_{Tail})$ *percentile* of X (i.e., the probability that X is less than or equal to the VaR is $1 - \alpha_{Tail}$). Commonly chosen values of α_{Tail} would include 0.10, 0.05, 0.01, etc.

The insensitivity of the VaR to the existence of a finite mean undoubtedly explains some of this risk measure's popularity in the finance and insurance literatures. However, knowing the VaR for only one (or even a few) fixed tail probabilities, α_{Tail}, leaves much to be desired in terms of characterizing the overall risk associated with a random variable. Percentiles can tell much about one tail of the distribution, but little or nothing about the center or other tail.

Certainly, if the VaR is known for all possible values of α_{Tail}, then one knows exactly how the random variable behaves; that is, this is equivalent to knowing the full PMF or PDF. However, the search for a single-quantity risk measure presupposes that working with entire PMFs or PDFs entails undesirable cognitive difficulties for human decision makers. Consequently, one must turn elsewhere for a comprehensive single-quantity measure of risk.

One robust risk measure that I like to promote is the *cosine-based standard deviation* (CBSD), developed in joint work with my son, Thomas Powers.[20] Taking advantage of the fact that the cosine function is bounded both below and above (unlike the power function, which is used in computing moments), this risk measure is applicable to all probability distributions, regardless of how heavy their tails are. Although the CBSD requires the selection of a parameter to calibrate the trade-off between information about the tails and information about the rest of the probability distribution, this parameter may be chosen to maximize information about the distribution *on the whole*. Then, for the symmetric Lévy-stable family, the risk measure is proportional to $2^{1/a} \times s$, where s is a positive dispersion parameter of the symmetric Lévy-stable distribution that corresponds to the standard deviation in the Gaussian case (i.e., when a equals 2). This expression has the intuitively desirable properties of increasing both as a decreases (i.e., as the tails become heavier) and as s increases. It also is directly proportional to the ordinary standard deviation in the Gaussian case.

To illustrate the usefulness of this particular risk measure, consider the simple problem of adding two random asset returns. Suppose, for example, that X_1 and X_2 denote the returns from investments in cotton on two successive days and that these two random variables are independent observations from a Gaussian distribution with mean m and standard deviation s (for which $a = 2$). In that case, the CBSD is proportional to $\sqrt{2} \times s$ for a single day and proportional to $2 \times s$ for the sum of two days (i.e., for a two-day period), so that

$$CBSD[X_1 + X_2] < CBSD[X_1] + CBSD[X_2].$$

This property, known as *subadditivity*, indicates that risk-reduction benefits may be achieved through diversification (i.e., risk pooling), a fundamental technique of risk finance (to be discussed in Chapter 7).

Alternatively, if X_1 and X_2 are independent observations from a symmetric Lévy-stable distribution with parameters m, s, and $a = 1$,[21] then the CBSD is proportional to $2 \times s$ for a single day, and proportional to $4 \times s$ for a two-day period, so that

$$CBSD[X_1 + X_2] = CBSD[X_1] + CBSD[X_2].$$

In this case, there is only simple *additivity*, and so diversification offers no risk-reduction benefits.

ACT 1, SCENE 3

[A basketball court. Young man practices shots from floor; Grim Reaper approaches quietly.]

REAPER: Good morning, Mr. Wiley. I'm the Grim Reaper.

MAN: I know who you are.

REAPER: Really? How so?

MAN: Your costume is rather . . . revealing.

REAPER: Yes, I suppose it is. Well then, you know why I'm here.

MAN: I suppose I do. But I'm a bit surprised that you don't speak with a Swedish accent.

REAPER: Ah! I think you've been watching too many movies. Next I suppose you'll want to challenge me to a contest to spare your life.

MAN: Well, is that permitted?

REAPER: Yes, it's permitted, but generally discouraged. There's no point in raising false hopes among the doomed.

MAN: But if it *is* allowed, what are the ground rules?

REAPER: Essentially, you can propose any challenge you like; and if I judge my probability of victory to be sufficiently great, I'll accept. But I must warn you, I've lost only once in the past 5,000 years.

MAN: Well, then, I think I have just the game for you: a free-throw challenge.

REAPER: That hardly seems fair, given the wonderful physical shape you're in.

MAN: Well, you didn't seem to think my "wonderful physical shape" was any obstacle to dying.

REAPER: [Laughs.] A fair point, indeed!

MAN: But in any event, the challenge won't be based upon our relative skill levels. Rather, you'll simply make a series of free throws, and I'll be permitted to live until you succeed in making one basket.

REAPER: [Confused.] But that's not much of a challenge. From the free-throw line, I'd estimate my chance of making a basket to be about 1/2. That means there's about a 1/2 chance it will take me one shot, about a 1/4 chance it will take two shots, about a 1/8 chance it will take three shots, and so on. Since those probabilities add up to 1, I'm destined to succeed.

MAN: Well, I'm thinking of something a little more challenging than that. My proposal is that you take your first shot from the free-throw line, with your regular chance of success: 1/2. However, if you don't make the first shot, then you have to move a little farther from the basket; just enough so that your chance of making the second shot goes down to 1/3. If you don't make the second shot, then you again have to move a little farther away, so that your chance of making the third shot becomes 1/4; and so on.

REAPER: That is a bit more challenging, I suppose. But you must realize, I'm fairly good at mathematics, so I can see that there's about a 1/2 chance it will take me one shot, about a 1/6 chance it will take two shots, about a 1/12 chance it will take three shots, and so on. Since those probabilities again add up to 1, I'm still destined to succeed.

MAN: Well, we'll see about that. Do you agree to my challenge?

REAPER: I certainly do.

[Young man passes basketball to Grim Reaper, who takes first shot from free-throw line, and misses. Reaper retrieves ball, takes second shot from slightly farther back, and again misses.]

MAN: It's not so easy, is it?

REAPER: [Smiles confidently.] Not to worry, it's just a matter of time until I win.

MAN: That's exactly right. Eventually, you'll win. But have you calculated how long it will take, on the average?

REAPER: [Stands silently as complacent expression turns to frustration.] Damn! On the average, it will take forever!

MAN: [Walks away.] Feel free to come for me when you're finished.

4

The Value of Experience
Independence and Estimation

In Chapter 2, we considered two pairings of probability interpretations and estimation methods: (1) the frequency/classical approach, called *frequentism*; and (2) the subjective/judgmental approach, called *Bayesianism*. In the present chapter, we will explore a number of concepts and methods employed in the former approach. The latter will be addressed in Chapter 5.

To present the standard frequentist paradigm, I will begin by defining the concept of a random sample, and then summarize how such samples are used to construct both point and interval estimates. Next, three important asymptotic results—the law of large numbers, the central limit theorem, and the generalized central limit theorem—will be introduced, followed by a discussion of the practical validity of the independence assumption underlying random samples. Finally, I will consider in some detail the method of hypothesis testing, whose framework follows much the same logic as both the U.S. criminal justice system and the scientific method as it is generally understood.

Point Estimators and Interval Estimators

The starting point for all statistical methods, whether frequentist or Bayesian, is a *random sample*. This is a collection of some number, n, of independent observations, all from the same probability distribution, and is denoted by $X_1, X_2, \ldots, X_n$. (As before, *independent* means that knowing something—or everything—about the values of one or more of the observations provides no new information about the other values in the sample.)

If the relevant probability distribution is known with certainty, then there is no need for statistical estimation. In our mortality example from Chapter 2, this would be equivalent to knowing the probabilities $p_{Male}(x)$ or $p_{Female}(x)$ for all ages x in Figure 1.1, rather than having to estimate them with $\hat{p}_{Male}(x)$ and $\hat{p}_{Female}(x)$. However, such complete information is not always available.

The simplest way to model unknown aspects of a probability distribution is to identify one or more parameters whose values are uncertain. For example, if a random sample comes from a Gaussian distribution (as shown in Figure 3.2), then there are two parameters—the mean, m, and the standard deviation, s—each of which may be known or unknown. For illustrative purposes, it will be assumed that only m is unknown and that the value of s is provided a priori.

There are two broad classes of estimators of an unknown parameter such as m: (1) *point estimators*, which are single real-valued numerical quantities that provide good guesses of the actual value of m; and (2) *interval estimators*, which provide (usually continuous) subsets of the real number line that are likely to contain the actual value of m. Each of these classes can yield a number of distinct estimators distinguishable from one another in terms of various optimality criteria. However, rather than delving into these differences, I simply will provide one example of each type of estimator.

In the case of a Gaussian random sample with unknown mean and known standard deviation, the most straightforward and commonly used point estimator of m is the *sample mean*, $(X_1 + X_2 + \ldots + X_n)/n$. This estimator is not only intuitively reasonable, but also enjoys certain desirable properties, as discussed in the next section. The most straightforward and commonly employed interval estimator of m is the symmetric *confidence interval* constructed by using the sample mean as midpoint, and then subtracting an appropriate multiple of the standard deviation of the sample mean to obtain the lower bound and adding the same multiple of the same standard deviation to obtain the upper bound; that is:

$$\text{Lower Bound: Sample Mean} - z_{\alpha/2} \times (s/\sqrt{n}) \text{ and}$$

$$\text{Upper Bound: Sample Mean} + z_{\alpha/2} \times (s/\sqrt{n}).$$

The length of the confidence interval, $2 \times z_{\alpha/2} \times (s/\sqrt{n})$, depends on the *confidence level*, $1 - \alpha$, with which one wants to capture m. This is governed by the factor $z_{\alpha/2}$ (the $100 \times (1 - \alpha/2)$th percentile of the Gaussian distribution with mean 0 and standard deviation 1), which increases as the confidence level increases. Typical values of $1 - \alpha$ are 0.90, 0.95, and 0.99, and the corresponding values of $z_{\alpha/2}$ are 1.645, 1.96, and 2.575, respectively. (Since 0.95 is a particularly common choice of $1 - \alpha$, it follows that the associated factor of 1.96—often rounded to 2—is correspondingly common, which is why people often speak of a confidence interval as consisting of "the sample mean plus or minus 2 standard deviations.")

A few further words need to be said about the meaning of the confidence level. Although this number certainly has the "look and feel" of a probability, it is not quite the same thing. I say "not quite" because it *is* in fact a probability before the actual values of the random sample are observed, but falls in stature once those values are known. This rather odd state of affairs arises from the restricted nature of the frequentist paradigm. Prior to observing the random sample, one can say that the lower and upper bounds of the confidence interval, which depend on the sample mean, are truly random variables, and therefore have a probability $(1 - \alpha)$ of capturing the unknown parameter m. However, once the random sample is observed, there is no remaining source of randomness because the elements of the random sample are *known* real numbers, and m is an *unknown* number. At that point, all one can say is that the confidence interval either *does* or *does not* capture m, without any reference to probability. In this context, confidence means the following: If one were to select a large number of random samples of size n and construct the same type of confidence interval from each sample, then one would tend to capture m about $100 \times (1 - \alpha)$ percent of the time.

Once a frequentist statistician has settled on a particular point and/or interval estimator of m, he or she can use the estimator to provide forecasts of future observations of the underlying random variable. For example, having observed the random sample $X_1, X_2, \ldots, X_n$, the statistician can use the sample mean as a good guess of the subsequent observation, X_{n+1}, and can construct confidence intervals for X_{n+1} as well.

Asymptotic Results

Not surprisingly, the frequentist approach affords great deference to *asymptotic* results—that is, mathematical theorems describing properties of statistical estimators as the sample size, *n*, becomes arbitrarily large. Three particularly important results of this type are the *law of large numbers* (LLN), the *central limit theorem* (CLT), and the *generalized central limit theorem* (GCLT), stated briefly below.

Law of Large Numbers

If E[X] is well defined, then as the sample size, n, approaches infinity, the sample mean must converge to the actual mean.

This result, sometimes called the *law of averages*, provides a mathematical statement of the very intuitive notion that the sample mean should become closer and closer to the actual mean as the random sample grows larger. From the perspective of frequentist estimation, this is very important because it means that all estimators based upon sample means tend to become more and more accurate as more data are collected. Naturally, the LLN requires that $E[X]$ be well defined; but it is very interesting to think about what happens to the sample mean in those cases in which $E[X]$ is either infinite (such as for values of *a* less than or equal to 1 in the Pareto family) or indeterminate (such as for values of *a* less than or equal to 1 in the symmetric Lévy-stable family). In the former case, the sample mean naturally tends to grow larger and larger without bound as *n* increases. In the latter case, the sample mean simply "bounces" around the real number line, never settling down at any particular value.

Central Limit Theorem

If SD[X] is well defined, then as the sample size, n, approaches infinity, the distribution of the sample mean must converge to a Gaussian distribution with mean E[X] and standard deviation SD[X]/$\sqrt{n}$.

For a random variable that possesses a finite standard deviation, the CLT expands on the LLN by describing the random behavior of the sample mean as it gets closer and closer to the actual mean for large sample sizes. Essentially, this result says that the sample mean approaches the actual mean in a smooth and systematic way, such that, for a large value of the sample size, the sample mean will have an approximately Gaussian distribution (that is consequently both approximately symmetric and light-tailed) about the actual mean with a standard deviation shrinking to 0.

Generalized Central Limit Theorem

As the sample size, n, *approaches infinity, there exists a coefficient,* c_n, *such that the distribution of* $c_n \times$ (Sample Mean) *must converge to a (four-parameter) Lévy-stable distribution.*

For clarification, the *four-parameter* Lévy-stable family is a generalization of the three-parameter symmetric Lévy-stable family, in which the additional parameter allows for asymmetry. The GCLT generalizes the CLT in the sense that the CLT represents a special case in which the coefficient c_n equals 1 and the sample mean approaches the Gaussian distribution with mean $E[X]$ and standard deviation $SD[X]/\sqrt{n}$.[1] The GCLT goes well beyond the CLT by addressing *all* random variables that possess a limiting distribution, including those for which the standard deviation is infinite (e.g., those having a Pareto distribution with *a* less than or equal to 2).

The Meaning of Independence

In defining a random sample, I stated that the individual observations had to be independent of one another in the sense that knowing something (or everything) about the values of one or more of the observations provides no new information about the other values in the sample.[2] Since this assumption is fundamental to frequentist (as well as Bayesian) analysis, it seems worthwhile to explore its meaning a bit further. To begin, I will clarify the relationship between statistical independence, on the one hand, and statistical *uncorrelatedness*, on the other.

Independence Versus Uncorrelatedness

Let us consider two random variables, Y_1 and Y_2, both from the same probability distribution. If they are independent of one another, then knowing something about Y_1 (e.g., Y_1 is less than 10) or even knowing *everything* about Y_1 (e.g., Y_1 equals 5), implies nothing about Y_2, and vice versa. On the other hand, if the two random variables are uncorrelated (denoted by $Corr[Y_1, Y_2] = 0$), then knowing that Y_1 is particularly high (or low) does not imply that Y_2 will tend to be particularly high (or low), and vice versa. Since the definition of uncorrelatedness is weaker than the definition of independence, it follows that independence logically implies uncorrelatedness;

that is, if Y_1 and Y_2 are independent, then they must be uncorrelated. However, it is important to note that uncorrelatedness does *not* imply independence.

As an example, suppose that a location is selected at random, and with uniform probability, from all points on the surface of the earth, and consider the statistical relationship between the following two random variables: Y_1, the distance (measured along the surface of the earth) from the North Pole to the randomly chosen location; and Y_2, the average annual temperature at the same location. Making the simplifying assumption that average annual temperatures decrease symmetrically as a point moves (either north or south) away from the equator, it follows that Y_1 and Y_2 must be uncorrelated (because knowing that Y_1 is particularly high and knowing that Y_1 is particularly low *both* imply that Y_2 will tend to be particularly low), but dependent (because knowing that Y_1 is particularly high does imply *something* about Y_2, i.e., that it must be particularly low).

Of course, one also can look at things from the perspective of positive or negative correlation. Specifically: (1) Y_1 and Y_2 are *positively correlated* (denoted by $Corr[Y_1, Y_2] > 0$) if knowing that Y_1 is particularly high implies that Y_2 will tend to be particularly high and knowing that Y_1 is particularly low implies that Y_2 will tend to be particularly low; and (2) Y_1 and Y_2 are *negatively correlated* (denoted by $Corr[Y_1, Y_2] < 0$) if knowing that Y_1 is particularly high implies that Y_2 will tend to be particularly low and knowing that Y_1 is particularly low implies that Y_2 will tend to be particularly high. Here, positive or negative correlation logically implies statistical *dependence*, but dependence does not require either positive or negative correlation.

An Intriguing Intuition

Returning to the role of independence in a random sample, I would note that the relationship between independence and the LLN is not entirely intuitive. In fact, students of introductory statistics often sense a contradiction therein because the idea that the sample mean of the first n trials must converge to a fixed constant (i.e., the actual mean) seems to belie the fact that the outcome of the nth trial has nothing to do with the previous $n-1$ trials. Along these lines, one might ask: How can the simple average of a series of random variables be required to become arbitrarily close to the actual mean unless the individual random variables are forced to offset each other in some way? Or more precisely: How can the LLN be true unless the successive random variables are somewhat *negatively correlated*, with a relatively low value of one observation being offset by a relatively high value of a later one, and vice versa?

Usually, such naïve questioning is quickly nipped in the bud by the deft explanations of an experienced instructor. However, in some refractory cases (including my own) the intuition simply retreats underground, finding sanctuary in the brain's subconscious. Then, while the individual's conscious mind embraces the orthodox tenets of independence and the LLN, the subconscious surreptitiously nurtures the view that convergence results must imply negatively correlated outcomes in a random sample. After an indefinite period of time—several years or perhaps even decades—this secret conviction may cause one to engage in such superstitious behaviors as: buying talismans to ward off the "evil eye" (when things are going well) or to change one's luck (when things are going badly); or more prosaically, betting heavily on red (after a long string of black) or on black (after a long string of red) in casino roulette.

In inquiring after the source of this strange intuition, I would note that certain negative-correlation structures—such as assuming that $Corr[X_1, X_2]$, $Corr[X_2, X_3]$, $Corr[X_3, X_4]$, etc. equal some negative constant and that all other pairs of observations are uncorrelated—can cause the sample mean to converge to the actual mean faster than it would under the assumption of independence.[3] In other words, such structures might be used to justify a "law of not-so-large numbers" (LNSLN). Therefore, it seems reasonable to believe that some people may confuse the LLN with some sort of LNSLN.

This sort of confusion is not difficult to imagine because the LLN is asymptotic in nature and thus can never truly be experienced in real life. Although most potential LNSLNs are also asymptotic, there is one particular LNSLN that applies to finite samples and not only can be experienced, but also is ubiquitous. I therefore would argue that this particular convergence result likely forms the basis for the intuition of negative correlations.

Remembrance of Fair Divisions Past

Consider a finite sequence of N random variables from the same probability distribution, whose sum is some constant (i.e., $X_1 + X_2 + \ldots + X_N$ equals some fixed number k). Regardless of the value of the standard deviation of these random variables, it is easy to show that the correlation between any two of them is given by $-1/(N-1)$, and that the following LNSLN applies: *As the sample size,* n, *approaches* N, *the sample mean must converge to the actual mean.* This constant-sum sampling model is intrinsic to the fair division of limited resources—a problem that would have been at least as familiar to our primitive human ancestors as it is to us today.

For example, consider what might have happened when N cooperative primitive hunters returned to their village after killing a single deer.[4] Assuming that the carcass had to be divided equally among the hunters' respective families, it is immediately obvious (to anyone with even the most cursory knowledge of cervine anatomy) that this division problem would have been rather difficult. Even if N is just 2, in which case the deer's exterior bilateral symmetry would have provided a convenient guide for carving, the animal's internal asymmetry would have rendered the division of flesh into truly equal parts—whether according to weight, nutritional value, or some other measure—somewhat random.

Without delving too deeply into the grisly details, let us assume that the weight of edible flesh was used as the measure for division and that a single deer yielded a total of 75 pounds. Assuming a total of five hunters, and letting X_1 denote the weight allocated to hunter 1, X_2 denote the weight allocated to hunter 2, and so on, it follows from the constant-sum model described above that the random variables $X_1, X_2, \ldots, X_5$ come from the same distribution, with mean $75/5 = 15$ pounds and pairwise correlations $-1/4$. In short, each hunter would have been acutely aware that his actual share of the deer carcass was only approximately equal to his "fair share" (i.e., 15 pounds), and that his random gain (or loss) would have subtracted from (or added to) the shares of the other hunters.

Such fair-division problems would have been ubiquitous in primitive societies.[5] Besides game meat, other resources that would have required careful partitioning include fruit and vegetable gatherings, favorable land for housing, and sometimes even human chattel (e.g., captives from raids on neighboring villages). In each case, the close connection between the negative correlations of the allocated shares and the convergence of the sample mean to a fixed constant would have been apparent.

Given the likely importance to social harmony of a good knowledge of fair division, a strong intuitive understanding of the statistical properties of constant-sum sampling should have provided a natural survival advantage. Thus, it seems reasonable to expect biological evolution to have imprinted human cognition with an intuitive awareness of the connection between negative correlations and the convergence of the sample mean.

Hypothesis Testing

One of the most important and widely used techniques of frequentist statistics is hypothesis testing. As will be seen in Chapter 14, this methodology also provides a conceptual framework for the scientific method as it is
generally understood.

The formulation of any hypothesis test is based upon two statements:
(1) a *null hypothesis* (denoted by H_0) that describes the current state of
belief regarding some quantifiable problem; and (2) an *alternative hypothesis* (denoted by H_1) that provides the state of belief that naturally would
follow if one were to reject the null hypothesis. In most statistical problems, each hypothesis is stated in the form of an equation. For example, in
the Gaussian parameter-estimation problem discussed above, one might
be interested in performing a formal hypothesis test in which the null hypothesis is given by H_0: "*m* equals 10," and the alternative hypothesis by H_1:
"*m* does not equal 10."

To carry out a hypothesis test, two further items are needed: (1) a *test
statistic*, whose value provides information about the relative credibilities
of the null and alternative hypotheses; and (2) a *level of significance*, which
enables one to identify those values of the test statistic for which the null
hypothesis should be rejected (called the *critical region*). To test H_0: "*m*
equals 10" against H_1: "*m* does not equal 10," the most straightforward test
statistic is the sample mean minus 10, for which smaller absolute values
provide more support for the null hypothesis, and larger absolute values
provide less support. The level of significance, denoted by α, is analogous
to the complement of the confidence level $(1 - \alpha)$ discussed above and represents the greatest probability with which the statistician is willing to
reject the null hypothesis under the assumption that the null hypothesis is
true. This probability is also called the probability of *type 1 error*. (In contrast,
the probability that the statistician retains the null hypothesis under the assumption that the alternative hypothesis is true is called the probability of
type 2 error. Interestingly, the latter probability is not fixed in advance because hypothesis testing embodies an institutional bias in favor of keeping
the probability of type 1 error below a certain threshold, even at the expense
of permitting a much greater probability of type 2 error.)

For a given level of significance, the *complement* of the critical region
is constructed in a manner analogous to a confidence interval, but using
the value of *m* under the null hypothesis (i.e., 10) as midpoint. Subtracting
an appropriate multiple of the standard deviation of the sample mean to

obtain the lower bound and adding the same multiple of the same standard deviation to obtain the upper bound, the complementary region is given by:

$$\text{Lower Bound: } 10 - z_{\alpha/2} \times (s/\sqrt{n}) \text{ and}$$

$$\text{Upper Bound: } 10 + z_{\alpha/2} \times (s/\sqrt{n}).$$

Consequently, the critical region itself consists of the portions of the real number line below the lower bound and above the upper bound. If the test statistic falls within this critical region, then it is said to be *statistically significant*, and the null hypothesis must be rejected.

Commonly chosen values of α are 0.10, 0.05, and 0.01, and the corresponding values of $z_{\alpha/2}$ are 1.645, 1.96, and 2.575, respectively. However, it is not unusual for statisticians to avoid the final step of declaring whether or not a particular null hypothesis is rejected at a given level of significance and instead to provide only the *p-value* (i.e., probability of type 1 error) associated with the observed test statistic. Given this quantity, one can determine whether or not to reject the null hypothesis at any proposed level of significance, α, simply by comparing the *p*-value to α. If the *p*-value is smaller, then the null hypothesis is rejected; if the *p*-value is larger, then the null hypothesis is retained.

The Criminal Justice Analogue

Rather remarkably, there exists a pronounced parallel between the methodology of hypothesis testing and the dialectical nature of criminal jurisprudence in the United States and many other nations. Beginning with the selection of the null hypothesis, H_0: "The defendant is not guilty," and the alternative hypothesis, H_1: "The defendant is guilty," the analogy proceeds to the choice of a level of significance (i.e., "beyond a reasonable doubt"), as well as the institutional bias in favor of keeping the probability of type 1 error small, even at the expense of permitting a much greater probability of type 2 error (i.e., "it is better to let ten guilty people go free than to convict one innocent person").

Regrettably, I have not had the opportunity to serve on a criminal (or civil) jury. Although I possess no hard evidence in the matter, I speculate that my lack of experience in this area arises from the common desire of both prosecution and defense attorneys not to have individuals who identify themselves as statisticians sitting in the jury box. My impression is that attorneys on both sides prefer to have jurors with few preconceived notions regarding quantitative methods of decision making, presumably to ensure that the jury's final verdict is more directly related to the quality of the lawyers' courtroom presentations than to the intrinsic quality of the evidence. Although this may be fine for those with complete confidence in the adversarial system's ability to arrive at the truth, I must admit that I am less than sanguine about the process. One simply need consider how frequently well-publicized jury trials result in outcomes that are surprising to both the prosecution and the defense to realize the high level of uncertainty inherent in a system that, inter alia, forbids the final decision makers (i.e., the jurors) to ask questions of witnesses or in some cases even to take notes.

Testing Hypothesis Testing

Despite my unfortunate lack of jury service, I have been fortunate enough to have had the opportunity to employ a critical "life or death" hypothesis test firsthand. Unfortunately, it was *my* life that was on the line at the time. More than two decades ago, I was informed that I would need to undergo several months of chemotherapy for a nasty tumor that had begun metastasizing through my body. Fortunately, the type of cancer involved (which, not coincidentally, was the same as that experienced by our 27-year-old man in Chapter 1) was highly curable, although there were always the usual potentially life-threatening complications of aggressive chemotherapy.

After consulting with various doctors, and reading a number of relevant medical journal articles, I was faced with a decision that required some formal statistical analysis. Although the particular cocktail of chemicals to be used in my treatment was fairly standard, there remained the basic question of whether I should undergo therapy in a geographically distant research hospital, where the health care providers would have had more experience with the treatment protocol, or in a nearby nonresearch hospital, where I might be the first patient to undergo the prescribed regimen.

Fortunately, before I had to make my decision, I came across a journal article that provided data on the very issue I was considering.[6] As summarized in Table 4.1, the article presented a comparison of chemotherapy outcomes, using the specific protocol I would be having, in both research and nonresearch hospitals.

Table 4.1
Chemotherapy Survival Analysis

	Patients Surviving	Patients Dying	Totals
Research Hospitals	48	8	56
Nonresearch Hospitals	54	13	67
Totals	102	21	123

Source: Williams et al. (1987).

What was particularly interesting (or perhaps I should say "challenging") about using these data was that the observed proportion of treatment survivals at research hospitals (48/56, or approximately 0.86) was clearly larger, on an absolute basis, than the proportion of treatment survivals at nonresearch hospitals (54/67, or approximately 0.81). Therefore, at first blush, a research hospital would have seemed a substantially better choice. However, the true value of statistical analysis in this type of setting is to determine whether or not such absolute numerical differences—even if fairly large—are statistically meaningful. In the case at hand, this can be accomplished by a formal test of H_0: "The treatment survival rates at research and nonresearch hospitals are equal," against H_1: "The treatment survival rates at research and nonresearch hospitals are not equal."

Given the data in Table 4.1, one can apply a standard hypothesis test called a *chi-squared test,* which yields a test statistic of 0.5635 and an associated p-value of 0.4529. Therefore, for any reasonably small level of significance, the null hypothesis should be retained, suggesting that hospital type has no real impact on treatment survival rate.

Of course, the bottom line question is: When one's life is at stake, is one willing to accept the dictates of an impersonal hypothesis test? In this case, my initial reaction was "Of course not! The research hospitals give a 5 percent better chance of survival, regardless of what the test says." But then, after some agonizing, I decided that it would represent a profound betrayal of my formal statistical training to reject the entire methodology of hypothesis testing so early in my career. Consequently, I ended up selecting a local, nonresearch hospital that was logistically more convenient.

Although I survived the necessary treatment and am comfortable that my decision was the right one, I now must acknowledge, in retrospect, that it was poorly informed. As pleased as I was to have found the data in Table 4.1,

I never noticed that they were from an *observational study*, rather than a *randomized controlled study*. In other words, the comparison of outcomes from research and nonresearch hospitals was based upon a set of patients who presumably had some choice as to which type of hospital they would use for treatment, rather than being assigned to one type or the other randomly. As will be discussed at some length in Chapter 12, this experimental design essentially vitiated any hypothesis test based upon the data, since there easily could have been other unobserved variables—such as a greater likelihood of healthier patients choosing nonresearch hospitals—that confounded the results.

ACT 1, SCENE 4

[The Garden of Eden. Adam and Eve stand before Tree of Life, as God (unseen) speaks from above.]

GOD: Adam and Eve, I'm very disappointed in both of you.

ADAM: Yes, Lord. We know that You commanded us not to eat from the Tree of Knowledge, and we're very sorry.

GOD: Are you sorry for disobeying Me or simply for getting caught?

ADAM: Uh, I'm not sure what You mean, Lord. I—

EVE: [Interrupting.] He means we're sorry for *disobeying* You, Lord.

GOD: *Really?* Well, no matter. It isn't just that you disobeyed the *letter* of My command in this particular instance; it's also the ways in which you've disobeyed the *spirit* of My commands on many occasions. For example, there are forty-five varieties of fruit on the Tree of Life, each representing a different virtue: Faith, Hope, Empathy, Courage, Patience, Kindness, . . . I could go on and on. And if you recall, I told you to maintain a balanced diet of all those different fruits—to eat a mixture, to *diversify*. But what did you do? Eve, you ate only the fruit called Deference; and Adam, you ate only the one called Acceptance.

ADAM: Yes, Lord. But once I tried Acceptance, I found I was quite happy with it.

EVE: And in my case, Lord, I would have explored beyond Deference, but the Serpent told me not to bother.

GOD: Ah, yes—the Serpent! Now, that brings Me to the other fruits: the forbidden ones. Unlike the Tree of Life, each fruit on the Tree of Knowledge is unique. And of all the thousands of different fruits growing there, Eve, which two did you pick?

EVE: I believe they were called How to Damage Things and How to Shift Responsibility, Lord.

GOD: Yes. What a sorry pair of choices those were! I notice that you passed up all sorts of more useful alternatives: How to Know Whom to Trust, How to Learn from One's Mistakes, How to Predict the Future from the Past—even How to Make a Fruit Salad would have been better.

EVE: Well, Lord, it's not entirely my fault. You see, the Serpent suggested that we try those two.

GOD: Ah, the Serpent again! Every time you mention the Serpent, it damages My heart to see you shifting responsibility.

ADAM: We're sorry, Lord. We won't mention the Serpent again.

GOD: Adam, will you ever stop making promises you can't keep?

ADAM: Uh, I'm not sure how to answer that, Lord. I—

GOD: [Interrupting.] Then go! Just go! [Sighs.] Leave My sight! You are hereby banished from paradise!

[Adam and Eve turn and walk sadly away, out the gates of Eden.]

SERPENT: Banished from paradise? That's quite a harsh punishment, isn't it?

GOD: Yes. I'm afraid I had to make an example of those two so that others will benefit from their experience.

SERPENT: Hmm. How to Damage Things and How to Shift Responsibility. I can imagine starting an entire industry based upon those two concepts someday.

GOD: [His mood shifting.] What? Insurance?

SERPENT: No. I was thinking of civil litigation.

5

It's All in Your Head
Bayesian Decision Making

The chances are your chances are . . . awfully good.
—AL STILLMAN AND ROBERT ALLEN (*CHANCES ARE*,
RECORDED BY JOHNNY MATHIS, 1957)

From certain remarks in the previous chapter, the reader will have an inkling of the serious shortcomings of the frequentist paradigm. Despite its rigorous mathematical basis, frequentism remains unable to answer some of the most basic questions a person is likely to pose when encountering uncertainty. For example, given a random sample $X_1, X_2, \ldots, X_n$, one might ask: What is the probability that the next observation, X_{n+1}, will be less than 10? Rather remarkably, this very natural type of question is off-limits to the frequentist statistician except in the most trivial of cases. The frequentist can offer only an estimate of the desired probability, without answering the question directly.

The Bayesian paradigm provides an elegant framework for resolving such problems by permitting one to treat all unknown parameters as random variables and thus impose prior probability distributions over them. In the present chapter, I will begin by showing how this approach allows one to make explicit statements about the probability distributions of future observations, and then argue in favor of a "fundamentalist" (or "literalist") Bayesian approach to generating prior probability distributions. Next, I will introduce the expected-utility principle in a Bayesian context and explain how it leads to a very natural system for making decisions in the presence of uncertainty. Finally, I will show how the Bayesian decision framework is sufficiently powerful to address problems of extreme (Knightian) uncertainty.

Frequentist Shackles

Let us recall the Gaussian parameter-estimation problem from the previous chapter. In that example, we observed a random sample from a Gaussian distribution with unknown mean, m, and known standard deviation, s, and were interested in estimating m. We saw first that this could be done by constructing either a point estimate or an interval estimate and, subsequently, that statements about m could be evaluated using the method of hypothesis testing.

Now suppose that a frequentist statistician were asked the question posed above: What is the probability that the next observation, X_{n+1}, will be less than 10? Clearly, if he or she were to try to answer this question prior to observing $X_1, X_2, \ldots, X_n$, then the probability offered would have to be a function of m, which can be denoted by

$$\text{Probability } X_{n+1} \text{ Is Less Than 10, Given } m.$$

Since m is unknown, this probability would be unknown as well. However, after observing the random sample, the frequentist could estimate the desired probability by inserting the point estimate of m—that is, the sample mean—obtaining

$$\text{Probability } X_{n+1} \text{ Is Less Than 10, Given } m \text{ Equals Sample Mean.}$$

Unfortunately, this expression does not provide an answer to the question asked, because it is not the true probability. If the sample mean happens to be close to the actual value of m, then this estimated probability is likely to be close to the true probability. However, it will not be the correct probability unless the sample mean is exactly equal to m, and this cannot be verified except in the trivial case when s equals 0.

In fact, there is only one way to compute the probability that X_{n+1} is less than 10 without knowing m exactly, and that is to possess a probability distribution over m. Once such a distribution is available, the desired probability may be expressed as

$$E[\text{Probability } X_{n+1} \text{ Is Less Than 10, Given } m],$$

where the expected value is taken over the distribution of m. That is, instead of inserting a single estimate of m into

Probability X_{n+1} Is Less Than 10, Given m,

one can take an *average* of all possible values of this expression using the distribution of m. If the distribution of m is provided before the random sample is observed, then it is called a *prior distribution*; if it is determined after observing the random sample, then it is called a *posterior distribution*. To obtain the latter distribution from the former, one can use the mathematical equation

$$\text{Posterior PDF of } m = \text{constant}$$
$$\times (\text{PDF of Random Sample, Given } m) \times (\text{Prior PDF of } m).$$

This result was first developed by British mathematician Thomas Bayes and was published in 1764, a few years after Bayes's death.[1]

Bayesian Liberation

Bayes's theorem gives its name to the Bayesian (i.e., subjective/judgmental) approach to estimation. Using this approach, all that is needed to answer the question "What is the probability that the next observation, X_{n+1}, will be less than 10?" is a prior PDF of m. Consistent with the presentation in Chapter 2, this prior PDF may be constructed by some type of (more or less sophisticated) judgment. Although there are different schools of Bayesianism, some of which impose more restrictive forms of judgment than others, I believe that a "fundamentalist" (or "literalist") viewpoint, requiring the statistician to use those estimates that he or she personally believes are most valid (assuming that they satisfy the basic axioms of mathematical probability; e.g., probabilities must be nonnegative and "add up" to 1), is itself most valid logically.[2] At the very least, implementing a belief that beliefs must be implemented is logically consistent.

To illustrate how this fundamentalist perspective can be applied in practice, I will consider a number of estimation problems far removed from the capabilities of the frequentist paradigm. In these examples, the parameter m denotes a probability with regard to the state of the world (expressed as the truth of some event or phenomenon) and thus is restricted to values in the interval from 0 to 1 (see Table 5.1). For each event or phenomenon listed in the leftmost column, I offer my prior beliefs regarding this probability, expressed as both a point estimate (in the middle

Table 5.1
Prior Probabilities of Various Events or Phenomena

Event or Phenomenon (By Category)	Point Estimate (Prior Mean)	Prior Beta Probability Distribution
A. Historical Controversies		
1. Soviets/Cubans killed J. F. Kennedy	0.550	Mean = 0.550, SD = 0.100
2. Mobsters killed J. F. Kennedy	0.550	Mean = 0.550, SD = 0.200
3. U.S. planned 9/11 attacks	0.005	Mean = 0.005, SD = 0.005
B. Future Events before 2025		
1. Female becomes U.S. president or VP	0.925	Mean = 0.925, SD = 0.075
2. Nuclear attack occurs somewhere	0.150	Mean = 0.150, SD = 0.100
3. Alien intelligence is confirmed	0.900	Mean = 0.900, SD = 0.050
C. Speculative Science		
1. Bigfoot or Yeti exists	0.250	Mean = 0.250, SD = 0.250
2. "Face" on Mars is true artifact	0.005	Mean = 0.005, SD = 0.005
3. Life on Mars exists or existed	0.950	Mean = 0.950, SD = 0.050
D. The Paranormal		
1. Astrology has predictive value	0.005	Mean = 0.005, SD = 0.005
2. Clairvoyance has predictive value	0.750	Mean = 0.750, SD = 0.100
3. Ghosts exist	0.500	Mean = 0.500, SD = 0.100
E. Religion		
1. Supreme Being exists	0.975	Mean = 0.975, SD = 0.025
2. Angels exist	0.500	Mean = 0.500, SD = 0.200
3. Afterlife awaits	0.995	Mean = 0.995, SD = 0.005

column) and a full probability distribution (in the rightmost column). These probability distributions are from the two-parameter *beta* family, whose sample space consists of the real numbers from 0 to 1, and each is completely determined by knowing its mean and standard deviation. Their corresponding PDFs are plotted in Figure 5.1.

The events and phenomena in Table 5.1 were selected deliberately because they are controversial and likely to be viewed by many as beyond the domain of scientific inquiry. My purpose is to show that if one can provide logically consistent quantitative measures of one's beliefs in such extremely subjective contexts, then it should be even easier to do so in more mundane matters. Furthermore, as a fundamentalist Bayesian, I would argue that as long as one is capable of formulating such estimates, to refrain from using them—even in the most subjective of contexts—is intellectually dishonest. In short, it is only *logically inconsistent* beliefs, not *crazy* beliefs, that are dangerous to science.

Having raised the issue of inconsistency, I think it worthwhile to address a few of the estimates in Table 5.1 that may, at first sight, appear problematic.

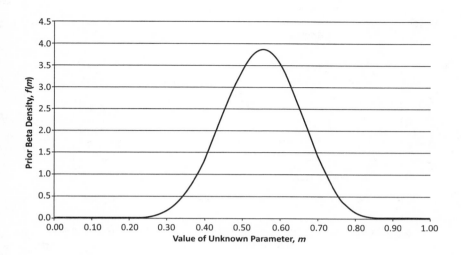

Figure 5.1 (A1)
Prior PDF of m = Probability Soviets/Cubans Killed J. F. Kennedy

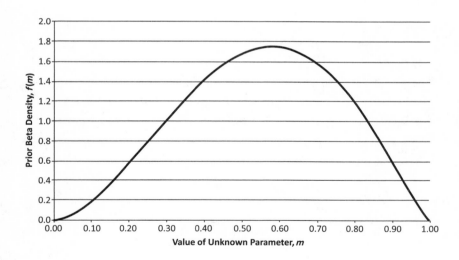

Figure 5.1 (A2)
Prior PDF of m = Probability Mobsters Killed J. F. Kennedy

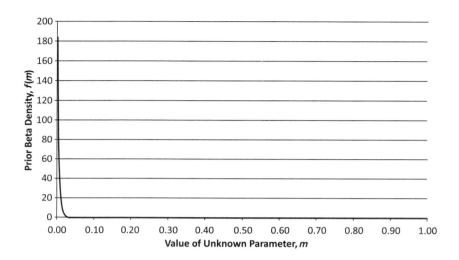

Figure 5.1 (A3)
Prior PDF of m = Probability United States Planned 9/11 Attacks

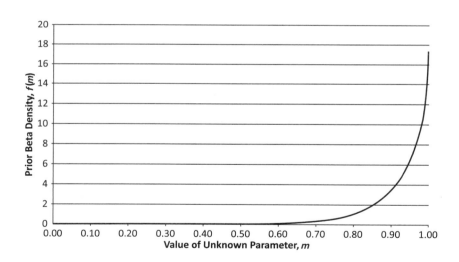

Figure 5.1 (B1)
Prior PDF of m = Probability Female Becomes U.S. President or Vice President before 2025

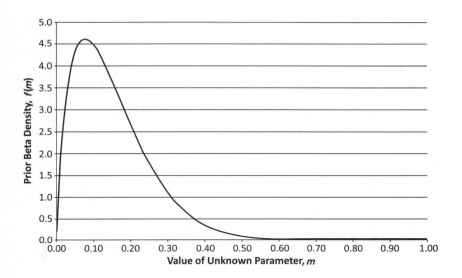

Figure 5.1 (B2)
Prior PDF of m = Probability Nuclear Attack Occurs Somewhere before 2025

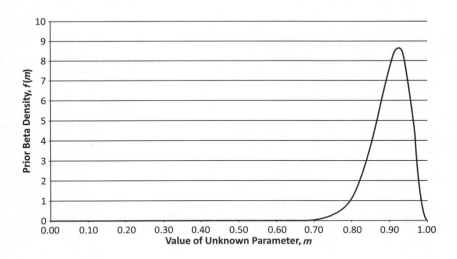

Figure 5.1 (B3)
Prior PDF of m = Probability Alien Intelligence Is Confirmed before 2025

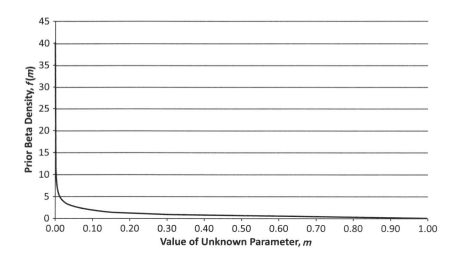

Figure 5.1 (C1)
Prior PDF of m = Probability Bigfoot or Yeti Exists

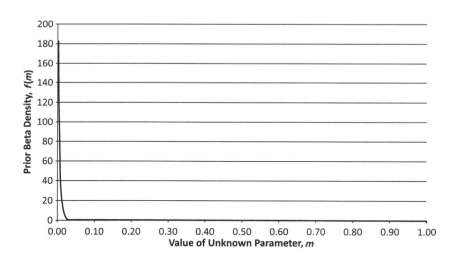

Figure 5.1 (C2)
Prior PDF of m = Probability "Face" on Mars Is True Artifact

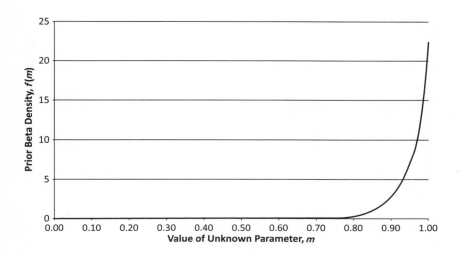

Figure 5.1 (C3)
Prior PDF of m = Probability Life on Mars Exists or Existed

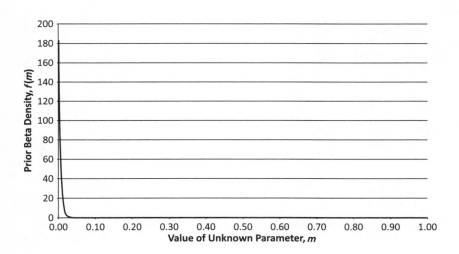

Figure 5.1 (D1)
Prior PDF of m = Probability Astrology Has Predictive Value

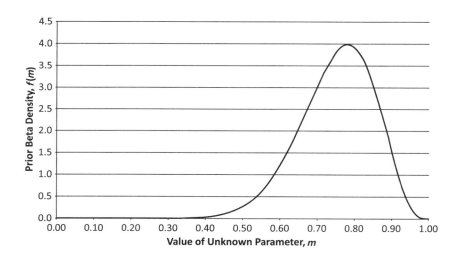

Figure 5.1 (D2)
Prior PDF of m = Probability Clairvoyance Has Predictive Value

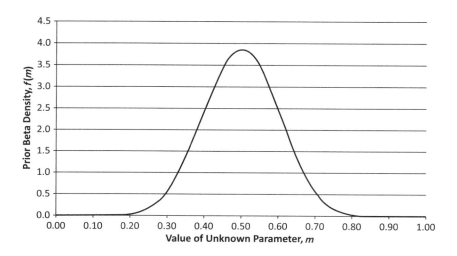

Figure 5.1 (D3)
Prior PDF of m = Probability Ghosts Exist

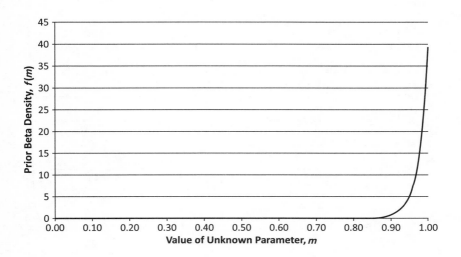

Figure 5.1 (E1)
Prior PDF of m = Probability Supreme Being Exists

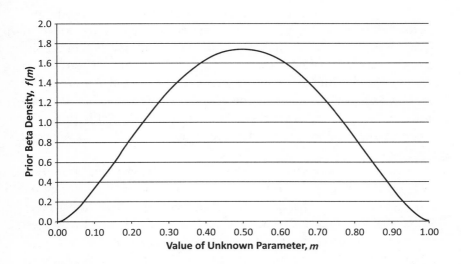

Figure 5.1 (E2)
Prior PDF of m = Probability Angels Exist

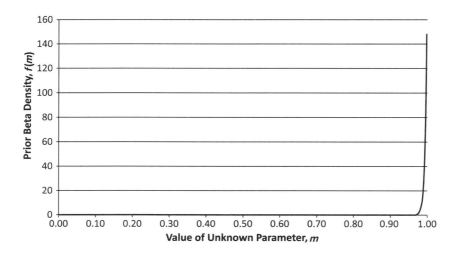

Figure 5.1 (E3)
Prior PDF of m = Probability Afterlife Awaits

In category A (Historical Controversies), for example, I have allocated a probability of 0.55 to the event that President Kennedy was killed by agents of the Soviet Union and/or its Cuban allies and another probability of 0.55 to the event that he was killed by organized criminals. Clearly, these two probabilities sum to a number greater than 1; nevertheless, this does not imply a logical inconsistency because there is a chance that both parties were working together and—more intriguingly—that both parties were working independently and happened to choose the same time and place for their attacks.

Furthermore, in category E (Religion), I have assigned a probability of 0.995 (near certainty) to the existence of an afterlife while according the existence of a supreme being (God) a somewhat lower probability of 0.975. Rather than being inconsistent, these choices simply indicate that I reject the fairly common notion that the existence of heaven (or hell, or purgatory, or whatever) implies the existence of God. To my mind, the existence of God almost certainly implies the existence of an afterlife (although this is clearly not the view of all of the world's established religions), but I also can imagine the possibility of an afterlife without the existence of a divine entity.

What Is Happiness?

One of the most powerful and important models of human decision making is the *expected-utility* paradigm.[3] This framework, which is widely used in both statistics and economics, does not require a Bayesian setting; however, in conjunction with Bayesianism, it provides a comprehensive and consistent approach to decision making in the face of uncertainty.

The notion of expected utility traces its development to the classical solution of Swiss mathematician Nicholas Bernoulli's St. Petersburg Paradox. This problem, originally posed in 1713 while Bernoulli held an academic appointment in the eponymous Russian city, contemplates a game in which a fair coin is tossed until it comes up Heads. The player is told that a prize of X units of some currency (e.g., *ducats* in the original problem) will be awarded, where X equals:

> 1 if Heads occurs on the first toss;
> 2 if Heads occurs on the second toss;
> 4 if Heads occurs on the third toss;
> 8 if Heads occurs on the fourth toss; and so on;

and then is asked how many units he or she would be willing to pay to play the game.

At Bernoulli's time, as today, most people would be willing to pay only a very few units to play the game. However, this result was seen as paradoxical by mathematicians of the early eighteenth century because they were accustomed to using *expected value* as the basic measurement of worth in decisions involving uncertainty. Applying this criterion to the St. Petersburg game yields an expected value of

$$1 \times (1/2) + 2 \times (1/4) + 4 \times (1/8) + \ldots,$$

which is infinite. Clearly, there is something puzzling about a game whose expected value is infinite, but which could command only a very small admission fee.

The classical solution to the St. Petersburg puzzle was provided by Daniel Bernoulli (a cousin of Nicholas) in 1738.[4] This solution is based upon the observation that most decision makers are characterized by *decreasing marginal utility* of wealth—that is, a decision maker's utility (or happiness, as measured in abstract units called *utiles*) typically increases

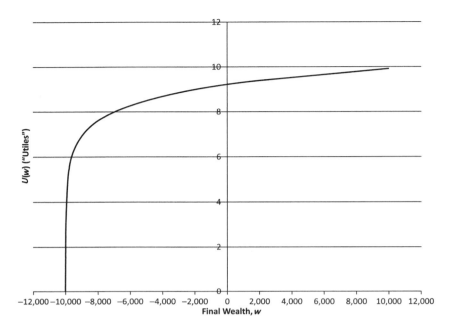

Figure 5.2
Natural Logarithm as Utility Function (with Initial Wealth of 10,000)

with each unit of wealth gained, but the incremental increases in utility become progressively smaller as wealth increases.

To determine the true value of the proposed game, one therefore must transform the player's *final wealth*, W (that is, the sum of the player's initial wealth and the random outcome, X) by an increasing and concave-downward *utility function, U(w)*, before computing the expected value. D. Bernoulli suggested using the natural-logarithm function, which is depicted in Figure 5.2. Employing this function yields the expected utility

$$\ln(\text{Initial Wealth} + 1) \times (1/2) + \ln(\text{Initial Wealth} + 2) \times (1/4)$$
$$+ \ln(\text{Initial Wealth} + 4) \times (1/8) + \ldots.$$

Assuming that the player has an initial wealth of 10,000 units, this expected utility is equal to the utility produced by a fixed award of about 7.62 units. In other words, the expected-utility analysis appears to explain quite well why the game's actual value is only a few units.

It is important to note that there are a number of sound alternative explanations to the St. Petersburg problem:

- Human concepts of value are bounded above, and thus it is meaningless to speak of a game offering an *infinite* expected value—or *infinite* expected utility, for that matter. In fact, Austrian mathematician Karl Menger showed that D. Bernoulli's solution must be modified by requiring that the utility function be bounded, or else the paradox can be made to reappear for certain payoff schemes.[5]
- The game lacks credibility, and is in fact unplayable, because no individual or organizational entity is able to fund the arbitrarily large prizes X associated with arbitrarily long streaks of Tails in the coin-tossing sequence.
- Decreasing marginal utility addresses only the impact of the payoff amounts and not the impact of the outcome probabilities. As has been noted by Israeli cognitive scientists Daniel Kahneman and Amos Tversky in their development of *cumulative prospect theory*, decision makers often misestimate the probabilities of low-frequency events.[6] Clearly, this type of effect could substantially lower the perceived expected value of N. Bernoulli's game.

Interestingly, the third bullet point is consistent with an argument that is often made by my own actuarial science students: that a principal—if not *the* principal—reason the St. Petersburg game seems unappealing is that it is very difficult to believe that any of the larger values of X will ever be achieved, given that their probabilities are so small. This highly intuitive phenomenon would be especially significant in the context of heavy-tailed outcome distributions, such as those encountered with certain insurance and asset-return risks. It also offers the advantage of not requiring the assumption of decreasing marginal utility, which, while a thoroughly reasonable hypothesis, seems strangely extraneous to problems of decision making under uncertainty.

Given that I interpret my students' argument correctly, the issue of misestimating the probabilities of low-frequency events can be addressed by positing a simple mathematical model. Specifically, one can assume that every decision maker is characterized by an *apprehension function*, $A(x)$, rather than (or perhaps in addition to) a utility function, which can be used to create a subjective probability distribution over the random outcome, X, by taking the product of this new function and the true underlying PMF, $p(x)$.

I will assume further that most decision makers are *risk pessimistic* in the sense that they tend to underestimate the probabilities of large positive

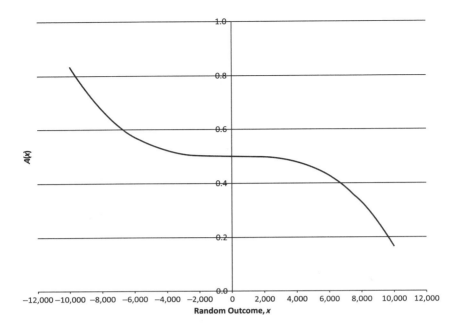

Figure 5.3
Hypothetical Apprehension Function (Characterized by Risk Pessimism and Impatience)

outcomes and to overestimate the probabilities of large negative outcomes. This behavior is modeled by requiring that the apprehension function be a positively valued decreasing function that is flat at the expected value of the outcome. In other words, the smaller the outcome, the greater the decision maker's apprehension concerning that outcome; however, in a neighborhood of the mean outcome—that is, for "typical" values of X—there is very little discernable change in the relative adjustments applied to the PMF. In addition to risk pessimism, it seems reasonable to assume that many decision makers are characterized by what might be called *impatience*: the property of increasing marginal apprehension below the mean and decreasing marginal apprehension above the mean; in other words, the apprehension function is concave upward below the mean and concave downward above the mean. Figure 5.3 provides a sketch of a hypothetical apprehension function for a risk-pessimistic and impatient decision maker with an expected outcome of 0 units.

To apply the apprehended-value principle to the St. Petersburg game, first note that the expected outcome is infinite, implying that a risk-pessimistic decision maker with impatience would have an apprehension function resembling only the left-hand portion of the curve in Figure 5.3; that is, $A(x)$ would be decreasing and concave upward. Essentially, this means that the smaller payoffs would be given substantially more weight relative to the larger payoffs, and so, for an appropriate selection of the apprehension function, the *apprehended value* of N. Bernoulli's game could be made arbitrarily close to 0.

Risk Versus Uncertainty?

In his influential 1921 treatise, *Risk, Uncertainty, and Profit*, American economist Frank Knight distinguished between the concepts of risk and uncertainty as follows:[7,8]

> Uncertainty must be taken in a sense radically distinct from the familiar notion of Risk, from which it has never been properly separated. The term "risk", as loosely used in everyday speech and in economic discussion, really covers two things which, functionally at least, in their causal relations to the phenomena of economic organization, are categorically different. . . . The essential fact is that "risk" means in some cases a quantity susceptible of measurement, while at other times it is something distinctly not of this character; and there are far-reaching and crucial differences in the bearings of the phenomenon depending on which of the two is really present and operating. . . . It will appear that a measurable uncertainty, or "risk" proper, as we shall use the term, is so far different from an unmeasurable one that it is not in effect an uncertainty at all. We shall accordingly restrict the term "uncertainty" to cases of the non-quantitive type.

In short, Knight argued that risks are predictable from empirical data using formal statistical methods, whereas uncertainties cannot be predicted because they have no historical precedent. This distinction is often used to explain: (1) *uninsurability*—that is, the refusal of insurance companies to underwrite certain types of exposures because of anticipated, but actuarially intractable, structural changes in loss distributions (such as those caused by more generous civil justice awards);[9] and (2) *flights to quality*—that is, the abandonment of certain asset or derivative markets by traders perceiving forthcoming, yet unforecastable structural changes in return distributions. In both contexts, the structural changes often are described in terms of potentially unprecedented variations in the tail-heaviness of the relevant probability distributions.

While there certainly exists a *qualitative* difference between the concepts of predictable risk and Knightian uncertainty, it is not immediately clear why, from a *quantitative* standpoint, this difference is anything more than a simple distinction between "lesser risk" and "greater risk." In particular, one might ask: Is it possible to forecast and make decisions regarding such uncertainties using formal statistical methods? To examine this question more closely, let us consider a representative example from insurance underwriting.

One of the insurance industry's most worrisome lines of business is pollution liability, in which individual losses often are modeled using heavy-tailed probability distributions. For the purpose at hand, let us assume that the total loss amount covered by a particular insurance company's pollution liability policy, recorded in millions of dollars, is captured by a Pareto random variable, X. As was previously discussed, this random variable possesses an infinite standard deviation if the a parameter is less than or equal to 2 and an infinite mean if a is less than or equal to 1. To make the implications of Knightian uncertainty especially poignant, let us assume further that: (1) throughout the insurance company's historical experience, the value of a has always remained fixed at 2.5 (for which both the mean and standard deviation are finite); but (2) the insurance company's actuaries now anticipate a major structural change in civil justice awards that is likely to cause a to shrink dramatically and in a manner without historical precedent.

For the insurance company to continue writing its pollution liability coverage, its actuaries must be able to forecast the random variable X for the post-change period and also to estimate an associated decision-making criterion, such as the company's expected utility. If the actuaries are frequentist statisticians, then they must estimate a with some value $\hat{a}$ in the interval from 0 to 2.5 to compute

Expected Utility of (Initial Wealth + Premiums − X), Given $\hat{a}$;

whereas if they are Bayesian statisticians, then they must provide a probability distribution over a on the sample space from 0 to 2.5 to compute

E[Expected Utility of (Initial Wealth + Premiums − X), Given a].

Interestingly, it is not the computational differences between the frequentist and Bayesian approaches that are most critical in the context of Knightian uncertainty. Rather, it is the fact that frequentist actuaries would be entirely unable to construct $\hat{a}$ because they have no formal procedure for saying anything about a in the absence of relevant historical data, whereas Bayesian actuaries would have no trouble positing a probability distribution for a because they are used to selecting prior distributions based largely—and sometimes entirely—upon judgment. Note further that, even in extreme cases in which such a prior distribution places substantial weight on values of a less than 2 (for which the standard deviation and possibly even mean are infinite), there is no obstacle to calculating the expected utility as long as the utility function is bounded.[10] Thus, the qualitative difference between risk and Knightian uncertainty poses a quantitative conundrum for frequentists, but not for Bayesians.

It is rather instructive to note that insurance actuaries often use Bayesian methods precisely because of data limitations and the necessity of incorporating human judgment into the decision-making process.[11] Therefore, in the context of the present discussion, one actually could argue that Bayesian methods are not only resistant to issues of Knightian uncertainty, but also specifically motivated by, and designed to resolve, such issues.

This leads to an interesting question: To a Bayesian, is Knight's distinction between risk and uncertainty ever of real significance? Somewhat surprisingly, I would argue that it is. Specifically, Knight's use of the terms *measurable* and *unmeasurable* to distinguish between risk and uncertainty, respectively, is quite valid in a Pickwickian sense.

Although Knight employed *unmeasurable* to mean a random outcome without historical precedent, a similar term—*nonmeasurable*—is used in probability theory to describe a mathematical set that cannot be used as the sample space of a proper random variable (because there is no way to distribute probability in a nontrivial way across such a space). Consequently, if one were to contemplate a random outcome a that must take values from a nonmeasurable set, then not even the most fundamentalist Bayesian could construct a legitimate prior distribution for a, and further analysis would be impossible.

Fortunately, such problems have not (yet) arisen in insurance or financial markets, or other quotidian realms of human activity, where conventional discrete and/or continuous sample spaces appear quite sufficient. However, things are not so clear-cut at the epistemological edge of human speculation. For example, as I will argue in Chapter 12, related issues actually do arise in attempting to place a prior distribution over all possible configurations of an infinite set of explanatory variables in a statistical-modeling setting.

Non-Expected-Utility Theory

At the end of Chapter 2, I noted that there exist alternative theories of probability that will not be considered in this book because I find them insufficiently intuitive. I now wish to make a similar point regarding alternatives to the expected-utility paradigm. Although it is true that one alternative to expected utility (i.e., apprehended value) already has been considered, my purpose in that case was primarily to show that sometimes a simple intuitive model may offer as good an explanation as a classically accepted model. I thus will make no attempt to address the vast field of academic inquiry that goes by the name of *non-expected-utility theory*, except to point out below the sort of weaknesses that it is intended to address.

One of the most compelling arguments against the expected-utility framework was presented by French economist Maurice Allais in 1953 and is often called the Allais paradox.[12] In this problem, a decision maker is given the following two choices:

Choice 1: Which of alternatives A1 or B1 would you prefer?

A1: {$1,000,000 with probability 1

B1: $\begin{cases} \$5,000,000 \text{ with probability } 0.10 \\ \$1,000,000 \text{ with probability } 0.89 \\ \$0 \qquad \text{ with probability } 0.01 \end{cases}$

Choice 2: Which of alternatives A2 or B2 would you prefer?

A2: $\begin{cases} \$1,000,000 \text{ with probability } 0.11 \\ \$0 \qquad \text{ with probability } 0.89 \end{cases}$

B2: $\begin{cases} \$5,000,000 \text{ with probability } 0.10 \\ \$0 \qquad \text{ with probability } 0.90 \end{cases}$

Essentially, Choice 2 is the same as Choice 1, except that $1,000,000 is subtracted from each of the items in Choice 1 with probability 0.89 to obtain the corresponding items in Choice 2. Therefore, according to the expected-utility criterion, anyone who prefers A1 to B1 in Choice 1 also should prefer A2 to B2 in Choice 2, and vice versa. However, experimental evidence shows that in practice, most people prefer A1 to B1 (presumably because they like the idea of gaining $1,000,000 with certainty, and do not want to accept even a 0.01 chance of getting $0 in return for a potential outcome of $5,000,000) and B2 to A2 (presumably because the 0.01 increase in the chance of getting $0 is not very significant when there is already a 0.89 chance of getting $0, and so it is worth taking this chance in return for the $5,000,000 potential).

So is this a failure of expected utility? Certainly, the experimental evidence discredits the *descriptive* value of the theory—that is, its value as a positive-economic model of what people actually do in certain circumstances. However, I would argue that there is no reason to believe that such evidence undermines the *prescriptive* value of the theory—that is, its value as a normative-economic model of what people should do in certain circumstances.

To a large extent, I agree with the assessment of American (Bayesian) statistician Leonard Savage, who, having selected inconsistent responses when first presented with Allais's problem, determined that he had simply made an irrational choice and that further thought enabled him to reconcile his two choices.[13] In my own case, I certainly would have selected A1 over B1 and B2 over A2 when I first saw the Allais problem some years ago, but now would choose B1 over A1 and B2 over A2. The principal reason for this change is that the potential regret that could arise from getting $0 after choosing B1 over A1 now strikes me as a somewhat irrational psychological concern that I would like to eliminate from my own decision making if possible. In summary, then, I find the Bayesian expected-utility worldview a comprehensive and cogent framework for prescriptive decision making.

ACT 1, SCENE 5

[A spacious and well-appointed office. Middle-aged man sits at large wooden desk; Grim Reaper approaches quietly.]

REAPER: Good afternoon, Mr. Wiley. I'm the Grim Reaper. Do you remember me?

MAN: Why yes, of course I do. How long has it been, Reaper? Twenty-five years? Thirty years?

REAPER: It's been a little more than thirty-three years.

MAN: Well, I can't say that I'm pleased to see you again so soon. But I would've been even less pleased to see you sooner. I guess you finally succeeded in making one of your free throws. How many tries did it actually take?

REAPER: If you must know, it was something over 17 million.

MAN: I see. Well, 17 million is a large number, but it's nothing compared to infinity. In the great scheme of things, I'd say you did relatively well.

REAPER: Yes, of course you're right. And you also seem to have done quite well for yourself.

MAN: [Looks around office modestly.] I can't complain. Professional statisticians are in great demand these days.

REAPER: [Sighs.] And no one demands you more than I.

MAN: Well, then, shall we go?

REAPER: [Unenthusiastically.] Yes, I suppose so.

MAN: Reaper, you don't seem your old self. I hope there are no hard feelings between us. If it would make you feel better, I'd be happy to offer another challenge: "double or nothing," so to speak. What I mean is, if I win, you don't come back for another thirty-three years, but if you win, I have to gather up one of your victims for you—say, a heartbreaking case, an innocent child, perhaps.

REAPER: [Eyes light up.] Really, would you? It would be somewhat irregular, of course. But I'd relish the chance to get even. What do you propose?

MAN: [Smiles, takes out two pieces of paper and two letter-sized envelopes.] OK, here's the challenge: I'm going to choose a positive real number, and write it down on one of these two pieces of paper without letting you see what it is. Let's call that number X. I'm then going to toss a fair coin and allow you to see the outcome: Heads or Tails. If the coin comes up Heads, I'm going to write $2 \times X$ on the other piece of paper—without letting you see it, of course; but if it comes up Tails, I'm going to write $(1/2) \times X$ on the other piece of paper—again without letting you see it. I'm then going to seal the two pieces of paper in the two separate envelopes, mix them up behind my back, and return them to my desk. You will get to choose one of the envelopes, open it, and look at the number inside. Given this number, you will have to tell me whether, on the average, the number in the other envelope is greater than, less than, or equal to the one you have just seen.

REAPER: How appropriate. Another problem involving averages. Well, I'm certainly up for that. Let's proceed.

[Man writes down first number, tosses coin (which comes up Heads), writes down second number, seals both numbers in envelopes, mixes up envelopes and returns them to desk. Grim Reaper chooses envelope and opens it to reveal "1".]

REAPER: OK. This is easy. Since your coin came up Heads, the number in my envelope must be either X or $2 \times X$. It doesn't matter what number I actually observed that number to be—in this case, it happened to be

1—because, by symmetry, either envelope is equally likely to contain the smaller number, X. Therefore, *on the average*, the number in the other envelope must be exactly equal to the number in my envelope.

MAN: Are you sure about that?

REAPER: Quite sure.

MAN: Good. Now let's look at things another way. As you noted, since my coin came up Heads, the number in your envelope must be either X or $2 \times X$. If X equals 1, then the other number must be 2, but if $2 \times X$ equals 1, then the other number must be 1/2. Therefore if, after observing the number 1, we determine that that 1 is equally likely to be either X or $2 \times X$, then the expected value of the other number is $2 \times (1/2) + (1/2) \times (1/2)$, which equals 1.5. But that, on the average, is greater than the 1 you observed.

REAPER: [Nervously.] But both conclusions can't be right—

MAN: Correct. Your error was in assuming that any number you observed was equally likely to be either X or $2 \times X$. For any particular number observed—say, the number 1—we can make that assumption. But if that assumption is made for all numbers that could be observed, then we find that our original X has to be chosen from a uniform distribution over the set of all positive real numbers—and that simply can't be done.

REAPER: Damn! Double damn!

MAN: Yes; it's certainly one or the other.

2

The Realm of Insurance

6

Aloofness and Quasi-Aloofness
Defining Insurance Risks

For he maketh his sun to rise on the evil and on the good, and sendeth rain on the just and on the unjust.
—GOSPEL OF SAINT MATTHEW, 5:45 (KING JAMES VERSION)

The question "What is insurance?" can be approached from two very different perspectives, each of which is crucial to a complete description of the concept. On the one hand, seeing insurance as a category of financial instrument for managing risk transforms the question to: What types of risks are appropriate for insurance products? On the other hand, viewing insurance as an established sector of the financial services industry leads to the alternative: What exactly constitutes an insurance company? The first of these two queries will be addressed in the present chapter; the second in Chapter 7.

To provide some institutional background, I will begin by reviewing a few salient points in the history of insurance markets, as well as the several sectors into which these markets are often divided. I then will develop a formal distinction between conventional insurance risks and noninsurance financial risks, showing that the former category derives from a set of random processes that is qualitatively different from that underlying the latter. Although I will not argue that the difference between these two categories of risk is so profound as to prohibit the convergence of financial markets, I do believe that this difference serves as a useful touchstone for insurance companies, investment entrepreneurs, and government regulators in evaluating various financial markets.

A Brief History of Insurance

The notion of an insurance contract traces its earliest historical roots to the use of *bottomry* contracts in Babylonian society of the third millennium B.C.[1] Under this type of arrangement, a land or marine trader would take out a loan of merchandise or money from a merchant, agreeing to a high rate of interest (usually at least 100 percent). If all went well, then the principal and interest would be paid at the end of the trading expedition; however, if the merchandise or money were lost or stolen, then the principal and interest would be forgiven. The merchant was compensated for assuming the risk of the trading venture through the large interest payment. The bottomry contract illustrates the concept of *risk transfer*, in which one party cedes responsibility for an uncertain outcome to another party, which party assumes the risk in return for some financial compensation.

A somewhat different practice developed among Chinese marine traders at around 3000 B.C. Rather than simply transferring all risk from one party to another, groups of traders established reciprocal arrangements in which each trader's store of merchandise was subdivided into small equal shares, each of which was carried on a different ship. In this way, no trader would be completely devastated by the sinking of one ship. This type of arrangement illustrates the concept of *risk pooling*, in which each member of a group cedes responsibility for small shares of its own uncertain outcome to the other members of the group and in return assumes similar shares of risk from the other members.

Throughout the ancient world of the Mediterranean, the Near East, and Asia, contracts of risk transfer and risk pooling permitted the growth and development of society and commerce. In ancient Greece and Rome, bottomry contracts for marine cargo became more formalized, and active markets developed in which bankers and merchants exchanged information on various risks, such as war, weather, and piracy. Greece and Rome also saw the creation of fraternal societies in which deceased members were provided a decent burial in return for their dues.

With the fall of the Roman Empire and the associated decline in trade, insurance activity also went into decline and did not evolve further until the fourteenth century. The oldest known "modern" insurance contract was issued in 1343 in Genoa.[2] In return for a premium payment, the insurer agreed to pay a stated sum to the insured if the latter's ship did not complete its voyage successfully. Over the next several centuries, the market for marine insurance grew and developed throughout the various Italian city-states and was exported to England by the sixteenth century.

Two events in seventeenth-century England further precipitated the development of the insurance industry as we know it today: (1) the establishment of Edward Lloyd's coffeehouse as a venue for merchants, bankers, and insurance underwriters to exchange information and negotiate marine insurance contracts; and (2) the Great Fire of London in 1666, which generated demand for fire insurance. In 1720, the first two modern fire insurance companies—the London Assurance Corporation and the Royal Exchange Assurance Corporation—were chartered as stock companies. Success in the fire insurance market spurred interest in life insurance, and in 1762, the first modern life insurance company—the Equitable Assurance Society—was formed as a mutual company (i.e., an enterprise owned by its policyholders). Lloyd's of London was organized as a formal association of marine underwriters in 1769 and exists to this day as an association of insurance and reinsurance syndicates whose investors provide capital and bid for insurance contracts through their underwriters.[3]

In colonial America, insurance companies were established in both the stock- and mutual-company forms. The growth of domestic fire insurers was assisted by the fact that the London Assurance and Royal Exchange Assurance corporations, which enjoyed a statutory monopoly in England, were not permitted to insure property in the colonies. In 1752, American scientist and statesman Benjamin Franklin participated in forming the first successful colonial fire insurance company—the Philadelphia Contributorship for the Insurance of Houses from Loss by Fire—as a mutual firm. In 1759, Franklin assisted the Presbyterian Church in organizing the first colonial life insurance company—the Presbyterian Ministers' Fund— also as a mutual. Following the American Revolution, the first two stock insurance companies were chartered by the Pennsylvania legislature in 1794: the Insurance Company of North America and the Insurance Company of Pennsylvania.

In recent decades, the international insurance industry has evolved in several directions. Since the 1960s, the *alternative insurance* market, composed of self-insurers, risk-retention groups, and captive insurance companies, has grown and matured. The 1980s and 1990s witnessed major changes in the nature of health insurance in the United States, with an increasing emphasis on managed-care delivery systems such as HMOs and PPOs. Current worldwide trends include the integration of traditional insurance with other financial services products and the globalization of insurance markets as various nations embark on the deregulation of their financial sectors.

Insurance Today

In the United States and most other industrialized nations, insurance companies are generally licensed to sell either: (1) *property-liability* insurance; or (2) *life-and-health* insurance. Although regulatory requirements may prevent one company from being licensed in both categories, corporate insurance groups frequently include members from both sectors. Although the lines of business written by property-liability and life-and-health insurance companies are substantially different, one area of overlap is the writing of *accident-and-health* insurance. Accident-and-health insurance also may be provided by various nonprofit health insurers, HMOs, PPOs, and similar health care delivery systems, as well as by self-insured employers.

Property-Liability Insurance

Property-liability insurance encompasses all lines of business associated with damage to property (including theft and loss) and injury to individuals (including occupational disease). Claim payments can be made on either a *first-party* basis to an affected policyholder[4] or on a *third-party* basis to compensate victims of a policyholder in tort cases. Although first-party benefits for loss of life generally fall within the domain of life insurance, such death benefits may be offered by property-liability insurance companies in certain relevant contexts, such as for automobile collision deaths covered by an automobile insurance policy.

The principal lines of property-liability insurance include: private passenger and commercial automobile; workers compensation; general, professional, and product liability; homeowners, commercial, and farmowners multiple peril; fire and allied lines; inland and ocean marine; and surety and fidelity. In addition, property-liability insurers write a substantial amount of accident and health coverage.

The various lines of property-liability insurance are often classified as either *personal lines,* for which the policyholders are individuals, or *commercial lines*, for which the policyholders are organizations. Personal lines include private passenger automobile and homeowners multiple peril, as well as personal fire, inland marine, and accident-and-health insurance. Commercial lines encompass most other property-liability products.

Property-liability policies often include restrictions limiting the amount of loss that the insurance company will pay to compensate the policyholder. These restrictions are of three general types: (1) *deductibles*, which require the policyholder to pay loss amounts up to a certain level, after which the insurance company takes over; (2) *limits*, which place a cap on the total amount that the insurance company will pay; and (3) *copayments*, which require the policyholder to pay a certain percentage of each loss amount, with the balance paid by the insurance company. The purpose of deductibles and copayments is generally to reduce problems of moral hazard and morale hazard (that is, situations in which the presence of insurance provides a financial incentive for the policyholder to increase risk),[5] whereas the purpose of limits is to protect the insurance company from unlimited, and therefore less predictable, losses. However, deductibles also are commonly used to eliminate smaller claims for which the administrative expense of processing the claim composes a significant portion of the total claim amount.

Life-and-Health Insurance

The life-and-health insurance sector includes lines of business associated with payments for loss of life, injury, and disease on a first-party basis and frequently encompasses annuity savings plans as well. The pure life insurance market is commonly broken down into three types of products: individual, group, and credit.

Individual life insurance includes traditional whole life, term life, and endowment and retirement income policies, as well as interest-sensitive universal life and variable life plans. Although usually purchased by individuals, these products also may be purchased by businesses that depend on the financial earnings of certain key employees. Life insurance offered by fraternal benefit societies is also counted in this category.

Group life insurance is purchased by individuals at a group rate made available through an employer, professional association, labor union, etc. Premiums for the group policy take into account the risk characteristics and operational expenses associated with the group as a whole, and premium payments for individual members (certificate holders) are usually lower than premiums for comparable individual life insurance policies. In employer-based groups, premiums may be paid, at least in part, by the individual's employer. Employees often can retain their life insurance coverage after retirement by paying premiums directly to the life insurance company.

Credit life insurance is purchased by individuals who have incurred debt to finance a major purchase, such as a house or an automobile. The credit insurance policy protects both the policyholder's beneficiaries and the lender by paying the debt in the event that the borrower dies before the loan is discharged. This type of life insurance can be bought on either an individual or a group basis.

As noted above, accident-and-health insurance is written by a variety of insurers other than property-liability and life-and-health insurance companies. These entities include nonprofit health insurers, HMOs, PPOs, and similar health care delivery systems. Like life insurance, accident-and-health coverage may be provided on either an individual or group basis.

Fundamental Types of Risk

The role of insurance products and firms within the broader financial services industry is frequently discussed and debated.[6] A number of scholars and practitioners have argued that the integration of financial services is inevitable because there is little meaningful distinction between insurance risks and other financial risks. According to this view, one should expect to see, inter alia: an increasing role for banks, with their large customer databases, in both commercial and personal insurance transactions; a growing number of insurance-based financial securities, bundled in a manner similar to mortgage-backed securities, trading on various financial exchanges; and the creation of insurance-linked debt instruments, such as *catastrophe bonds*,[7] by leading investment firms.

Institutional realities, however, cast some doubt on this assessment. The much-anticipated expansion of bancassurance has made only limited progress despite the reduction of regulatory barriers, and *property-catastrophe derivatives*—highly touted as an inexpensive and capacious alternative or supplement to reinsurance in the mid-1990s—were traded only briefly by the Chicago Board of Trade (CBOT) and the Bermuda Commodities Exchange before fizzling out. Although a reasonably serious catastrophe bond market has emerged, it remains rather modest in scope and has not substantially altered the overall landscape of the insurance/

reinsurance sector. So what are the essential differences between insurance and other financial services? And will these differences persist into the future?

Traditionally, distinctions between insurance and other financial risks have relied on either: (1) regulatory definitions and institutional terminology/jargon; or (2) attempts to draw a theoretical difference between the categories of *pure* risks (characterized by the negative outcomes—i.e., losses—common to insurance) and *speculative* risks (characterized by both positive and negative outcomes).[8] Although the latter approach may be intuitively attractive, it possesses little mathematical rigor. All that is needed to transform a pure risk into a speculative risk is to subtract its expected value; then, like a market price, it will have the potential of both increasing and decreasing.

As an alternative to the pure risk/speculative risk dichotomy, I would distinguish between the "aloof" and "quasi-aloof" risks of insurance and the "non-aloof" risks of other financial services markets. To this end, let us consider a theoretically exhaustive set of *financial random processes* and define *aloof* and *quasi-aloof random processes* as special subsets of this original set that can influence all financial random processes as they propagate through time, but are themselves relatively immune to the effects of non-aloof random processes. *Risks* are then defined as the random fluctuations in the various underlying processes at a given point in time. After showing in some detail that conventional insurance products are generally based upon aloof and quasi-aloof risks, I will explore the usefulness of the aloof risk/non-aloof risk dichotomy in the context of relevant applications.

Financial Random Processes

To motivate formal definitions of financial random processes and risks, let us consider the role of financial markets in the global economy. In a thoughtful and comprehensive essay on the role of money and financial institutions, mathematical-institutional economist Martin Shubik made the following observation:[9]

> The dynamic that triggers the actions of the financial system comes from many sources. It is consistent with scenarios such as that sketched by Schumpeter (1961);[10] the large literature on business cycles (see Minsky, 1986); or in more mathematical form has been suggested in

a shift in expectations caused by exogenous events such as sunspots (see Cass and Shell, 1983).

In short, the financial system exists to address the inevitable and ongoing deviations from market equilibrium as they emerge over time. Thus, it is only natural to define financial random processes and risks as the fundamental causes of market disequilibrium.

To this end, consider a global economy consisting of some large number of goods and services, and let **X** denote the set of all *fundamental financial random processes*, X, that can affect market equilibrium at some time t.[11] Naturally, this set is extremely abstract. In some cases, its individual elements may be represented conveniently by observable numerical time series (e.g., if X denotes the indexed value of a specific currency at time t). In other cases, however, the elements may exist only theoretically and at best be represented by real-world proxies (e.g., if X denotes the level of litigiousness in a given society at time t).

Since it is often more convenient to speak of risks than random processes, the former quantities will be defined as random fluctuations in the underlying random processes at a specific point in time. For a given X, the random deviation between this process and its conditional expected value taken just prior to time t, $\tilde{X}$, will be called the *financial risk* associated with X.

Degrees of Aloofness

Let us now define the concept of *aloofness*, which forms the basis for differentiating between insurance and noninsurance risks. Any element Y of a proper subset **Y** of **X** will be called an *aloof random process* if and only if all of the relevant statistical information about Y that exists just prior to time t is contained in **Y**. Gathering the Y over all possible subsets $\mathbf{Y_1}$, $\mathbf{Y_2}$, $\mathbf{Y_3}$, ... yields the set $\mathbf{Y_{All}}$ of all aloof random processes, as illustrated in Figure 6.1. For any given Y, the corresponding random deviation $\tilde{Y}$ will be called the *aloof risk* associated with Y.

The above definitions reveal that the set of aloof random processes is a very special subset of the set of all fundamental financial random processes, that is, a subset possessing the interesting property that its elements at time t are not statistically dependent on any elements of its complement at time t. Intuitively, this means that aloof random processes can influence all financial random processes as they move through time, but are themselves

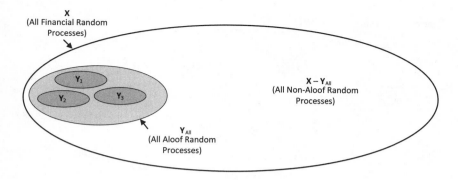

Figure 6.1
Aloof and Non-Aloof Random Processes

immune to the effects of non-aloof processes. Although the set of aloof processes may be thought of as *exogenous* to the set of non-aloof processes, it is important to keep in mind that individual aloof processes may not be exogenous to one another. It is for this reason that the term *aloof*, rather than the more familiar *exogenous*, is used to describe them.

Note that a given set **Y** may contain as few as one random process; and in fact, there is not yet any assurance that such sets even exist. To address this point specifically, I would propose the sunspots mentioned by Shubik above as a cogent example of an aloof risk. With their potentially deleterious impact on satellite and other telecommunication systems, but vast spatial displacement from terrestrial financial markets, there is little doubt that sunspots can affect, but not be affected by, other financial risks. Another aloof risk that is closely related to sunspot activity is solar-flare activity. Thus, the two random processes, Y_{Spots} and Y_{Flares} (based upon the numbers of "significant" sunspots and solar flares, respectively, in a given time interval), along with any other purely sun-generated processes, would constitute a nonsingleton set of aloof random processes, Y_{Sun}.

Realistically, of course, most insurance random processes are not as detached from terrestrial financial markets as those of Y_{Sun}. In fact, if one simply considers the loss payments associated with sunspot activity at time t, it can be seen that the financial random process associated with the currency unit of each loss payment becomes relevant. Thus, even if all loss payments may be expressed in U.S. dollars, the amounts of the actual payments will be affected by the value of that currency at time t—a random

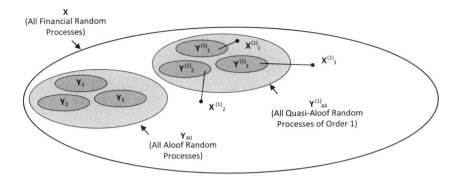

Figure 6.2
Quasi-Aloof Random Processes of Order 1

process that clearly is non-aloof in nature. Consequently, to build a theory of insurance risks that both recognizes the concept of aloofness and provides a reasonably accurate reflection of the real world requires that the aloofness concept be weakened somewhat.

To this end, let each element $Y^{(1)}$ of a subset $\mathbf{Y}^{(1)}$ of all non-aloof random processes be called a *quasi-aloof random process of order 1* if and only if all of the information about $Y^{(1)}$ that exists just prior to time t is contained in $\mathbf{Y}^{(1)}$ and/or $\mathbf{X}^{(1)}$, for some set $\mathbf{X}^{(1)}$ of exactly 1 non-aloof random process that is outside of $\mathbf{Y}^{(1)}$. This concept is illustrated in Figure 6.2.

More generally, each element $Y^{(k)}$ of a subset $\mathbf{Y}^{(k)}$ will be called a *quasi-aloof random process of order k* if and only if all of the information about $Y^{(k)}$ that exists just prior to time t is contained in $\mathbf{Y}^{(k)}$ and/or $\mathbf{X}^{(k)}$, for some appropriately chosen set $\mathbf{X}^{(k)}$ of exactly k non-aloof random processes. For any k, the set of non-aloof random processes $\mathbf{X}^{(k)}$ associated with the set of quasi-aloof random processes $\mathbf{Y}^{(k)}$ will be called the *attendant set* of $\mathbf{Y}^{(k)}$. For small values of k, the above definitions show that the set of quasi-aloof random processes of order k is similar to the set of aloof random processes in that its elements at time t are statistically dependent on only very few elements of its complement at time t.

Let us now turn to the relationship between aloof (and quasi-aloof) risks and the financial risks traditionally covered by insurance products. Although I do not believe that these two sets of risks are necessarily identical, I will argue that aloof and quasi-aloof risks form the core of the insurance industry.

Insurance Risks

The heuristic argument in support of the aloof/non-aloof dichotomy is quite simple. Insurance risks (such as solar flares, vehicle collisions, and individual deaths) are detached from other financial risks and thus cannot be financed through the use of correlated investments from the financial markets. These risks therefore must be addressed through insurance products. Conversely, noninsurance financial risks (such as stock, bond, and currency-index returns) are quite easily managed through the financial markets and so have little need for insurance.

Table 6.1 presents breakdowns of two different financial random processes associated with each of a number of the most common sources of insurance risk. The sources are listed along the leftmost column and arranged in four general categories: (A) Extraterrestrial and Meteorological Events; (B) Other Unintentional Events; (C) Intentional Events and Moral Hazards; and (D) Negligence. The two financial random processes considered for each source are: (1) claim frequency, expressed as the number of loss events per exposure unit; and (2) loss severity, expressed as the dollar amount of damages per claim. For a given underlying source along the left column, the cells under the two random processes list the relevant attendant random processes, along with the number (k) of attendant processes.

This table is intended for illustrative purposes only and does not necessarily provide a comprehensive or definitive list of the attendant random processes associated with each of the aloof and quasi-aloof random processes identified. However, the table does suggest, at least conceptually, that the random processes associated with traditional insurance products tend to be quasi-aloof processes of fairly low order (i.e., k is less than or equal to 6). On the claim-frequency side, the claim-count processes underlying insurance losses are sometimes influenced by a society's overall level of prosperity, as when a recessionary economy leads to fewer automobile collision claims (because of less driving) or more workers compensation and disability claims (because of the fear of unemployment). On the loss-severity side, all insurance payments, regardless of the line of business involved, are affected by the relevant currency, which is highly sensitive to a number of non-aloof financial risks (interest rates, currency exchange rates, etc.).

As an example, consider the first source in category A (Sunspots) for which there is one attendant random process—Technology—for the claim frequency and two attendant processes—Currency and Technology—for

Table 6.1
Insurance Frequency and Severity Random Processes (with Their Attendant Random Processes)

	Frequency and Severity Random Processes (with Attendant Random Processes in Italics,* and Value of k in Parentheses)	
Underlying Source	Claim Frequency (Number of Events per Exposure Unit)	Loss Severity (Dollar Amount of Total Damages per Event)
A. Extraterrestrial and Meteorological Events		*Currency* +
Sunspots	*Technology* ($k=1$)	*Technology* ($k=2$)
Solar flares	*Technology* ($k=1$)	*Technology* ($k=2$)
Asteroid/comet impacts	($k=0$)	($k=1$)
Earthquakes	*Construction* ($k=1$)	*Construction, Medicine* ($k=3$)
Storms	*Construction* ($k=1$)	*Construction, Medicine* ($k=3$)
Floods	*Construction* ($k=1$)	*Construction, Medicine* ($k=3$)
Droughts	*Planning* ($k=1$)	*Planning, Medicine* ($k=3$)
B. Other Unintentional Events	*Safety* +	*Currency* + *Medicine* +
House fires	*Construction* ($k=2$)	*Construction* ($k=3$)
Business fires	*Construction* ($k=2$)	*Construction* ($k=3$)
Vehicle collisions	*Construction* ($k=2$)	*Construction* ($k=3$)
Plane crashes	*Communication, Construction* ($k=3$)	*Construction* ($k=3$)
Personal injuries/deaths	($k=1$)	($k=2$)
Personal illnesses/deaths	*Wellness* ($k=2$)	*Wellness* ($k=3$)
Worker deaths	*Wellness* ($k=2$)	*Wellness* ($k=3$)
C. Intentional Events and Moral Hazards	*Safety* + *Law Enforcement* +	*Currency* + *Safety* + *Law Enforcement* +
Thefts/fraud	*Prosperity* ($k=3$)	*Prosperity* ($k=4$)
Vandalism	*Prosperity* ($k=3$)	*Prosperity* ($k=4$)
Terrorist attacks	*Politics, Construction* ($k=4$)	*Politics, Construction, Medicine* ($k=6$)
Assault injuries	*Prosperity* ($k=3$)	*Prosperity, Medicine* ($k=5$)
Murders/suicides	*Prosperity* ($k=3$)	*Prosperity, Medicine* ($k=5$)
Worker injuries	*Prosperity* ($k=3$)	*Prosperity, Medicine* ($k=5$)
Worker illnesses	*Prosperity, Wellness* ($k=4$)	*Prosperity, Wellness, Medicine* ($k=6$)
Disability	*Prosperity, Wellness* ($k=4$)	*Prosperity, Wellness, Medicine* ($k=6$)
D. Negligence	*Safety* + *Litigiousness* +	*Currency* + *Safety* + *Litigiousness* +
E&O liability	($k=2$)	($k=3$)
D&O liability	($k=2$)	($k=3$)
Vehicle liability	*Prosperity, Construction* ($k=4$)	*Prosperity, Construction, Medicine* ($k=6$)
Personal liability	*Prosperity, Construction* ($k=4$)	*Prosperity, Construction, Medicine* ($k=6$)

Table 6.1
(*Continued*)

	Frequency and Severity Random Processes (with Attendant Random Processes in Italics,* and Value of *k* in Parentheses)	
Underlying Source	Claim Frequency (Number of Events per Exposure Unit)	Loss Severity (Dollar Amount of Total Damages per Event)
D. Negligence	*Safety + Litigiousness +*	*Currency + Safety + Litigiousness +*
Commercial liability	*Prosperity, Construction (k = 4)*	*Prosperity, Construction, Medicine (k = 6)*
Product liability	*Prosperity, Construction (k = 4)*	*Prosperity, Construction, Medicine (k = 6)*
Pollution liability	*Prosperity, Construction (k = 4)*	*Prosperity, Construction, Medicine (k = 6)*
Medical liability	*Prosperity, Medicine (k = 4)*	*Prosperity, Medicine (k = 5)*

* The various attendant random processes appearing in the table may be interpreted as follows: *Technology* = average quality of technological devices produced by a society; *Construction* = average quality of building construction in a society; *Planning* = average quality of emergency planning by government and/or society in general; *Safety* = average level of safety practiced by society as a whole; *Wellness* = average healthiness of individuals in a society; *Law Enforcement* = average effectiveness of law-enforcement efforts by both government and individuals; *Prosperity* = average level of wealth of a society; *Politics* = political stability of a society; *Litigiousness* = average intensity of litigation in a society; *Medicine* = average effectiveness of medicine as practiced in a society; and *Currency* = value of the currency used.

the loss severity. This means that the claim-frequency random process is governed by only two underlying effects: the number of significant sunspots during a given time period and the average quality of exposed technological devices (e.g., satellites and other electronic communication equipment) during the corresponding period. Although the latter random process exists only abstractly (or approximately) in the real world, that is beside the point. The fact that one can identify a unique attendant process in addition to the sunspot process reveals that the claim-frequency process is nearly independent of all other financial processes; in other words, it is quasi-aloof.

A more complex example is afforded by the last source in category D (Medical Liability) for which the claim frequency possesses four attendant random processes—Safety, Litigiousness, Prosperity, and Medicine—and the loss severity possesses five—the four just mentioned plus Currency. Here again, several of the attendant random processes (especially those representing society's average levels of safety and litigiousness and the average effectiveness of medicine) exist only abstractly in the real world. In this case, the claim-frequency and loss-severity processes are clearly less aloof than those in the sunspots example.

Macro and Micro Risks

Although abstract in nature, the above separation of financial risks into aloof/quasi-aloof insurance risks versus non-aloof noninsurance risks offers a number of practical uses for insurance companies, derivative-product entrepreneurs, and government regulators. As new risks emerge, insurance firms and investment entrepreneurs (i.e., market makers) require an effective way of determining whether the new risk should be handled by traditional insurance, new derivative products, or perhaps both. Then, as new risk financing mechanisms are created, both insurance and securities regulators must have a clear and logical way of distinguishing between insurance products on the one hand and investment securities on the other. Finally, understanding the differences between insurance and noninsurance risks can help both insurance companies and investment entrepreneurs explore potential areas of synergy between traditional insurance products and other noninsurance financial products.

One intriguing example of a relatively new risk financing product is weather derivatives. Initially developed in the mid-1990s as over-the-counter securities primarily for power companies to stabilize cash flows, these instruments have become popular within a number of business sectors with weather-sensitive revenues (e.g., agriculture, construction, and travel/hospitality). In 1999, weather derivatives became exchange-traded when the Chicago Mercantile Exchange (CME) began offering futures and options based upon average monthly and seasonal temperatures. As of 2010, these derivatives were available for eighteen U.S. cities and a comparable number of non-U.S. cities.

Since weather in general, and urban temperature fluctuations in particular, represent relatively aloof risks, it is quite natural to ask: Why are these risks financed by noninsurance financial products rather than traditional insurance?

To answer this question requires a refinement of the aloof/non-aloof dichotomy. Specifically, it must be recognized that aloof and quasi-aloof risks come in very different "sizes." Consider, for example, the cases of solar-flare activity on the one hand and vehicle collisions on the other. When a major solar flare occurs, that single event can have broad, possibly catastrophic, implications as satellites and other communication devices around the world are affected. When two automobiles collide, however, the event is extremely limited both in location and magnitude.

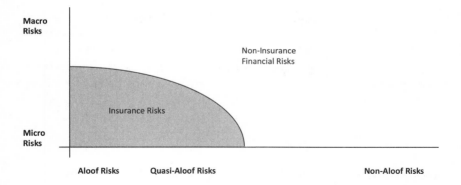

Figure 6.3
The Realm of Insurance Risks

Obviously, there is no clear demarcation between large aloof/quasi-aloof risks of the former type and small aloof/quasi-aloof risks of the latter. Nevertheless, it is easy to see that the more pervasive, or *macro*, risks—such as solar, meteorological, and seismic activity—afford the opportunity to create derivative indexes that can be used by numerous affected parties to offset such risks; whereas the more limited, or *micro*, risks—such as accidents, thefts, and individual mortality—do not. Consequently, although insurance and noninsurance financial markets have been divided historically along aloof/non-aloof lines, the enhanced technology of contemporary financial markets makes the creation of noninsurance financial products for macro aloof/quasi-aloof risks more likely, and perhaps inevitable. In short, I would anticipate that the future division between insurance and noninsurance financial markets will be governed by the schematic plot in Figure 6.3, in which the lower left corner, associated with micro aloof/quasi-aloof risks, will remain the domain of a clearly distinct insurance industry.

Given this analysis, it remains rather puzzling that the CBOT's exchange-traded property-catastrophe derivatives died out at just about the same time that the CME's market for exchange-traded weather derivatives was beginning to prosper. Although there are any number of possible explanations for this disparity—regulatory restrictions on the trading of catastrophe derivatives by insurance companies, trader skepticism about the transparency of catastrophe-loss indexes, etc.—probably the best explanation is simply one of institutional incumbency. In the case of property-catastrophe risk, a viable traditional insurance/reinsurance market already existed prior to the CBOT's initiative, and injections of capital into the reinsurance market in the 1990s were able to compete successfully with catastrophe derivatives; in the case of weather risk, no traditional insurance market existed prior to the CME's efforts, so the derivative market was uncontested in its development.

ACT 2, SCENE 1

[Same psychiatrist's office. Doctor sits in chair; patient sits on couch.]

DOCTOR: Mrs. Morton, it's good to see you again. How have things been?

PATIENT: Well, Doctor, I'm pleased to say that my hydraphobia is completely under control.

DOCTOR: I see. That's certainly good news. How did you manage the turnaround?

PATIENT: It was quite easy, really. I simply borrowed an idea from the field of risk management. You see, after identifying a risk, a risk manager is supposed to determine whether it's best to try to *mitigate* the risk—say, by taking preventive measures—or to *transfer* the risk—say, by purchasing insurance. If neither of those alternatives seems reasonable, then the risk manager may want to *avoid* the risk. So that's what I've done: I've decided to avoid hydras.

DOCTOR: *Avoidance*, eh? Mrs. Morton, I should advise you that, despite what might be the current fad in the world of ... what did you call it? "risk banishment"? ... we tend to frown on avoidance as a strategy in psychiatry. You see, once a phobic patient learns to avoid the source of her fear, she soon begins to avoid other sources of fear and difficulty ... and her world becomes smaller and smaller. For example, today you may decide to avoid water—

PATIENT: What? Not water—*hydras*.

DOCTOR: Yes, hydras, which, of course, live in water. So today you may decide to avoid ponds because of hydras, then tomorrow you may decide to avoid lakes because of water nymphs, and the next day you may decide to avoid oceans because of sea serpents.

PATIENT: I don't quite understand, Doctor. Hydras exist, whereas water nymphs and sea serpents are mythological.

DOCTOR: But so are hydras ... I believe. Wasn't there a story about Hercules killing a nasty hydra, or some such thing?

PATIENT: Yes. [Pauses.] Permit me to change the subject for a moment. I think I see your point about the limitations of avoidance as a strategy. And that actually leads me to the main problem I wanted to discuss today.

DOCTOR: And what would that be?

PATIENT: Unfortunately, it appears that I've developed another phobia: a fear of asteroid impacts. You know, like the one that killed the dinosaurs millions of years ago.

DOCTOR: I see—a fear of asteroids. Perhaps we should call it "asterophobia." Yes, asterophobia—what do you think of that, eh?

PATIENT: I suppose it's a fine name for my problem. But I was hoping you could suggest a way of dealing with it.

DOCTOR: Well, tell me, when did you first notice this particular phobia, asterophobia—yes, I like that!—emerge?

PATIENT: Ah, that's very interesting. It actually was triggered by something you said during my last visit. You had suggested that perhaps my death wasn't the worst thing that could happen; and as I thought about it, I realized you were quite right. I certainly should have been thinking more about others than about myself. So that caused me to consider just how bad it would be if everyone died—if the human race became extinct, so to speak. And that's when I first began to worry about asteroid impacts.

DOCTOR: Hmm. A phobia brought about by a discussion with me. A condition caused by one's doctor. There's a word for that, you know: *iatrogenic*. It means "caused by one's doctor." [Pauses.] Say, you're not thinking of suing me for that, are you?

PATIENT: No, of course not. The idea never crossed my mind . . . until now. [Pauses.] But anyway, Doctor, returning to the point: How do you suggest I deal with my fear of asteroids?

DOCTOR: Yes, your asterophobia—your iatrogenic asterophobia, to be precise. Well, in cases such as this, I always recommend the same thing.

PATIENT: And what would that be?

DOCTOR: Oh, it's quite simple. Just avoid the problem.

PATIENT: Avoid? But I thought you said earlier—? [Pauses.] But how could I avoid the problem of asteroid impacts anyway, unless I had a spaceship or something?

DOCTOR: No, no, no. You've missed my point entirely. I'm not suggesting that you can avoid an asteroid impact. Heavens, what do you take me for, a nutcase?

PATIENT: Uh—

DOCTOR: No, no. I was just pointing out that the best way to deal with phobias is always the same: simply avoid *thinking* about them!

7

Trustworthy Transfer; Probable Pooling
Financing Insurance Risks

People Who Do Things exceed my endurance;
God, for a man that solicits insurance!
—DOROTHY PARKER ("BOHEMIA," *SUNSET GUN*, 1928)[1]

I now wish to turn to the issue of what constitutes an insurance company. From the previous chapter, it is evident that such a firm somehow must engage in financial transactions involving aloof and quasi-aloof risks. However, the exact nature of these transactions is not absolutely clear. One fundamental ambiguity is whether a firm must engage in *both* risk transfer *and* risk pooling—that is, the two fundamental risk finance transactions that have been with us since the dawn of history—to be an insurance company. As will be seen, this question is fundamental to the legal definition of insurance as refined in U.S. case law.

I will begin by examining the basic organizational forms and operational functions of insurance companies as encountered in the most common institutional settings. Although these characteristics are fairly well defined in traditional insurance markets, they become less evident in the so-called alternative markets. Not surprisingly, it is in such less-traditional markets that a clear, guiding definition of an insurance company is most desirable.

Insurance Institutions

Organizational Forms

An insurance company may have one of a variety of ownership structures: *stock, mutual, reciprocal exchange, syndicate,* or *nonprofit.*[2] Stock insurance companies, like other stock corporations, are owned by shareholders who have purchased common stock and have the right to vote for members of the firm's board of directors. Mutuals and reciprocal exchanges are owned by their policyholders—the former existing as incorporated entities in which the policyholders elect the board of directors, and the latter as agreements among the policyholders formalized by a power-of-attorney transfer to the firm's management. Syndicates, like those of Lloyd's of London, are owned by groups of investors whose underwriters bid for insurance contracts against other syndicates. Nonprofit insurance companies operate much as other nonprofit organizations, but may be formed in accordance with laws and regulations designed specifically for nonprofit insurance entities.

Company Operations

With regard to business operations, there may be substantial diversity among insurance companies within a given market. However, general patterns of institutional practice reveal that certain operations are intrinsic to the insurance business. These include:

1. *writing contracts of insurance,* through which the responsibility for financial loss from an aloof or quasi-aloof risk is transferred to the insurance company in return for a premium payment made by the policyholder;
2. *bearing risk,* by taking ultimate responsibility for the payment of random loss amounts that may be substantially greater than premiums collected;
3. *complying with insurance regulation,* by securing company and agent licenses necessary to sell insurance, by satisfying required solvency standards, and by receiving the approval of policy forms and rates subject to regulatory authority;

4. *pricing*, by selecting premium levels to achieve a certain profit given an anticipated portfolio of policyholders;

5. *underwriting*, by selecting a portfolio of policyholders with various risk characteristics, where the losses generated by the selected policyholders are expected to allow a certain profit given current premium levels;

6. *claim management*, through which reported claims are evaluated to identify appropriate payments and loss reserves, unreported claims are forecast to establish additional loss reserves, paid losses may be offset by salvage and subrogation efforts, and potential fraud is investigated and challenged;

7. *loss control*, by designing products and setting prices to reduce moral hazard, morale hazard, and adverse selection and by working with policyholders to prevent and mitigate losses;

8. *financial management*, through which the insurance company's invested assets are managed to achieve the desired balance between risk and return, as well as the matching of investment income with future loss payments, all subject to regulatory constraints on the types of investments permitted;

9. *marketing*, through which new primary and reinsurance business is generated and old business is retained, in concert with the marketing efforts of any brokers and independent agents involved in the production of business; and

10. *administration*, through which the various operations of the company are coordinated and accounting, auditing, and legal functions are carried out.

Although most traditional insurance companies perform the above operations in-house, it is not unusual for companies to outsource one or more of these functions to specialty firms. This is particularly true within the alternative insurance market, consisting of self-insurers (i.e., corporations that estimate and set aside financial reserves to cover their anticipated losses from aloof and quasi-aloof risks), risk-retention groups (i.e., groups of corporations that join together to form collective self-insurance funds), and captive insurance companies (i.e., subsidiary companies formed primarily to write insurance for their parent corporations). Interestingly, however, the risk bearing practices of these alternative entities do not deviate dramatically from those of traditional insurance companies. Although the alternative market does tend to place greater emphasis on the bearing of risk by policyholders, this is conceptually no different from what is commonly found in the mutuals and reciprocal exchanges of the traditional market.

Enterprise Risk Management

Whatever the particular corporate form and internal systems of an insurance company, its financial bottom line is given by its total rate of return (TROR), which may be expressed as follows for a fixed accounting period:

$$\text{Total Rate of Return} = \frac{\left(\begin{array}{c}\text{Earned Premiums} - \text{Incurred Losses} - \text{Earned} \\ \text{Expenses} + \text{Investment Gains} - \text{Income Taxes}\end{array}\right)}{\text{Average Net Worth}}.$$

The TROR represents the insurance company's earnings, net of taxes, as a proportion of the capital (net worth) invested in the insurance enterprise and is a random quantity that fluctuates with the company's underwriting and investment results. The process of managing the company's TROR—called *enterprise risk management* (ERM)—is a fundamental responsibility of the company's officers and directors and often is accomplished by optimizing the trade-off between the TROR's expected value and standard deviation (i.e., by *mean-standard deviation optimization*) supplemented by scenario-based stress testing using VaR and other tail-sensitive risk measures. If the tail of the TROR's probability distribution is too heavy for the standard deviation to be finite, then mean-standard deviation optimization obviously cannot be used, and one must rely on alternative measures such as those discussed in Chapter 3.

To provide an overview of an insurance company's ERM program, I will assume that the expected value of the TROR is well defined and that it possesses a fixed "target" expected value, thus leaving the company with the issue of minimizing the TROR's variability. The ERM process then consists of four basic steps: (1) *risk identification*; (2) *risk assessment*; (3) *risk control*; and (4) *risk finance*.[3]

Risk Identification and Assessment

Quite naturally, the first step is the identification of all risks—aloof, quasi-aloof, and non-aloof—that the insurance company faces. Given the particular components of insurance operations summarized above, it is clear that these risks consist primarily of the losses paid to policyholders according to the terms of the various policy contracts sold, as well as the investment returns earned on both net worth and the premium-income stream prior to the payment of losses.

After all significant risks have been identified, an insurance company must assess the overall importance of each risk in terms of its potential impact on the firm. For the aloof and quasi-aloof risks associated with insurance underwriting, this is accomplished by estimating the expected value and variability of both the claim frequency and loss severity associated with each policyholder, along with statistical dependencies among policyholders (e.g., two buildings in the same coastal region may be vulnerable to damage from the same hurricane and therefore have positively correlated frequencies and severities). For non-aloof investment risks, the company similarly must estimate the expected values and variabilities of individual returns, as well as statistical dependencies among returns. In the case of investments, positive and negative correlations often play a much larger role, as would be expected from the fundamental character of non-aloof risks.

Risk Control and Finance

Figure 7.1 provides conceptual guidelines for controlling an insurance company's aloof and quasi-aloof underwriting risks through the techniques of *frequency mitigation*, *severity mitigation*, and *avoidance*.

If a given exposure possesses a high expected frequency, but only a low or modest expected severity, then frequency mitigation is appropriate. For example, an insurance company offering property coverage for a low-value apartment building with numerous individual units—each of which could be the source of an accidental fire—is likely to address the high expected frequency by requiring the owner to install fire extinguishers and sprinkler systems. However, if an exposure possesses a high expected severity, but only a low or modest expected frequency, then severity mitigation is appropriate. For example, an insurance company writing medical malpractice liability coverage for a hospital with a small maternity ward—and therefore the potential of expensive "damaged baby" claims—is likely to address the high expected severity by taking an active role in claim set-

High	**SEVERITY MITIGATION**		**AVOIDANCE**
Expected Severity			
Low	**(Not Applicable)**		**FREQUENCY MITIGATION**
	Low		**High**

Expected Frequency

Figure 7.1
Risk Control for Aloof/Quasi-Aloof Risks (Conceptual)

tlement negotiations. Finally, if an exposure is characterized by both a high expected frequency and high expected severity, then total avoidance is likely the best approach. An example of this is the writing of asbestos liability coverage for a large asbestos-manufacturing plant with a poor safety record.

For non-aloof investment risks, the paradigm of Figure 7.1 is less directly applicable because investment returns generally cannot be broken down so neatly into separate frequency and severity components. However, one certainly could equate severity mitigation and/or avoidance with deliberate efforts to eschew highly volatile investments, such as financial options, junk bonds, and certain categories of real estate.

Figure 7.2 summarizes "textbook" guidelines for reducing the variability of an insurance company's aloof and quasi-aloof underwriting risks through the methods of *diversification* (via risk pooling) and *hedging* (via risk transfer).[4] Having avoided (during the risk control step) those unacceptably costly exposures with both high expected frequencies and high expected severities, an insurance company can focus on the exposures exhibiting high expected frequencies or high expected severities alone. In the former case, the likely presence of a great number of similar and statistically independent claims permits the company to take advantage of the law of large numbers (LLN) by risk pooling/diversification.[5] In the latter case—which includes regional catastrophes such as hurricanes, earthquakes, and even terrorist attacks—there presumably is an insufficient number of claims to diversify successfully, so the insurance company is more likely to employ risk transfer/hedging by purchasing reinsurance

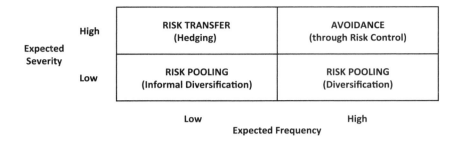

Figure 7.2
Risk Finance for Aloof/Quasi-Aloof Risks (Conceptual)

from another company. For exposures with both relatively low expected frequencies and relatively low expected severities, the insurance company will continue to pool (retain) these risks, but will do so informally (i.e., with less explicit contemplation of the LLN).

Although the scheme indicated by Figure 7.2 seems intuitively plausible, it presents two conceptual difficulties:

• By indicating risk transfer for exposures with low expected frequencies but arbitrarily high expected severities, the conventional paradigm suggests that there is always some reinsurance company willing to assume (and presumably pool) those catastrophe losses. However, this is inconsistent with actual market experience, in which certain types of catastrophe exposures—for example, damages from terrorist attacks—are not readily covered by private reinsurance.

• There is an apparent inconsistency between the effect of increasing expected frequencies on losses with low expected severities and those with high expected severities. In the former case, diversification appears to apply because risk pooling is effective for higher expected frequencies, whereas in the latter case, diversification does not appear to work because the firm must resort to avoidance. One possible explanation for this discrepancy is that losses with higher expected severities also possess heavier tails, thus inhibiting diversification. However, there is no obvious theoretical or empirical reason this should be true.

To reconcile Figure 7.2 with the above two objections requires the formal mathematical modeling of loss portfolios and a careful study of the

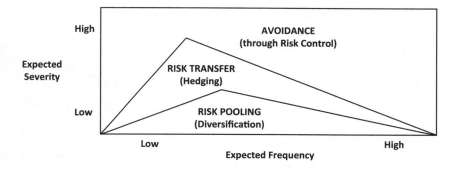

Figure 7.3
Risk Finance for Aloof/Quasi-Aloof Risks (More Realistic)

boundaries separating the regions of risk pooling, risk transfer, and avoidance. Given the potentially significant role of heavy tails, it is particularly important to evaluate the decreasing benefits of risk pooling as the tails of the relevant loss distributions become heavier.

One such analysis, based upon a Lévy-stable approximation to a sum of Pareto losses, and employing the CBSD risk measure discussed in Chapter 3, yields Figure 7.3 as a more realistic and conservative alternative to Figure 7.2.[6] Essentially, the new paradigm favors the safer alternative (i.e., avoidance over risk transfer, risk transfer over risk pooling) whenever there is ambiguity as to the optimal risk financing method. Therefore, beginning with the apex of either boundary (i.e., the upper one between avoidance and risk transfer, or the lower one between risk transfer and risk pooling), the indicated boundary must be *increasing on the left* as the relative efficacy of diversification grows over expected frequency for light-tailed losses and *decreasing on the right* as the relative efficacy of diversification diminishes over expected frequency for heavy-tailed losses.

For non-aloof investment risks, Figure 7.3 is less directly applicable because, as mentioned above, investment returns generally cannot be broken down into separate frequency and severity components. Consequently, the financing of investment risks is typically handled by selecting optimal diversification and hedging strategies in a risk-vs.-return analysis. This type of approach, like Figure 7.3, must account for the presence of heavy-tailed return distributions as necessary.

A Simple Model of Risk Finance

Given the complexities of modern insurance and other financial markets, it is rather remarkable that the financing of an insurance company's aloof, quasi-aloof, and non-aloof risks is based largely upon only *two* fundamental tools: diversification and hedging.[7] Interestingly, these two methods match precisely the two earliest forms of "insurance" attributed to the ancients: the division and swapping of cargoes among ships (diversification through risk pooling) and the use of bottomry contracts (hedging through risk transfer). To explore the properties of these two methods more deeply, and also to highlight the importance of a *third* tool of risk finance that is often overlooked, I will consider a simple analysis of the variability of a random loss or investment portfolio with finite standard deviation as the portfolio undergoes diversification and/or hedging.

Conceptually, diversification describes the marginal reduction in variability that occurs when the individual components of a portfolio become *less positively correlated* with each other, whereas hedging describes the marginal reduction in variability that arises when the individual components become *more negatively correlated* with each other. In both cases, it is assumed that these processes are implemented while keeping the overall expected value unchanged. Also, the qualification "marginal" is used to indicate that, although both processes should contribute toward some reduction in variability, there is no guarantee that either process, by itself, will reduce the portfolio's total variability.

Mathematically, both processes can be captured using a simple "before-and-after" description of the portfolio. I will begin by modeling the initial portfolio as a random variable, X, which may be viewed as the sum of any number of distinct random components (e.g., insurance losses, stocks, cash, etc.) that can be mutually statistically independent or dependent. I then will assume that a portion of this portfolio, to be called X_{Out}, is removed, and that another component, called X_{In}, is simultaneously added. In short, the "before" portfolio consists of X, and the "after" portfolio consists of $X - X_{Out} + X_{In}$.

Now, if one wants the exchange of X_{In} for X_{Out} to reduce the total variability (as measured by the standard deviation), then $SD[X - X_{Out} + X_{In}]$ must be less than $SD[X]$. Defining the subportfolio X_{Keep} as the difference $X - X_{Out}$, it can be shown that there are a number of ways this reduction in variability can be accomplished based upon the relationships among the three standard deviations—$SD[X_{Keep}]$, $SD[X_{Out}]$, and $SD[X_{In}]$—and the two pairwise correlations—$Corr[X_{Keep}, X_{Out}]$ and $Corr[X_{Keep}, X_{In}]$.

Devilish Diversification

Formally, one can say that diversification occurs if $Corr[X_{Keep}, X_{Out}]$ is positive and greater than $Corr[X_{Keep}, X_{In}]$—in other words, if the portfolio is changed so that the resulting components are less positively correlated with each other. (Note that although $Corr[X_{Keep}, X_{In}]$ is often nonnegative in practice, there is no reason to make this a strict requirement of the definition of diversification.) As previously noted, one example of diversification is the retention of uncorrelated aloof/quasi-aloof risks by an insurance company (i.e., risk pooling). However, it is crucial to point out that such pooling must be accompanied by concomitant increases in the company's invested capital so that the standard deviation of the total loss amount per ownership share decreases. This is analogous to increasing the number of boats as the total amount of cargo increases in the Chinese marine-trader story. If the amount of invested capital does not increase, and the insurance company simply pools a growing number of exposures, then this is comparable to stacking more and more cargo in a fixed number of boats, and a type of "false diversification," in which the standard deviation actually *increases*, takes place.

For an insurance example in which it is unnecessary to assume increasing invested capital, consider an insurance company with a fixed amount of capital that elects to swap part of a group of insured Florida property exposures (subject to hurricane catastrophe risk) for part of another company's insured California property exposures (subject to earthquake catastrophe risk). For non-aloof risks, an analogous example would arise from replacing some of the shares of one asset by those of another in an investment portfolio. Nevertheless, even with such simpler forms of diversification, there is still a devil lurking in the details. Specifically, $SD[X - X_{Out} + X_{In}]$ can easily be greater than $SD[X]$ if $SD[X_{In}]$ is too large compared to $SD[X_{Out}]$.

Heavenly Hedging

Next, one can say that hedging occurs if $Corr[X_{Keep}, X_{In}]$ is negative and less than $Corr[X_{Keep}, X_{Out}]$—that is, if the portfolio is altered so that the resulting components are more negatively correlated with each other. (In this case, note that $Corr[X_{Keep}, X_{Out}]$ often is 0 in practice because X_{Out} is cash that is used to purchase the hedging instrument X_{In}; however, there is no reason to impose this condition on the definition of hedging.) As noted above, an insurance company's purchase of a reinsurance policy to offset aloof/quasi-aloof risks constitutes one example of hedging (i.e., risk transfer). For non-aloof risks, purchasing one or more asset derivatives to offset part of an investment portfolio provides a comparable example of hedging.

With hedging, things generally are much more "blessed" than with diversification. This is because there is no obvious possibility of "false hedging," and $SD[X - X_{Out} + X_{In}]$ is generally likely to be less than $SD[X]$.

Purloined Pacification

Finally, one can say that *pacification* occurs if $SD[X_{In}]$ is less than $SD[X_{Out}]$—that is, if the portfolio is changed by replacing a portion with something less variable. This idea is quite simple and obvious, but—like Edgar Allen Poe's purloined letter—appears to be overlooked by being "hidden in plain sight."[8] I have chosen the term "pacification" to suggest the calming or tranquilizing influence of the process on a portion of the original portfolio, and the process is essentially the opposite of gambling—that is, the taking of unnecessary risks for excitement.

The fundamental importance of pacification is seen very clearly by noting that: (1) neither the process of diversification nor that of hedging, by itself, can guarantee a reduction in a portfolio's total variability, even with $Corr[X_{Keep}, X_{Out}]$ as large as possible (i.e., 1) in the former case, and $Corr[X_{Keep}, X_{In}]$ as small as possible (i.e., −1) in the latter case; (2) diversification and hedging, taken together, are still insufficient to guarantee a reduction in a portfolio's total variability, even with $Corr[X_{Keep}, X_{Out}]$ as large as possible and $Corr[X_{Keep}, X_{In}]$ as small as possible;[9] *but* (3) either diversification or hedging, taken together with pacification, *is* sufficient to guarantee a reduction in a portfolio's total variability.

A Taxing Tale

In the United States, the legal definition of an insurance company has arisen repeatedly in the context of the government's tax treatment of insurance premiums paid to captive insurance companies.[10] This is not surprising, given that the notion of a captive insurance company seems, at first consideration, somewhat absurd. After all, how can a parent company buy insurance from (i.e., transfer risk to) a company that it owns? In this section, I will use certain observations regarding the captive insurance tax controversy to refine the definition of insurance.

Under U.S. federal law, the authorization to deduct certain types of business expenses derives from the Internal Revenue Code (IRC). An expense is commonly deductible in the computation of taxable income if either: (1) the expense is specifically identified by a section of the IRC; or (2) the expense is ordinary, necessary, reasonable in amount, and incurred in connection with a trade or business, and the expense is not a capital expenditure, personal expenditure, or an expenditure related to tax-exempt income or contrary to public policy.

Insurance tax policy has consistently favored transfers of risk to traditional insurance companies over alternative risk management methods, most notably self-insurance. This bias goes back as far as the Tariff Act of 1909 and has persisted through subsequent laws to the present. The principal advantage given to traditional insurance over self-insurance is that commercial insurance premiums paid to traditional insurance companies are tax deductible as general business expenses, whereas self-insurance reserves are not.

In attempting to establish whether or not a transaction with a captive insurance company constitutes insurance, one encounters a fundamental conflict between two goals of federal tax policy: (1) respecting the legal separateness of corporate entities within an affiliated group of companies; and (2) challenging the economic substance of intercompany transactions that appear to be for no purpose other than minimizing taxes. These two goals collide in the case of captives because risk is being transferred to an affiliated corporation in a manner that may resemble self-insurance.

Economic-Family Theory

To avoid conflict with the doctrine of legal separateness while still denying the tax deductibility of premiums paid to captives, the IRS advanced its *economic-family* theory in 1977, which treated the parent and the captive as one unit for purposes of evaluating the economic impact of reductions in loss variability. Under this theory, no insurance transaction between a parent company and its captive insurance subsidiary results in any transfer of risk outside the corporate family, so such transactions do not justify tax deductions.

Clearly, the economic-family theory is intuitively appealing. It is hard to argue that buying insurance from a wholly owned captive provides any meaningful transfer of risk when every insurance loss paid by the captive results in an equivalent decrease in the value of the captive on the parent's balance sheet. In effect, the economic-family theory seems reasonable because it questions the *efficiency* of risk transfers between a parent and its captive.

However, the credibility of the economic-family theory was severely strained in litigation with U.S. retailer Sears after the IRS denied tax deductions for premiums paid by Sears to its then wholly owned subsidiary Allstate Insurance Company.[11] Although it was true that every insurance loss paid by Allstate simply decreased the value of Allstate on Sears's balance sheet, it also was true that more than 99 percent of Allstate's business came from unrelated risks, and it was difficult to see why Sears's transaction with Allstate was really any different from a comparable transaction with any other major insurance company.

Variability-Reduction/Unrelated-Business Theory

Seeking to develop a coherent approach capable of respecting arrangements that intuitively look like insurance while still denying tax deductions in the case of wholly owned *pure* captives (i.e., wholly owned captives that write insurance for *only* their parents), the courts resorted to a definition of insurance advanced by the U.S. Supreme Court in the case of *Helvering v. LeGierse*.[12] Although the facts of that particular case were far removed from the context of captives, the federal courts relied on the Supreme Court's description of insurance as consisting of "risk shifting" (i.e., risk transfer) and "risk distribution" (i.e., risk pooling).[13] This terminology is consistent with what is found in many conventional textbooks; however, there is not general agreement as to whether or not both of these characteristics are necessary in order for a transaction to qualify as insurance.

In a series of rulings in 1991 (including that of the Sears case), the U.S. tax courts looked for both risk transfer and risk pooling and rejected the IRS's economic family theory in favor of the *variability-reduction/ unrelated-business* theory.[14] Specifically, the courts determined that the writing of unrelated exposures composing a significant portion of a captive's business (as little as 29 percent of premiums in one case) caused substantial pooling of risk over the insurance premiums originating outside the corporate group and that this risk pooling in turn caused risk transfer to occur, thereby justifying tax deductions.

In these cases, the courts heard testimony from taxpayers' experts to the effect that certain measures of "relative risk" or "average risk"—such as the ratio of the standard deviation of total insured losses to total insurance premiums—capture the statistical effects of risk pooling and decrease to 0 as the number of exposure units from unrelated business increases to infinity. Accepting this type of argument, the courts concluded that if a captive writes a significant amount of unrelated business, then that will cause risk to be pooled over the premiums originating outside the corporate group and thereby transferred.

Apparently, the courts at that time were attracted by the intuitively reasonable approach of using unrelated business as a requirement for insurance. This approach is appealing because it appears to explain why the Sears/Allstate transaction should be treated as insurance, even though the risk transfer from Sears to Allstate is not efficient (i.e., losses are not removed from the parent's balance sheet). However, by focusing on the statistical effects of unrelated exposure units, the courts overlooked the fact that "relative-risk" or "average-risk" ratios manifest the same statistical behavior with respect to the number of exposure units, regardless of whether those exposure units come from related or unrelated business. In contrast, an earlier (1989) federal appeals court decision in a case involving health service provider Humana, Inc., correctly observed that the statistical effects of risk pooling can be achieved through both related and unrelated business.[15]

Transfer-Efficiency/Market-Forces Theory

In the case of Humana, the government had sustained a setback on a different front. Initially, the IRS had denied the tax deductibility of premiums paid by both a parent and a number of brother/sister subsidiaries to a captive insurance company owned largely by the parent. Relying on a version of the economic-family theory commonly known as the net-worth approach, the government argued that risk and premium never leave the corporate group, so insurance purchased from the captive is tantamount to self-insurance. However, on appeal, the Sixth Circuit Court decided to allow tax deductions for premiums paid by brother/sister subsidiaries, but not for premiums paid by the parent.

The appellate court's reasoning was based upon a balance-sheet analysis recognizing that from the perspective of a brother/sister subsidiary, risk is transferred because losses paid by the captive are not reflected in the subsidiary's financial statement. In permitting tax deductions for brother/sister premiums, the court's opinion effectively recognized that tax deductibility could be justified by the extent to which: (1) losses are removed from the policyholder's balance sheet; and (2) the policyholder makes an independent decision to purchase insurance from the insurance marketplace.

This approach afforded the starting point for the *transfer-efficiency/ market-forces* theory, which my colleague Moshe Porat and I developed together.[16] According to this theory, tax deductions for transactions between a parent (or brother/sister) company and a captive can be justified by the degree to which the risk transfers are economically efficient in removing losses from the policyholder's balance sheet. This efficiency in turn is ensured by the degree to which the captive is constrained by market forces to operate in the manner of a traditional insurance company.

Essentially, this theory provides a definition of an insurance company based upon the following refined notions of the roles played by risk transfer and risk pooling:

- Risk transfer involves the shifting of responsibility for the payment of losses from a ceding party (the policyholder) to an assuming party (the insurance company). In this process, risk is transferred efficiently if the assuming party provides a reasonable assurance that it will pay for losses.
- Risk pooling refers to increases in the stability of an insurance company or other financial entity primarily by increasing the number of uncorrelated exposure units and the operation of the LLN. In the case of a simple risk pool, in which each individual member cedes one exposure unit to the pool and assumes responsibility for paying a proportional share of the pool's total losses, an increase in the number of members reduces the variability of each member's loss payment. In the case of an insurance company, in which increased stability is associated with a smaller probability of insolvency, an increase in the number of exposure units must be accompanied by an appropriate adjustment in the level of invested capital.[17] The manner in which the company does this will be dictated by market forces.

To summarize, I would offer the following definition: *An insurance company is an enterprise engaged in the business of assuming financial responsibility for the transfer of aloof/quasi-aloof risks in an economically efficient manner by operating subject to the forces of the marketplace for transferring such risks.*

ACT 2, SCENE 2

[Offices of Trial Insurance Company. Head clerk and supervisor both stand by clerk's desk.]

BOSS: Mr. Sorter, it's my pleasure to welcome you to your first day of employment at Trial Insurance. I suppose you've heard our motto: "If it's not a Trial, it's not a policy." [Pauses.] And this, of course, is your desk. It's rumored to have been used by Mr. Kafka, many years ago, naturally.

CLERK: Do you mean *Franz* Kafka, the writer?

BOSS: Yes. He's one of many luminaries to have graced the insurance world— along with composer Charles Ives, poet Wallace Stevens, tenor Luciano Pavarotti, and course, psychic Edgar Cayce.

CLERK: Really? Edgar Cayce worked in insurance? Who would have predicted that? [Smiles.] What was he, an actuary?

BOSS: [Wags his finger facetiously.] Oh, Mr. Sorter, I can see that your dry sense of humor will be appreciated here.

CLERK: Thank you. Now I suppose I should get to work. But my desk appears empty, sir.

BOSS: Not for long. [Picks up tall stack of paper from side table and sets it definitively on Sorter's desk.] This is today's incoming mail. It consists of application forms, claim forms, complaint letters, advertisements for reinsurance, etc.

CLERK: And my job?

BOSS: Your job, as Trial's head clerk, is to sort them into seven piles according to their area of relevance: Underwriting, Claim Adjustment, Accounting, Actuarial, Legal, Miscellaneous, and *Other.*

CLERK: I see. But what's the difference between Miscellaneous and Other?

BOSS: [Looks around to make sure he is not overheard.] *Miscellaneous* actually means "Other," and *Other* actually means "Suspicious." That is, you should place any items that seem suspicious—suspicious applications for coverage, suspicious claim forms, etc.—into the Other pile.

CLERK: I see. But wouldn't it be easier just to call Other "Other" and Suspicious "Suspicious"?

BOSS: Well, Mr. Sorter, you shall be forgiven because you are new to Trial Insurance. But the first thing you must understand is that the insurance business is like no other: We have no inventory; we have no physical product; all we sell is a promise that may or may not be acted upon, depending on circumstances. And those circumstances, Mr. Sorter—those circumstances are subject to manipulation!

CLERK: Manipulation?

BOSS: Yes, Mr. Sorter, manipulation. It's like fighting a guerrilla insurgency: you never know which customer is your friend and which is your enemy. As I said, the insurance business is like no other: We actually prefer *not* to do business with those who are most eager to do business with us. Instead, our job is to be eternally suspicious: suspicious of adverse selection, suspicious of moral hazard, suspicious of excessive medical treatments, suspicious of malingerers, suspicious of suspicious claims, and so forth.

CLERK: Suspicious.

BOSS: Yes, Mr. Sorter, suspicious. But despite the fact that we are suspicious, we don't want to be perceived as suspicious. It's not good for our reputation, you understand. Legitimate customers wouldn't want to do business with us if they felt that securing a policy or getting a claim paid were a *trial*, so to speak.

CLERK: I, I believe I understand, sir. But how do we form our suspicions? How do I know when to place something in the *Other* pile and when not to?

BOSS: A very good question, Mr. Sorter. And the answer can be summed up in *one word*: intuition—judgment—instinct—discernment—perceptivity—divination—precognition. Indeed, those are the characteristics of a truly great insurance executive. Now, Mr. Sorter, are you ready to do battle?

CLERK: I am, sir!

BOSS: Good. Then go to work!

[Sorter does not move toward papers on desk.]

BOSS: Mr. Sorter, I said it was time to work. What are you waiting for?

CLERK: Sir, I believe I'll need to see your identification.

8

God-Awful Guessing and Bad Behavior
Solvency and Underwriting

I believe that insurance is well positioned to be the glamour industry of the 1990s.

—SAUL P. STEINBERG (SPEECH DELIVERED AT TEMPLE UNIVERSITY, APRIL 9, 1992, AS RECALLED BY THE AUTHOR)

In preceding chapters, we have considered definitions of insurance both in terms of what constitutes an insurance product and in terms of what constitutes an insurance company. To summarize, I have argued that: (1) an insurance product is a financial contract that transfers an aloof or quasi-aloof risk from one party to another; and (2) an insurance company is an enterprise engaged in the business of assuming financial responsibility for such transferred risks in an economically efficient manner by operating subject to marketplace forces.

Of course, insurance companies throughout the world are generally subject to some form of government regulation, and such oversight—in addition to market forces—can have a powerful effect on a company's internal risk management. In the present chapter, I will provide a brief overview of government regulation of insurance company solvency, and then discuss, in some detail, the most pernicious risks encountered by insurance firms as they build their portfolios of exposures.

Role of Government

The role of government in insurance markets differs greatly from nation to nation and often from one line of business to another within a given nation.[1]

At one extreme, government may take a *laissez-faire* approach, relying on market forces to set prices and "thin the herd" of weak insurance companies. At the other extreme is the establishment of a government monopoly as the sole provider of insurance. Government activity may originate at either the national or subnational (i.e., state or provincial) level. In some cases, both national and subnational governments may be involved with regulating or offering insurance coverage in a particular line of business. In the United States, most regulation of insurance is carried out by state governments, whereas important government insurance programs operate at both the federal and the state levels.

Solvency Regulation

The goal of *solvency* regulation is to protect the financial interests of insurance consumers by enhancing the ability of insurance companies to make good on their obligations to pay claims. This type of regulation is a fundamental activity of insurance regulators throughout the world and is seen as the principal area for government involvement by many nations of Europe and states within the United States.

Governments have a number of tools at their disposal for regulating the solvency of insurance companies:

1. *restrictions on licensing*, which can be used to require that insurance companies establish a certain minimum level of capitalization before writing business in a given market and which also can be used (or abused) to protect currently licensed companies from competition by limiting the number of companies active in a market;

2. *solvency monitoring*, which involves the close review of annual financial statements, financial ratios, and risk-based capital methods (to be discussed below), so that financially weak insurance companies are directed to take prompt actions to correct their shortcomings;

3. *company rehabilitation*, in which regulators take control of the day-to-day operations of an insurance company to save it as a viable corporate entity;

4. *company liquidation*, in which regulators take control of the assets and liabilities of a unsalvageable insurance company and

manage all payments to creditors to make sure that policyholders are treated fairly; and

5. *guaranty funds*, which use assessments of financially healthy insurance companies to ensure the payment of claims (subject to certain prespecified limits) of policyholders whose insurance companies have gone into liquidation.

In the United States, the ultimate measure of an insurance company's solvency is its *surplus* (i.e., *net worth*, or *assets* less *liabilities*), as calculated according to the insurance accounting system known as Statutory Accounting Principles (SAP). All insurance companies are required to file annual financial statements with regulators in their domiciliary state, prepared on a SAP basis, and stock insurers also must file annual financial (10K) statements with the Securities and Exchange Commission on a Generally Accepted Accounting Principles (GAAP) basis.

Generally speaking, the SAP result in a more conservative (lower) calculation of net worth than do the GAAP because the SAP: (1) require certain expenses to be debited earlier and certain recoveries and tax assets to be credited later; (2) impose restrictions on the discounting of loss reserves as well as on credits for "unauthorized" reinsurance; and (3) exclude certain nonliquid assets, such as furniture and fixtures. These differences arise from the fact that the SAP seek to measure the liquidation value of an insurance company, whereas the GAAP measure the value of the company under a "going-concern" model.

Financial Ratios and Risk-Based Capital

The analysis of various *financial ratios*—for example, the ratio of written premiums (net of reinsurance) to surplus—has been a major component of solvency monitoring by regulators in many nations for many decades. In the United States, the review of financial ratios was formalized by the National Association of Insurance Commissioners (NAIC) in its Early Warning System, created in the early 1970s. In the 1980s, this system evolved into the NAIC's Insurance Regulatory Information System (IRIS), based upon the calculation of eleven financial ratios for property-liability insurance companies, and twelve financial ratios for life-and-health companies.

With a spate of major insurance company insolvencies in the late 1980s, the IRIS ratios, as well as the entire system of solvency regulation at the state level, came under sharp criticism. The main statistical criticisms of the IRIS ratios were: (1) that the particular ratios used had been chosen subjectively, as opposed to being identified through a formal discriminant analysis of solvent and insolvent insurance companies; and (2) that the "normal" ranges for the individual ratios also were chosen subjectively, rather than through a formal statistical procedure.

In the early 1990s, in response to criticisms of IRIS, the NAIC implemented the more sophisticated Risk-Based Capital (RBC) system as its primary statistical tool for solvency monitoring. The RBC analysis (modeled after a similar approach applied by the Securities and Exchange Commission to commercial banks) identifies various categories of risk for insurance companies, and then computes a minimum surplus requirement associated with each category as the product of a specified annual statement item and a subjective factor. The insurance company's overall minimum surplus—called the *authorized control level* RBC—is then calculated as the sum of the individual surplus requirements for the various risk categories, with adjustments for correlations among the different risks.[2]

Under the RBC approach, regulators may require an insurance company to perform financial self-assessments and/or develop corrective-action plans if its surplus falls below 200 percent of its authorized control level RBC. Furthermore, regulators are authorized to take direct action (e.g., company rehabilitation) if the insurance company's surplus falls below this minimum RBC and are required to take action if the insurance company's surplus falls below 70 percent of the minimum level. Outside the regulatory arena, the RBC methodology often is used by insurance companies, insurance rating agencies, and policyholders as part of any comprehensive evaluation of company solvency.

An Insurance Paradox

Throughout the risk-and-insurance literature, the premium-to-surplus (P/S) ratio—that is, the ratio of an insurance company's annual net premiums to its average surplus (net worth)—is viewed as a fundamental measure of financial leverage.[3] Consequently, one would expect this ratio to provide some evidence of the benefits of the law of large numbers (LLN). In particular, one might anticipate that the P/S ratio tends to increase as a function of premiums, since insurance companies with more premiums—and hence a larger number of policyholders—should enjoy greater finan-

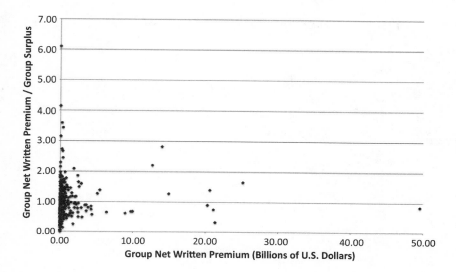

Figure 8.1
Premium-to-Surplus Ratio vs. Premium (U.S. P-L Insurance Groups, Calendar Year 2009) Source: A. M. Best Company (2010).

cial stability through diversification and thus be able to operate at a higher leverage.[4] However, a simple analysis of real-world data belies this intuition.

The scatter plot in Figure 8.1 presents the P/S ratio vs. premiums for all U.S. property-liability insurance groups doing business in calendar year 2009.[5,6] Although a cursory inspection of these data might suggest an inverse power relationship, this type of model would give too much credence to a few outliers—namely, the points from the highly unusual groups with rather small premium volumes and large P/S ratios. To get a better idea of the true relationship between the P/S ratio and premiums, one can truncate the data by removing all groups whose P/S ratio is greater than 3 and whose annual premiums are greater than $7 billion. Although the latter set—that is, those groups with a premium volume greater than $7 billion—clearly constitute many of the most successful and stable insurance groups in the U.S. market, their removal helps to clarify what is going on within the cluster of smaller groups at the left of the plot and does not alter any conclusions.

From Figure 8.2, it can be seen that the relationship between the P/S ratio and premiums is essentially a constant function, with slightly positively

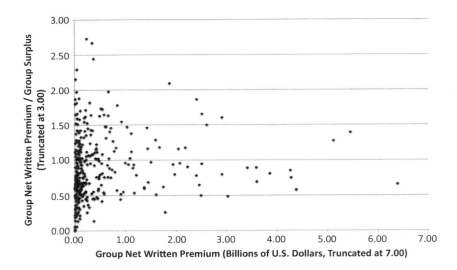

Figure 8.2
Premium-to-Surplus Ratio vs. Premium (Truncated Data, U.S. P-L Insurance
Groups, Calendar Year 2009) Source: A. M. Best Company (2010).

skewed random fluctuations above and below an overall average of about
1. In other words, a group's premium volume has no systematic impact on
the magnitude of its overall leverage, and the only discernible effect of
premium volume is on the variation of the P/S ratio: as groups write more
business, there is less statistical dispersion among their leverage ratios.
This last effect is unsurprising; after all, one would expect smaller groups
to be either: (1) less-established enterprises that are naturally somewhat
removed from market equilibrium; or (2) niche players that intentionally
deviate from market norms. However, the complete absence of any increase in the P/S ratio is surprisingly counterintuitive.

So how can this paradox be resolved?

Effects of Increasing Writings

To seek an answer, one must look for the presence of other, less benign effects arising from an increase in an insurance company's number of policyholders. A quick list of phenomena associated with increased writings
would include the following positive and negative effects:

Positive Effects

- **Law of large numbers.** As more policyholders join the insurance company's risk pool, the variability of the average loss amount tends to shrink, enhancing the stability of the company's financial results through diversification.
- **Reduced actuarial pricing error.** As more historical data are collected, the insurance company's actuaries are able to make better forecasts of the premiums necessary to offset losses and expenses.[7]
- **Reduced classification error.** As more policies are written, the insurance company's underwriters gain greater experience in evaluating the risk characteristics of policyholders and make fewer mistakes assigning them to their proper risk classifications.
- **Reduced information deficiencies.** As more policies are written, the problem of asymmetric information from self-selecting policyholders with private information about their own loss propensities is diluted.
- **Capital accretion.** As profit loadings are collected from more policyholders, the insurance company's surplus increases, providing a greater financial buffer against insolvency.

Negative Effects

- **Increased classification error.** As more policies are written, the insurance company's underwriters begin to encounter less-familiar types of policyholders (from new demographic backgrounds and/or new lines of business) and have trouble assigning them to the proper risk classifications.
- **Increased information deficiencies.** As more policies are written, the insurance company's underwriters begin to encounter less-familiar types of policyholders, and the problem of unobservable—*not* asymmetric—information becomes more significant.
- **Decline in impact of initial net worth.** As more policyholders join the insurance company's risk pool, the impact of the financial buffer provided by the company's initial surplus, on a per-exposure basis, diminishes.

Naturally, it is not the number of negative effects that is determinative, but rather their relative significance. As any experienced insurance regulator knows, the first two items on the negative list frequently lead to insolvency when an insurance company attempts to expand its book of business too rapidly through new types or new lines of exposures that it cannot underwrite effectively.

For a classic example, one need look no further than the insurance group mentioned at the beginning of this chapter. In 2001, Saul Steinberg's Reliance Group Holdings (RGH) filed for bankruptcy, barely making it through the decade Steinberg had foreseen as "glamorous" for insurance. Having taken control of RGH through a leveraged buyout in 1968, Steinberg gained notoriety as a corporate raider in the 1980s with attempts to take over Disney, Quaker Oats, and other companies. Ultimately, however, it was not these forays into high finance that killed RGH, but rather the careless underwriting of its largest insurance subsidiary, the Reliance Insurance Company. Sadly, this nearly 200-year-old Pennsylvania insurance company succumbed to the massive unfunded liabilities generated by its indiscriminate writing of a novel type of workers compensation "carve-out" reinsurance.

What is particularly interesting is that the data from Figures 8.1 and 8.2 strongly suggest that many insurance companies—not just those unfortunate enough to end up insolvent—engage in these same activities. This behavior may well be described as a sort of Peter Principle for insurance markets.[8] In other words, insurance companies frequently convert the benefits of the LLN (and other positive effects of writing increased numbers of policyholders) into economic subsidies for expanded writings, investing in less-familiar categories of business until their P/S ratios approach the market average.

Why this apparent inefficiency exists is an interesting question and one that has not been investigated sufficiently by insurance researchers. One obvious possibility is that insurance companies derive economic benefits from increased market share that offset the disadvantages of less-effective underwriting. Whatever its origin, such an industry practice is unlikely to be challenged by those who monitor the distribution of P/S ratios most closely: government regulators. Although clearly concerned with all threats to insurance company solvency, regulators invariably find it politically difficult, if not impossible, to impede voluntary company efforts to expand the availability of insurance products for consumers.

The *Real* Risks of Insurance

As noted above, a common way for insurance companies to get into financial trouble is by expanding their portfolios so rapidly that underwriting procedures are overwhelmed by classification errors and information deficiencies. In a very real sense, therefore, it can be argued that it is these underwriting uncertainties, and not the more commonly discussed risks of actual losses and actuarial forecasts, that are most important to the insurance enterprise.

Table 8.1 provides a brief summary of how underwriting failures can occur, with the information problems divided into two subcategories (*asymmetric information* and *unobservable information*, respectively) and each type of underwriting issue broken down according to three possible causes (*active behavioral factors, passive behavioral factors,* and *nonbehavioral factors*).

A classification error occurs whenever an insurance company mistakenly identifies a particular policyholder as belonging to one risk classification when the policyholder actually belongs to a different one. Naturally, this is more of a problem for the insurance company when it assigns the policyholder to a lower-risk classification than is deserved, resulting in an inadequate premium. In most cases, such errors are attributable to honest human mistakes made either by the policyholder in completing a policy application or by the insurance company in evaluating the application. Sometimes, however, policyholders intentionally withhold or falsify

Table 8.1
How Underwriting Can Fail

		Information Deficiencies	
	Classification Error	Asymmetric Information (Adverse Selection)	Unobservable Information
Active Behavioral Factors	Material Misrepresentations	Planned Fraud	Moral Hazard, Opportunistic Fraud, Litigiousness
Passive Behavioral Factors	Application Oversights	General Carelessness	Morale Hazard
Nonbehavioral Factors	Insurance Company Mistakes	Other Private Information	Other Hidden Information

required information in completing their applications. For example, a life insurance applicant might claim to be a nonsmoker, when in fact he or she is a heavy smoker. Such *material misrepresentations* form a type of insurance fraud that is usually treated as a civil contract violation (rather than a criminal act) and can result in the abrogation of the insurance company's responsibilities under the policy.

Information deficiencies refer to a larger and more complex class of problems, many of which are extremely difficult to prevent or manage. Essentially, they occur when a policyholder poses a significantly higher risk than that associated with the classification to which the policyholder is (correctly) assigned. In other words, although the policyholder's overt characteristics indicate a specific classification, the policyholder possesses other, difficult-to-observe characteristics that make the policyholder's risk to the insurance company greater than what is expected.

The problem of asymmetric information arises whenever a policyholder possesses some private information about the policyholder's own propensity to generate losses of which the insurance company is unaware. This phenomenon is also frequently called *adverse selection* (although the plain meaning of this term could be applied equally well to the problem of unobservable information as an insurance company increases its book of business). Asymmetric information most commonly involves nonbehavioral factors—as when a life insurance applicant knows that a close family member has just been diagnosed with a life-threatening genetic illness—or passive behavioral factors—as when an automobile insurance applicant knows that he or she often uses a cell phone while driving. Cases of *planned fraud*—such as insuring an expensive piece of jewelry and then pretending that it has been stolen—are rarer and generally can be prosecuted as criminal felonies.

Unobservable information simply means that neither the insurance company nor the policyholder knows some critical information about the policyholder's propensity to generate losses. As with asymmetric information, it most commonly involves nonbehavioral factors—as when a life insurance applicant has an undiagnosed malignant tumor—or passive behavioral factors. However, in the case of unobservable information, any behavioral factor, whether passive or active, has the special property that it is triggered by the purchase of insurance (rather than being present prior to the insurance purchase). For this reason, insurance specialists use the terms *morale hazard* and *moral hazard* to describe the passive and active factors, respectively.

Morale hazard denotes an increase in the policyholder's carelessness with regard to the covered peril that is prompted by the purchase of insurance. For example, after purchasing a homeowners insurance policy that provides coverage for stolen contents, an individual may be less attentive to locking his or her door when leaving the house. Moral hazard, on the other hand, denotes a type of insurance fraud that is planned after the purchase of insurance but before the occurrence of a loss event. A classic example is that of a homeowner who wants to sell his or her house, but finds that the current market price is below the value for which the house is insured, so he or she proceeds to ignite an "insurance fire."

It is interesting to note that most professional economists see little meaningful distinction between morale hazard and moral hazard and tend to use the latter term to describe both phenomena. Clearly, this is a good example of the power of abstraction, although not necessarily an example of a good use of such power. By failing to distinguish between these two terms, one essentially equates a negligent act with a premeditated crime.

In addition to moral hazard, there are two other active behavioral factors that fall under the category of unobservable information. Unlike moral hazard, which involves an action taken after the purchase of insurance but before a loss event, the other two factors—*opportunistic fraud* and *litigiousness*—both arise after a loss event occurs.

Opportunistic fraud describes a decision by the policyholder to "pad the bill" for his or her insured losses. For example, after a burglary, the policyholder might report certain expensive items stolen that never were owned in the first place. Like planned fraud and instances of moral hazard, opportunistic fraud generally may be prosecuted as a felony, but often is more difficult to prove.

Litigiousness refers to the filing of unjustified third-party claims and easily can raise costs for the policyholder's own insurance company, as well as the insurance company of the party being sued. For example, after an automobile collision, one driver (the "victim") might try to build a case for pain and suffering compensation as a result of dubious soft-tissue injuries caused by another driver. To build his or her case for such compensation, the victim first must seek extensive medical treatments to demonstrate the seriousness of the injury. Since finding a friendly doctor or chiropractor is rarely a problem, there is little that can be done to stop this type of behavior, short of enacting no-fault insurance laws. It is indeed very instructive that one often hears the almost whimsical term *frivolous lawsuit* used to describe what is in fact highly destructive tort fraud.

A Tree Falls

Some years ago, a "friend of mine" moved to the greater Philadelphia metropolitan area. Owning two automobiles, he quickly decided that, given the high price of automobile insurance in southeastern Pennsylvania,[9] and the lack of sufficient off-street parking at his new house, he would reduce his personal fleet to just one car. In short, he would keep the newer car and dispose of the older one.

There was one problem with this plan, however. Quite simply, my friend was too lazy to go through the hassle of selling his older vehicle. Starting with the best of intentions, as time went on he found himself hesitating and delaying and postponing and demurring and procrastinating, all the while paying the extra insurance premiums for a second vehicle that he rarely drove.

One day my friend's attention was drawn abruptly to a different insurance problem: He experienced a psychological premonition that the large maple tree standing by the sidewalk in front of his house would break apart during a storm, posing a danger to passers-by. The source of this inkling is hard to pin down, but it may have arisen from one or more of the following: a barely hidden animosity toward the tree for producing so many leaves during the previous fall; a strange paranormal experience involving a tree that occurred earlier in his life; the recent death of a young child in a neighboring town who was killed by a falling tree branch; and the presence of numerous attorneys on his street.

So now, in addition to trying to get rid of his car, my dilatory friend had to decide what to do with his dangerous tree. To complicate matters, he rented his house, so the tree technically did not belong to him. However, knowing something about the world of insurance and litigation, my friend was well aware that his lack of ownership would not protect him in the case of a serious injury. Although a falling tree branch is about as close to an act of God as one can find, an injured victim in today's America generally is not satisfied complaining to God. Rather, he or she is likely to want to file a legal claim against anyone with a potential connection to the tree's downfall—which, in a civil justice system where scientific causality is often irrelevant, would mean the owner of the property, the tenant, and perhaps even a neighbor whose dog was observed urinating on the tree trunk shortly before the incident.

In any event, it was not long before my friend decided that the wisest course of action was to contact his landlady and report his concern about the tree to her. By informing her properly, he hoped to construct a possible legal defense in the case of an accident—that is, that he had done all he could be expected to do as a tenant about the hazard. Of course, my friend's character had not changed much, so, having reached a firm decision, he promptly procrastinated regarding its implementation. Nevertheless, after a few weeks of prodding from his wife and a few nights of fitful sleep, he finally called the tree's owner.

Suffice it to say that the landlady dealt with the matter rather expeditiously. Neither excessively anxious nor unduly insouciant, she quickly made arrangements for a professional tree surgeon to evaluate the tree's health. When the expert suggested that all that was needed was a light trimming, she was content to accept this advice and proceeded with the recommended work.

Fortunately, the landlady's action provided some assurance to my friend. Although it in no way dispelled his premonition, it did seem to comfort him that there were now two additional parties—the landlady and the tree surgeon—who stood ahead of him in line to be sued. It was thus with a certain measure of relief that he returned to the problem of having one car too many.

By now, the insightful reader will have noted that a new option had presented itself. Instead of selling his unwanted car, my friend simply could park it under the aforementioned maple tree and wait for the inevitable falling branch to destroy it. Just because the landlady and her tree surgeon did not believe the tree posed any real danger, this had not altered my friend's confidence in the impending disaster one bit. So, being the procrastinator he was, he decided to undertake this most passive and optimistic of options—and simply waited.

Interestingly, he had to wait less than a year (which is nothing for an experienced procrastinator), until an early spring ice storm indeed knocked a large branch from the tree, crushing the front end of the unwanted car. No longer wasting any time, my friend immediately called his insurance company and was very pleased to hear from the accommodating claim adjustor that the car truly was "totaled."

Thinking about this strange sequence of events, I find myself having a difficult time fitting it into the categories afforded by Table 8.1. Certainly this was not an issue of classification error, and certainly it was not a problem of adverse selection (since my friend possessed no private information prior to purchasing his automobile insurance policy). That leaves only the rightmost column of the above table. Also, it seems fairly clear that my friend did manifest rather unusual behavior—parking his car under the maple tree—that ultimately resulted in the car's demise. That leaves two possibilities: moral hazard (i.e., planned fraud encouraged by the purchase of insurance) and morale hazard (i.e., carelessness encouraged by having insurance coverage).

At this point, I am tempted to conclude that my friend's action was an instance of moral hazard; after all, he did park the car under the tree deliberately, not just as a matter of carelessness. But is it reasonable to believe that his desire for the tree to fall is equivalent to the commission of fraud? From the facts of the story, it appears that there was no meaningful evidence that the tree was likely to fall. So can my friend be guilty of a crime just by wishing it to happen?

ACT 2, SCENE 3

[A different insurance company office. Claimant sits across from claim adjustor at adjustor's desk.]

ADJUSTOR: Mr. Powers, who is this friend that you discuss in Chapter 8 of your book? You know, the one whose car was crushed by a tree?

CLAIMANT: He's someone very close to me. Someone I know well, both professionally and personally. But his particular identity isn't that important. He's supposed to be an Everyman type of character, like Adam and Eve in the earlier tree-related dialogue.

ADJUSTOR: I see. That's very interesting, but somewhat off point. Having read your book, I notice that you take great care with your use of punctuation: periods, commas, quotation marks, . . . , *ellipses*, etc.

CLAIMANT: Thank you. It's kind of you to say so.

ADJUSTOR: Yes. Then perhaps you could explain why you first introduce your close friend—the one you know both professionally and personally—as a "friend of mine," in quotation marks?

CLAIMANT: Hmm . . .

ADJUSTOR: And while you're thinking about that, I also would note that you mention your friend had "a strange paranormal experience involving a tree that occurred earlier in his life." Is that correct?

CLAIMANT: Yes . . . it is.

ADJUSTOR: Then, in Chapter 15, you go into some detail describing a strange paranormal experience involving a tree that you yourself had earlier in life. Is that true?

CLAIMANT: Yes . . . it is.

ADJUSTOR: Mr. Powers, let's stop beating around the bush. This "friend" of yours is none other than you, yourself, isn't it?

CLAIMANT: OK, OK. You've unmasked me; I admit it.

ADJUSTOR: So then, you also admit to committing willful insurance fraud by parking your car under the maple tree in your front yard?

CLAIMANT: No! Never! Fraud would require *moral* hazard, and I won't even acknowledge *morale* hazard.

ADJUSTOR: But you do confess that you parked your car under the tree?

CLAIMANT: Yes.

ADJUSTOR: And that you fully anticipated a large tree branch would fall on the car?

CLAIMANT: Yes.

ADJUSTOR: Well, then, how is that any different from intentionally parking your car in the middle of a junkyard where you know that a car compactor will pick it up and crush it?

CLAIMANT: It's completely different. In the case of the car compactor, everyone would agree that the car would be destroyed. In the case of the falling branch, even tree experts asserted that the car was perfectly safe.

ADJUSTOR: Tree experts, perhaps; but not you?

CLAIMANT: That's correct.

ADJUSTOR: Well, then, how would you describe your premeditated use of the tree?

CLAIMANT: That's easy. I'd say it was an example of a hedge.

ADJUSTOR: A *hedge*? But we're talking about a tree here.

CLAIMANT: I mean a *financial* hedge. You see, I believed that the tree branch would fall and that therefore I, as the resident tenant of the property, would be subject to a small probability of being found liable for someone's injury. So I essentially hedged—or offset—the chance of liability with the correlated chance of resolving my car problem. In other words, if the tree broke, then I would be exposed to a liability loss, but at the same time to the gain of getting rid of my car.

ADJUSTOR: Mr. Powers, I believe you're psychotic!

CLAIMANT: I'd prefer the term *psychic*. But let's wait until Chapter 15.

9

The Good, the Bad, . . .
The Role of Risk Classification

Even the Wicked prosper for a while, and it is not out of place for even *them* to insure.

—JAMES T. PHELPS (*LIFE INSURANCE SAYINGS*, 1895)[1]

Although not as universal as solvency regulation, rate (or price) regulation is used extensively by many nations of the world and often relied on for market stability by developing countries. In the United States, the purpose of rate regulation is twofold: (1) to protect insurance consumers from *excessive* premiums or *unfairly discriminatory* premiums (i.e., premium differences that cannot be justified by differences in risk characteristics among policyholders); and (2) to protect insurance companies (and therefore insurance consumers) from *inadequate* premiums that may threaten company solvency.

In the present chapter, I will offer a brief summary of the objectives and methods of rate regulation, and then probe one of the most controversial aspects of insurance: the risk classification used in underwriting and rating.

Rate Regulation

In the United States, most state governments regulate at least some insurance premiums, although the level of regulatory activity generally varies greatly from line to line.[2] Five categories are often used to describe the various types of *rate* regulation:

- *fix and establish*, under which the regulator sets insurance premium levels, with input from insurance companies and other interested parties;
- *prior approval*, under which insurance companies must secure regulatory approval before making any adjustments in premiums;
- *file and use*, under which insurance companies must notify regulators of premium adjustments a specified period of time *before* implementing them in the market;
- *use and file*, under which insurance companies must notify regulators of premium adjustments within a specified period of time *after* they have been implemented; and
- *open competition*, under which insurance companies can make premium adjustments without seeking authorization from or providing notification to regulators.

Under all of the above systems, regulators generally have the right to challenge—through an administrative or court hearing—premiums that are in violation of applicable rate regulatory and consumer protection statutes.

In some property-liability insurance markets around the world, rates are established through a *bureau* or *tariff* rating system, under which an industry or quasi-governmental agency collects statistical data from many or all insurance companies and computes *manual* rates that are then approved by the insurance regulator. Under a system of bureau rating, an individual insurance company often is permitted to deviate by a constant percentage from the manual rates based upon the company's historical losses and/or expenses. Price competition also may take place through dividends awarded by insurance companies to individual policyholders.

Another tool of government for addressing issues of insurance pricing, as well as insurance availability, is the establishment of *residual markets*. These "insurers of last resort" are generally industry-operated entities, commonly taking either of two basic forms: (1) an *assigned risk plan*, through which hard-to-place policyholders are allocated randomly among the insurance companies writing in a given market; or (2) a *joint underwriting association* or *insurance facility*, through which hard-to-place policyholders are provided insurance by a pooling mechanism that requires all insurance companies in the market to share the policyholders' total risk. In some cases, residual markets may be handled through government insurance programs.

Risk Classification

For most insurance companies, risk classification arises in two principal contexts: *underwriting* and *rating*.[3] Underwriting refers to the process by which an insurance company uses the risk characteristics of a potential policyholder to decide whether or not to offer that individual or firm an insurance contract. Rating is the process by which an insurance company uses a policyholder's risk characteristics to calculate a particular premium level once a contract has been offered. Naturally, in a well-organized insurance company the two facets of risk classification work hand-in-hand so that the company will not agree to a contract for a policyholder whose characteristics fall outside the firm's rating scheme and the company will not refuse a contract for a policyholder whose characteristics are comparable with previously rated policyholders.

The economic motivation for risk classification is quite simple: without it (or some effective substitute) voluntary markets will fail to cover all potential policyholders who desire insurance.[4] This can be seen by considering a hypothetical market for individual health insurance in which there are two types of potential policyholders: generally healthy people (GHs), who use $2,000 worth of medical services on average per year and compose 80 percent of individuals, and chronically ill people (CIs), who use an average of $32,000 worth of services annually and account for the remaining 20 percent. Assume further that no deductibles, limits, or co-payments apply to the reimbursement of medical claims and that insurance companies require a premium loading of 25 percent of expected losses to cover profits and various expenses.[5] Then, given that underwriting and rating are employed, GHs will pay an annual premium of $2,500, whereas CIs will pay a premium of $40,000. However, if risk classification is not used, and insurance companies offer contracts to all policyholders at one fixed price, then: (1) the insurance companies will have to charge a premium of at least $12,000 to break even (based upon a four-to-one ratio of GHs to CIs); and (2) many of the less risk-averse GHs will balk at such a high premium, not purchase insurance, and begin an adverse-selection "spiral" that leaves the insurance companies with only the CIs and a few very risk-averse GHs who are willing to pay a premium of about $40,000.

One way to prevent the adverse-selection spiral and ensure that all policyholders get covered for the same $12,000 premium is for government to make the purchase of health insurance mandatory, rather than voluntary. This is essentially what the new U.S. health care law (the Patient Protection and Affordable Care Act of 2010) proposes to do.[6] However, two important criticisms of this approach are immediately apparent. First, one might argue that by charging the CIs substantially less than their actuarially fair premium of $40,000, the government is encouraging morale hazard by removing an important incentive for less-healthy policyholders to engage in appropriate risk control behavior, such as reducing alcohol intake, improving diet, and exercising. Second, one could argue that, as a simple matter of social justice, the government should not force the GHs to be charged a premium that is so disproportionate to their underlying expected medical costs.

The first criticism—that of encouraging morale hazard—is clearly based upon more positive economic considerations than is the second, rather normative criticism. However, although it is readily apparent that risk control efforts can be very effective in many insurance lines, I would argue that individual health insurance is not one of them. This is because classification-based risk control incentives are effective only when either: (1) policyholders are commercial enterprises capable of long-term self-disciplinary measures and able to justify substantial premium reductions through their own historical costs; or (2) policyholders are able to obtain substantial premium reductions by making verifiable behavioral changes that result in lower costs—and individual health insurance fails to satisfy either of these conditions.

To make this point more compelling, consider a simple thought experiment: Imagine an individual policyholder with heart disease who chooses to eat more healthful foods primarily for the purpose of lowering his or her insurance premium rather than primarily for the purpose of avoiding surgery and living longer. Unlike an individual who ceases smoking and thus may qualify for a classification-based behavior-change discount (i.e., nonsmoker versus smoker), a heart patient who embraces an improved diet will benefit from decreased premiums only if he or she is joined in the effort by many other policyholders with heart disease (over whose diets the initial policyholder has no control) and after the passage of many years (that is, after the medical costs of all policyholders with heart disease can be shown to have decreased in the insurance company's database). Consequently, such an individual would have to be inhumanly optimistic and patient to make such a dietary change.

The second criticism—that of social injustice—raises some interesting issues. Superficially, the argument seems undeniably sound. After all, government does not require the owners of inexpensive automobiles to subsidize the owners of luxury cars; therefore, by analogy, why should government require those requiring less-expensive health insurance (i.e., GHs) to subsidize those requiring more-expensive policies (i.e., CIs)? One answer, of course, is that, unlike the owners of luxury cars, the CIs do not make an active decision to *choose* the more expensive product and thus should be afforded a certain degree of sympathy. Nevertheless, compassion alone does not provide an adequate basis for sound public policy.

The real problem with risk classification is that any attempted normative justification is meaningless at the level of individual policyholders. Since the particular individuals responsible for using medical services during a given policy period are not known with certainty in advance, it follows that a CI policyholder who pays $40,000 (under a voluntary policy) but does not use any medical services is substantially more aggrieved than a GH policyholder who pays $12,000 (under a mandatory policy) and generates no medical costs. The fact that there are fewer of the former than the latter is entirely irrelevant at the individual level. Hence, normative social justice considerations actually argue against, rather than in support of, risk classification systems.

To see this another way, consider a second thought experiment: Imagine a future time in which insurance companies can use a simple blood test to determine, in advance, exactly how many dollars in medical costs each individual policyholder will generate during the coming year. Under such an improved system, risk classification–based insurance obviously could not exist because each policyholder would occupy a unique risk classification and simply pay a premium equal to his or her medical costs plus an unnecessary 25 percent loading. Thus, the only reason risk classification–based insurance can exist today is that the classifications used are sufficiently coarse that there is still the possibility of some policyholders (e.g., the CIs and GHs who do not use any medical services) subsidizing others. In effect, by imposing the particular GH/CI breakdown, we are forcing certain CIs to provide huge subsidies (of up to $40,000), whereas under a system of uniform premiums, we would be forcing certain CIs and GHs to provide much smaller subsidies (of at most $12,000). Selecting the former alternative over the latter—given that mandatory coverage removes adverse-selection concerns and risk control considerations are not applicable—is therefore not only arbitrary, but also disproportionately punitive.

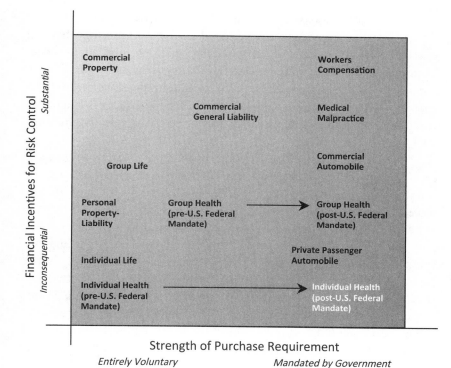

Figure 9.1
Usefulness of Risk Classification (Darker means less useful).

In summary, one can draw the following conclusions:

- In voluntary insurance markets, risk classification is generally necessary in order to succeed in covering most potential policyholders.
- In mandatory insurance markets, risk classification is not necessary in order to cover all potential policyholders, but it may discourage morale hazard by providing effective financial incentives to control risks in some cases (e.g., in commercial lines that permit policyholders to enjoy substantial premium reductions from their own improved loss experience and in any lines that permit policyholders to enjoy substantial premium reductions from verifiable behavioral changes).
- At the level of individual policyholders, normative social justice arguments oppose, rather than support, the use of risk classification systems.

The significance of the first and second bullet points is illustrated in Figure 9.1, which provides a simple paradigm for determining when risk classification is more or less useful.[7] In the upper left (unshaded) corner, insurance is voluntary and risk classification systems offer policyholders the possibility of obtaining substantial premium reductions through risk control efforts. In the lower right (shaded) corner, insurance is mandatory and risk classification systems afford little or no meaningful premium reductions through risk control.

Not to forget the third bullet point, I would observe that risk classification is more than simply "less useful" in the lower right corner; rather, it is particularly unjust to those lower-cost individuals who happen to be placed in more expensive classifications. Such policyholders not only are required by law to purchase insurance, but also are compelled to accept premiums based upon classifications that they cannot change through risk control efforts. For this reason, it is quite sensible for the new U.S. health care law to eliminate certain risk classifications in individual health insurance. This is also why risk classification schemes in private passenger automobile insurance (the "nearest neighbor" of individual health insurance in Figure 9.1) should always be subject to close scrutiny in jurisdictions where this coverage is required by law.

Controversies

In addition to the general issues discussed in the previous section, insurance regulators in the United States often must address specific problems of wide disparities in personal insurance premiums among different sociodemographic classes.[8] Whereas insurance industry actuaries generally consider rating systems to be fair if differences in *pure premiums* (i.e., premiums net of profit and expenses) reflect substantive differences in expected losses, regulators (and the public at large) may not find a correlation with expected losses sufficient justification for using certain sociodemographic variables in underwriting and/or rating. Issues of causality, controllability, and social acceptability often prevent policymakers from accepting the use of a proposed risk classification in a given line of personal insurance.

There are several fundamental reasons for skepticism regarding sociodemographic risk classification variables in personal insurance. These include:

1. **Doubts about actual correlation with risk.** For example, are younger drivers really more likely to have automobile collisions than older drivers? After all, one often hears about aged drivers with poor eyesight and/or slow reflexes causing collisions. If that is so, then why do senior citizen discounts exist?

2. **Doubts about actual causation of risk.** Granting that younger drivers actually are more likely to have collisions than older drivers, is age a true causal factor? Another obvious possibility is that driving experience provides the fundamental causal link. Should driving experience be used instead of age to avoid treating younger, but more experienced drivers unfairly?

3. **Doubts about complete causation of risk.** Assuming that age is a true causal factor because younger people are intrinsically less careful (and therefore more likely to drive fast, drive while intoxicated, etc.), should this factor be applied to everyone equally? For example, there may be younger drivers who are teetotalers and therefore never drive while intoxicated. Is it fair to use age as a factor, but not alcohol consumption?

4. **Doubts about individual fairness.** Assuming that age is a true causal factor that applies to everyone equally (i.e., without need for modification for such things as alcohol consumption), is it fair to penalize younger people for their age? After all, a younger person cannot take any action to reduce expected losses by changing his or her age, so the risk classification system simply imposes penalties for high expected losses, rather than providing financial incentives for reducing losses.

5. **Doubts about group fairness.** Finally, even if it is accepted that age is a true causal factor that applies to everyone equally and that it is reasonable to make younger people—as individuals—pay for their intrinsic carelessness (with no hope of reducing losses), does society really want to penalize younger people as a sociodemographic group? After all, younger people tend to be less affluent on the whole. Why not simply remove age as an underwriting and/or rating classification and thereby spread the losses over everyone?

When implementing a new risk classification, insurance companies must obtain the explicit or implicit approval of insurance regulators in regulated markets and at least the tacit agreement of consumers in competitive markets. As a result of concerns one through three above, companies may be expected to demonstrate not only an empirical correlation between the proposed risk classification and expected losses, but also a causal connection that is effective in predicting losses. Moreover, even when issues of correlation and causality have been successfully addressed, companies may encounter difficulties arising from concerns four and five when a risk classification is based upon a characteristic that is not within a policyholder's control. (For example, the make and model year of an automobile generally are not controversial factors in automobile insurance, whereas the gender and age of the driver may be.)

Premium Equivalence Vs. Solidarity

As mentioned above, it usually is desirable in voluntary insurance markets to employ one or more risk classifications for both underwriting and rating purposes. However, any insurance company establishing a risk classification system must confront a fundamental trade-off between the economic costs and the economic benefits associated with the system's degree of refinement. On the one hand, the use of smaller, more homogeneous classifications enables the company to price its product more accurately for specific subsets of policyholders, thereby reducing problems of adverse selection (in which lower-risk policyholders decline to purchase insurance because they perceive it to be overpriced for their levels of expected losses) and providing financial incentives for risk control (by lowering premiums for policyholders taking specific steps to reduce the frequency and/or severity of losses). On the other hand, the use of larger classes tends to make insurance more affordable for a greater number of individual policyholders (because premiums for higher-risk policyholders remain substantially lower than what is indicated by their actual losses). These two conflicting effects are captured, respectively, by the principles of *premium equivalence* and *solidarity*.

The principle of premium equivalence asserts that an insurance company's book of business should be partitioned into classifications that are homogeneous with respect to risk and that the total premiums collected from each group should be based upon the total expected losses for that group. Although this principle certainly makes intuitive sense, it actually describes an ideal that is impossible to implement in practice. This is because each individual policyholder possesses a unique constellation of risk characteristics, so *any* group of more than one policyholder must be somewhat heterogeneous. Instead, the best that insurance companies can do is to create a system of risk classifications in which the policyholders in each cell have *similar* risk profiles. In short, prospective policyholders representing approximately equivalent exposures are underwritten and rated in the same way.

Alternatively, the principle of solidarity asserts that individual policyholders should not be obligated to pay their specific losses, but rather that all policyholders should contribute equally to the payment of total losses. In a sense, this concept forms the basis for insurance; in other words, the "lucky" policyholders (i.e., those that do not experience a loss) subsidize the "unlucky" ones. In the case of complete solidarity, the insurance company represents the total pool of policyholders and assumes the risk of total losses.

To understand this issue more clearly, let us return to the example provided in item three above, in which it was assumed that age is a true causal factor of greater automobile insurance losses because younger people are intrinsically less careful (and therefore more likely to drive fast, drive while intoxicated, etc.). In that context, suppose that a young male policyholder realizes from anecdotal observations that a large number of automobile collisions among his peers are caused by individuals driving to or from parties where alcohol is served. Armed with this information, the young policyholder petitions his insurance company for a premium discount based upon the fact that he never attends such parties. However, the policyholder soon finds that his request is fruitless because the insurance company possesses no data to support his argument. When asked whether it has any plans to collect such data, the company responds that even if such data were available, it could not be used to create a risk classification for nonpartiers because anyone could declare membership in that category, and the company would not have the resources to audit such assertions.

In short, although the young policyholder would be better off with either a coarser risk classification scheme that ignored age or a more refined risk classification scheme that recognized both age and party attendance, he is stuck with the somewhat arbitrary status quo selected by insurance companies and regulators. For him, age is a controversial risk classification; for other policyholders in private passenger automobile and other personal insurance lines, different classifications might be controversial.

Causes of Controversy

Although all sociodemographic variables are subject to a certain degree of regulatory scrutiny, some—such as race/ethnicity and income—are more provocative than others. To explore the hierarchy of controversy among risk classifications, my former student Zaneta Chapman and I have found it useful to consider the fundamental sources of concern, which can be organized under rubrics of *causality, controllability,* and *social acceptability.*[9] For each of these categories, I will suggest a spectrum of sociodemographic variables ranked judgmentally from "most controversial" to "least controversial" for each of two important types of personal insurance: individual health and private passenger automobile.

Causality

Causality denotes the degree to which observed correlations between certain characteristics and expected losses arise from a true cause-and-effect relationship that can be used to predict losses effectively. For example, in items one through three above, the relationship between age and automobile insurance losses was questioned based upon doubts concerning, respectively: (1) the presence of a correlation; (2) the presence of actual causation; and (3) the presence of additional sources of causation that were omitted.

In Table 9.1, I rank by type of insurance seven salient sociodemographic variables by the level of causality-related controversy that they provoke. As already noted, these rankings are based entirely upon judgment; therefore, rather than attempting to justify each particular ranking, I will restrict attention to differences between the two types of insurance.

Unlike the case of health insurance, there is little compelling evidence that Race/Ethnicity, Current Health, and Health Behaviors are direct causal factors of private passenger automobile insurance losses—although if one had to guess, it seems reasonable to believe that certain Health Behaviors (like drinking and smoking) can raise the chance of a collision if they are carried out while driving. Also, it is important to note that the role played by Income in private passenger automobile insurance has more to do with the ability to pay premiums on time and financial incentives for fraud and/or litigation than with the probability of a collision. Residence,

Table 9.1
Level of Controversy Relating to Causality (Author's Judgment)

Level of Controversy	Individual Health Insurance	Private Passenger Automobile Insurance
High	Income	Race/Ethnicity
	Residence	Current Health*
	Race/Ethnicity	Health Behaviors*
	Gender	Income
	Age	Residence
	Health Behaviors*	Gender
Low	Current Health*	Age

* A distinction is made between Current Health conditions
(including genetic predispositions) and Health(-related) Behaviors
(such as smoking).

however, can impact both the chance of a collision (through association
with traffic density) and the potential for fraud and/or litigation (because
certain geographic areas are more disposed to this type of activity than
others).

Controllability

Controllability indicates the degree to which certain characteristics,
which may be causally related to expected losses, are subject to change by
policyholders that are interested in reducing their expected losses. For example, in item four above, the relationship between age and automobile
insurance losses was questioned not for reasons of causality, but rather for
the fairness of penalizing younger people for their ages, a characteristic that
cannot be changed. In Table 9.2, I judgmentally rank the seven sociodemographic variables from the previous table by the level of controllability-
related controversy that they create.

Since a policyholder's ability to control any particular sociodemographic factor is independent of the type of insurance purchased, the
rankings for individual health and private passenger automobile must be
identical. One notable difference between Table 9.2 and the prior table is
the tie among three variables—Age, Gender, and Race/Ethnicity—at the
highest level of controversy.

Table 9.2
Level of Controversy Relating to Controllability (Author's Judgment)

Level of Controversy	Individual Health Insurance	Private Passenger Automobile Insurance
High	Age, Gender, Race/Ethnicity	Age, Gender, Race/Ethnicity
	Current Health*	Current Health*
	Income	Income
	Residence	Residence
Low	Health Behaviors*	Health Behaviors*

* A distinction is made between Current Health conditions (including genetic predispositions) and Health(-related) Behaviors (such as smoking).

Social Acceptability

Social acceptability describes the degree to which certain characteristics, which may be causally related to expected losses but are not entirely controllable by policyholders, are viewed favorably in terms of normative social welfare considerations. For example, in item five above, the relationship between age and automobile insurance losses was questioned not for reasons of causality or controllability, but rather for the fairness of penalizing younger people, who constitute a less-affluent sociodemographic group. Table 9.3 provides judgmental rankings of the seven variables from the previous two tables by the level of controversy associated with social acceptability.

Although doubts have been raised at one time or another about most sociodemographic variables that are not entirely within the control of policyholders, Age and Gender generally have been found more acceptable than Race/Ethnicity and Income. These determinations probably arise from either (or both) of two considerations:

- *the likelihood of implicit cost averaging* (in particular, Age may be more acceptable because most individuals are both young and old policyholders at different times of their lives, and Gender may be more acceptable because higher insurance rates for a given sex in one line of business can be offset by lower rates in another line of business); and
- *support for social mobility/equality* (specifically, Race/Ethnicity and Income may be less acceptable because they are viewed as harming particularly disadvantaged segments of society).

Table 9.3
Level of Controversy Relating to Social Acceptability
(Author's Judgment)

Level of Controversy	Individual Health Insurance	Private Passenger Automobile Insurance
High ↑↓	Race/Ethnicity Current Health* Health Behaviors* Income Residence Gender	Race/Ethnicity Income Residence Current Health* Health Behaviors* Gender
Low	Age	Age

* A distinction is made between Current Health conditions (including genetic predispositions) and Health(-related) Behaviors (such as smoking).

In the two rankings of Table 9.3, the only differences are the placements of the variables Current Health and Health Behaviors. These differences are attributable to the fact that policyholders who are vulnerable because of either type of health status are highly likely to lose financially from being unable to purchase affordable individual health insurance, but less likely to lose financially from being unable to purchase affordable private passenger automobile insurance.

ACT 2, SCENE 4

[Offices of Trial Insurance Company. Head clerk sits at desk.]

CLERK: [Mumbles to himself as he reviews document.] Well, this is interesting: an application to insure a house for $500,000, when the house was just purchased for only $300,000. *Very* suspicious. Perhaps my first chance to use the Other pile?

FORM 1: Please, sir, I beseech you. Don't place me in the Suspicious pile.

CLERK: [Looks around in all directions.] Excuse me . . . who is speaking?

FORM 1: I, sir, the application form in your hand.

CLERK: Oh, really? I didn't realize the paperwork around here was in the habit of remonstrating. But then this is my first day on the job.

FORM 1: I'm sorry to disturb you, sir, but I want to assure you that there's no need to place me in the Suspicious pile.

CLERK: No need, eh? Hey, wait a minute, how do you know the purpose of the Other pile?

FORM 1: Well, I suppose I just surmised it from what you said: that I appeared to be "very suspicious."

CLERK: And now you're *talking*. That is *indeed* suspicious. But to get right to the heart of the matter, perhaps you'd care to explain why it is that you're asking for $500,000 of coverage on a house that's worth only $300,000.

FORM 1: Well, you see, sir, one can never be too careful. Perhaps the value of the house will increase faster than permitted by your company's inflation rider.

CLERK: Inflation rider? Uh, this is only my first day here. I'm afraid I'm not quite up to speed on all the relevant insurance jargon. [Relents.] Well, I must admit, you do sound sincere; so I suppose there would be no harm in simply sending you along to Underwriting. They can decide on your final disposition themselves.

FORM 1: Thank you, sir. You are most civilized.

CLERK: You're very welcome. [Picks up next document from pile.] And what do we have here? A claim form for a house fire—and the claim amount is $500,000. Well, that seems to be a popular figure today. Say, the street address is very familiar. [Gets up from chair to compare claim form with application form in Underwriting pile.] Yes, I thought so. It's the same as the address on that very polite application form. Now this is definitely suspicious!

FORM 2: [Gruffly.] You won't put me in the Suspicious pile if you know what's good for you!

CLERK: What? What did you say? Am I now being threatened by paperwork? This is certainly unacceptable!

FORM 2: You heard what I said. Unlike those polite application forms, we claim forms don't mince words. I have powerful friends. If you don't send me directly to Claim Adjustment, you'll regret it.

CLERK: Well, this is indeed quite intolerable! Into the Other pile you go! [Places claim form in Other pile.] That'll teach you to threaten me. [Picks up next document from pile as Boss enters.]

BOSS: Is something wrong? I thought I heard shouting.

CLERK: Nothing that I can't handle. A low-life claim form started making threats, that's all.

BOSS: Did it really? I've been told that Mr. Kafka used to speak of such things; but I always thought he was just being literal.

CLERK: Not to worry, in any case. I put the form in the Other pile.

BOSS: Very good, very good. I'm glad to see you have everything under control. [Begins to leave, then stops, holding out envelope.] Oh, I just received this by special courier. It's for you.

CLERK: What is it?

BOSS: It appears to be a subpoena of some sort. It seems you've been deposed in a legal matter regarding a homeowner's claim. [Leaves Sorter by himself.]

10

... And the Lawyerly
Liability and Government Compensation

Any one of us might be harmed by almost anything—
a rotten apple, a broken sidewalk, an untied shoelace, a
splash of grapefruit juice, a dishonest lawyer.

—STEPHEN G. BREYER (*BREAKING THE VICIOUS CIRCLE:*
TOWARD EFFECTIVE RISK REGULATION, 1993)[1]

The more active a nation's civil justice (tort) system, the more significant the liability component of its property-liability insurance market tends to be. In the United States, liability insurance premiums are extremely costly for many commercial policyholders, and at times, availability crises have arisen in lines such as pollution liability, general liability, and medical malpractice. Interestingly, even personal lines policyholders have been adversely affected—primarily by the high cost of private passenger automobile liability insurance.

The present chapter addresses several important aspects of a liability system. First, I will consider the loss event itself and how one can assign responsibility equitably for damages arising from two or more distinct sources. Next, I will discuss the concept of no-fault automobile insurance—one mechanism a society can use to reduce the costs of its liability system. Finally, I will suggest various ethical criteria for determining the ultimate financial responsibility of government as the "insurer of last resort."

Assessing Blame

In discussing any loss event in which liability is imputed, it is helpful to employ the somewhat legalistic term *tortfeasor* to refer to the party that is determined to be at fault and the term *victim* to refer to the party that suffers personal injury or property damage caused by the tortfeasor.[2] Naturally, it is possible for there to be more than one tortfeasor and more than one victim associated with a given event, and it also is possible for a tortfeasor to be a victim (of himself or herself and/or of another tortfeasor).

Laws dealing with the potential sharing of fault are called *comparative negligence* statutes. *Pure* comparative-negligence laws permit a victim to recover damages up to the percentage of fault for which a different tortfeasor is responsible, regardless of how much fault is attributable to the victim (e.g., in an automobile collision, if Driver A is 25 percent at fault and Driver B is 75 percent at fault, then A can recover 75 percent of his or her damages from B, and B can recover 25 percent of his or her damages from A). Statutes with *contributory negligence* restrictions permit a victim to recover damages only if his or her own contribution to fault is no more than that of the other tortfeasor (the 50 percent rule) or is strictly less than that of the other tortfeasor (the 49 percent rule).

In recent years, sophisticated techniques from the domain of mathematical game theory have been proposed for assessing and allocating fault. Although not all of these methods were available at the time I was in kindergarten, they are felicitously illustrated by the following story from those halcyon days, in which all but one of the names has been changed (not so much to protect the innocent as to avoid litigation).

A Finger-Paint Fiasco

On an apparently ordinary day in Ms. Chauncey's kindergarten class, the students had just completed their finger-painting projects and were getting ready for their mid-morning nap. As was common practice, three students—in this case, Mike, Larry, and Curly—were asked by the teacher to gather the plastic bottles of finger paint from around the classroom and to put them neatly away. Unfortunately, because of one simple careless act, what should have been a tranquil transition from digital artistry to manufactured slumber became an awful awakening from finger painting to finger pointing.

Since details are crucial whenever one attempts to assess blame, I shall try to be as clear as possible in describing the events of this case:

First, I would note that Ms. Chauncey had made the following assignments: Mike was to pick up the bottles of *blue* finger paint, of which there were four; Larry was to pick up the bottles of *red* finger paint, of which there were two; and Curly was to pick up the single bottle of *yellow* finger paint. Although Ms. Chauncey had not stated explicitly where the bottles were to go, she had pointed in the general direction of the back of the classroom where paints, brushes, construction paper, and various other arts and crafts supplies were stored on a large set of shelves.

Next, I would observe that each of the boys could carry only one bottle at a time, so both Mike and Larry had to make more than one trip from the front of the class to the back. As things transpired, the boys could not immediately find sufficient space for the bottles on the shelves, so they initially set their bottles on the floor in front of the shelves. Then, when all seven bottles had been transported there, the boys began looking for a place to put them. It was not long before they simultaneously noticed the same attractive free space: the flat top of a cardboard box containing valuable ceramic plates that was sitting on a small table next to the teacher's desk.

Each boy took his responsibility very seriously and thus maintained close custody of the bottle or bottles entrusted to him. First, Mike placed each of his four blue bottles carefully on the box. It then was Curly's turn, so he set down his single yellow bottle in a similar fashion. Unfortunately, it was this fifth bottle that "broke the box's back," so to speak. The moment Curly released his bottle, the box toppled over and crashed to the floor in a nasty pile of broken plates and running pigment.

In the interest of delicacy, I will provide no further details of that particular morning's events. However, suffice it to say that there was some discussion among the three boys and their teacher—as well as a few of the class's pre-lawyers—as to who was responsible for the disaster that pre-empted naptime. And that is indeed the question that will now be considered: Exactly who was responsible for the paint/plates tragedy?

I will begin by pronouncing, by authorial fiat, that Ms. Chauncey bore no significant responsibility for the disaster. Although I recognize that it has become vogue in certain quarters to assess primary responsibility to those with "deep pockets" and it is clear that the adult Ms. Chauncey possessed considerably deeper "emotional pockets" than did her young charges, the purpose of this discussion is to assess responsibility among those who were truly responsible rather than among those who are most able to bear the burden of responsibility.

So how should responsibility for the paint/plates disaster be assessed? Clearly, a number of intuitive approaches come to mind:

- Hold Curly entirely responsible, since it was his individual action—placing the single yellow bottle on the box—that precipitated the disaster. (Using the notation $[m, \ell, c]$ to indicate the proportions of responsibility attributable to Mike, Larry, and Curly, respectively, this approach gives [0, 0, 1].)
- Hold Mike entirely responsible, since it was his individual action—placing the first four bottles on the box—that initiated the sequence of events leading inevitably to the disaster (i.e., [1, 0, 0]).
- Hold Mike, Larry, and Curly equally responsible, since they all tacitly agreed to place the bottles on the box (i.e., [1/3, 1/3, 1/3]).
- Hold Mike, Larry, and Curly responsible in proportion to the numbers of bottles that they had placed on the box at the time of the disaster (i.e., [4/5, 0, 1/5]).
- Hold Mike, Larry, and Curly responsible in proportion to the numbers of bottles entrusted to them, whether or not the bottles had the opportunity to be placed on the box (i.e., [4/7, 2/7, 1/7]).

Rather remarkably, none of the above ad hoc procedures is equivalent to the most prominent solution concept offered by mathematical game theory—that is, the *Shapley value*. This allocation scheme, first proposed by American mathematician and economist Lloyd Shapley in 1953, would identify each boy's proportion of responsibility as the frequency with which his bottle causes the disaster when all possible sequences of bottle placements are considered.[3] Thus, listing these sequences as

    (a) Mike (4), Larry (2), Curly (1),
    (b) Mike (4), Curly (1), Larry (2),
    (c) Larry (2), Mike (4), Curly (1),
    (d) Larry (2), Curly (1), Mike (4),
    (e) Curly (1), Mike (4), Larry (2), and
    (f) Curly (1), Larry (2), Mike (4),

one finds that Mike is implicated in cases (c), (d), (e), and (f), Larry in case (a), and Curly in case (b). This yields the allocation [2/3, 1/6, 1/6].

Given that the Shapley value is defined in an intuitively reasonable way and that it also may be derived rigorously as the unique solution satisfying a set of reasonable axioms, it is tempting to settle on this particular allocation. However, the Shapley value does present one serious problem: If the boys are permitted to take turns placing their *individual* bottles on the box (rather than each boy's placing all of his bottles together in one bunch), then the calculation would have to be revised.

Without listing all 105 different sequences of individual bottles, it is fairly easy to see that this modification would result in a Shapley-value allocation of [4/7, 2/7, 1/7] because each boy's chance of setting down the critical fifth bottle would be given precisely by his share of the total complement of bottles.[4] Since there was no actual requirement that each boy place all of his bottles in one bunch and also since the allocation [4/7, 2/7, 1/7] appeals particularly strongly to intuition, this seems like an ideal choice. However, before jumping to a final conclusion, it might be prudent to ask: What would happen if the bottles were subdivided further? For example, what would happen if the boys had decided to take turns pouring single drops of their respective finger-paint stores onto the box?

This line of thinking leads to the Aumann-Shapley value (proposed by Israeli American mathematician Robert Aumann and Shapley in 1974), which evaluates each boy's responsibility as the frequency with which his paint causes the disaster when his entire store of paint is treated as an infinitely divisible continuum.[5] Without going into the necessary formalities from the calculus, it can be argued heuristically that the Aumann-Shapley approach also yields an allocation of [4/7, 2/7, 1/7] because on the margin, when the cumulative amount of finger paint poured onto the box is just short of five bottles' worth, each boy's chance of providing the next drop would be given by his share of the total number of bottles.[6]

That certainly seems like a considerable amount of work just to arrive at the obvious solution of [4/7, 2/7, 1/7]! But such precision is necessary because allocations of responsibility can involve very large monetary amounts when transferred to the real world.

An Oily Analogue

Consider, for example, three oil platforms in the Gulf of Mexico that each spill substantial amounts of oil as a result of damage from the same hurricane. Assume that the three platforms belong to three different oil companies—M Oil, L Oil, and C Oil—and (to maintain numerical consistency with our kindergarten story) that Platform M spills 4 million barrels, Platform L spills 2 million barrels, and Platform C spills 1 million barrels. Assume further that it has been determined by experts that a particular type of commercially valuable fish was rendered extinct by the first 5 million barrels to spill (with no additional damage caused by the remaining 2 million barrels). How should the three companies be required to compensate the fishing industry?

Given the above analysis of the kindergarten finger-paint fiasco, there are two obvious allocation schemes: (1) [2/3, 1/6, 1/6], if the oil from each platform were released in one discrete blob; and (2) [4/7, 2/7, 1/7], if the oil from each platform were released continuously. To offer an idea of the significance of this difference, suppose that the value of the exterminated fish population were determined to be $10 billion. In that case, M Oil's attorneys could save their client in excess of $950 million by convincing a court to select the second allocation scheme over the first.

No-Fault Automobile Insurance

The most direct way to reduce liability costs in the aggregate is to create recovery systems that compensate victims while avoiding the costly litigation necessary to determine fault.[7] Historically, the U.S. workers compensation system—in which employers are mandated to provide medical and wage-loss coverage to their employees in return for restrictions on employee-generated litigation—has stood for almost a century as worthy testimony to the potential benefits of such no-fault systems.

The no-fault concept was first proposed for automobile collision damages by American legal scholars Robert Keeton and Jeffrey O'Connell in 1965.[8] Its explicit purpose was to achieve improved efficiency and equity by compensating victims primarily through first-party personal injury coverages and by imposing certain barriers to litigation to limit the use of the liability personal injury coverages. In practice, this barrier to recovery, or *tort threshold*, typically takes one of two forms: (1) a *monetary threshold*, representing a specified dollar amount that must be reached by the victim's personal injury economic losses before he or she is permitted to seek noneconomic (pain-and-suffering) damages; or (2) a *verbal threshold*, representing a legal standard of seriousness that must be reached by the victim's injuries before he or she is permitted to seek noneconomic damages.

Massachusetts and Florida enacted the first automobile collision no-fault laws in the early 1970s. They were followed by a small flurry of others, resulting in a total of about a dozen by 1980. Over the years, numerous studies concluded that no-fault automobile insurance has, on the whole, achieved both the efficiency and equity goals for which it was proposed. Specifically, victims in mandatory no-fault jurisdictions are compensated more quickly than those in traditional tort jurisdictions, and when there is a strong barrier to tort recovery (such as a verbal or substantial dollar tort threshold), a far greater portion of insurance loss dollars are used to compensate economic losses under mandatory no-fault than under traditional tort.

In the last three decades, few states have enacted or rescinded no-fault statutes, so the overall picture in the United States has changed little. The most notable developments during this time period took place in New Jersey and Pennsylvania, where *choice no-fault* systems were enacted. Currently, only three of the fifty United States—Kentucky, New Jersey, and Pennsylvania—offer policyholders some form of choice no-fault. However, since 1997, legislation has been pending in the U.S. Congress to provide a federal mandate for this type of system.

Choice no-fault refers to any automobile collision recovery regime in which automobile insurance policyholders are afforded a choice between traditional tort recovery on the one hand, and some variant of no-fault—with a barrier to tort recovery and lower insurance premiums—on the other. Clearly, the choice no-fault movement represents an attempt to take advantage of the cost savings promised by no-fault while addressing the greatest perceived shortcoming of mandatory no-fault: the requirement that collision victims be restricted *involuntarily* from seeking recovery through the traditional tort system.

One crucial aspect of any choice no-fault system is the manner in which collisions involving different types of policyholders (i.e., both tort and no-fault electors) are resolved. Briefly, there exist three possible systems: (1) *tort-favoring*, in which both parties enjoy unrestricted tort rights; (2) *no-fault-favoring*, in which both parties are subject to restricted tort rights; and (3) *self-determining*, in which the tort elector enjoys unrestricted tort rights, but the no-fault elector is subject to restricted tort rights.

To develop a simple framework for describing the fundamental economic behaviors associated with choice no-fault, consider Figure 10.1, which portrays economic equilibrium in the market for first-party per-

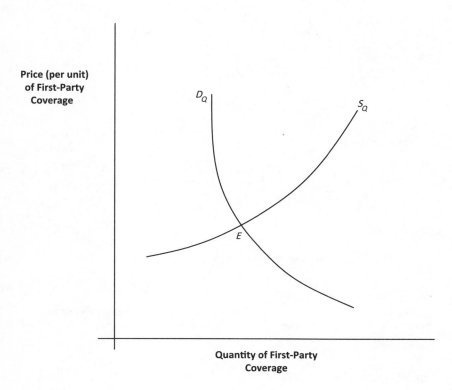

Figure 10.1
Equilibrium in a Market for First-Party Personal Injury Coverage Under Traditional Tort [Reprinted from page 20 of [3] with kind permission from Springer Science + Business Media B.V.]

sonal injury automobile insurance coverage under a traditional tort system. In this figure, the curve D_Q represents hypothetical market demand for this coverage, and the curve S_Q represents hypothetical market supply. Market equilibrium is found at the point E, the intersection of the two curves.

Now consider Figure 10.2, which depicts the anticipated impact of a transition from traditional tort to mandatory no-fault. Clearly, the basic effects of this transition are: (1) to shift the demand curve to the right (to D'_Q), to recognize the transfer in the policyholders' resources from the purchase of liability personal injury coverage to first-party personal injury coverage; and (2) to shift the supply curve to the right (to S'_Q), to recognize the insurance companies' increased capacity for first-party personal injury coverage as the market for liability personal injury coverage evaporates. The net result of imposing mandatory no-fault is thus to shift market

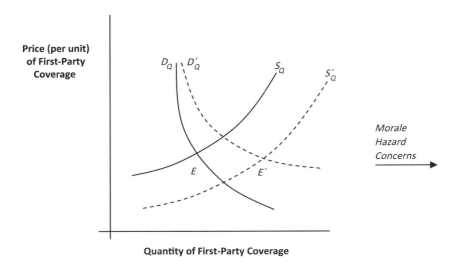

Figure 10.2
Equilibrium in a Market for First-Party Personal Injury Coverage Under Mandatory No-Fault [Reprinted from page 21 of [3] with kind permission from Springer Science + Business Media B.V.]

equilibrium from E to E', increasing the quantity of first-party personal injury coverage purchased, with an ambiguous effect on price.

As noted along the right-hand border of this figure, the region of increased first-party personal injury quantity is where problems of morale hazard are most likely to occur. In other words, as the equilibrium level of first-party personal injury coverage increases, policyholders are more likely to take risks in their driving, both because of enhanced first-party compensation and because of reduced liability risk.

To look more closely at the specific effects of a choice mechanism, I now will posit an entire continuum of mandatory no-fault systems existing between the extremes of traditional tort and mandatory pure no-fault. (For example, one could start with a monetary threshold of 0 and gradually increase its value through the positive real numbers to infinity.) In this model, the policyholders and insurance companies not only would be permitted to select the optimal amount of first-party personal injury coverage to buy and sell, respectively, but also would be permitted the choice of the optimal trade-off between reliance on traditional tort (with liability personal injury coverage) and pure no-fault (with only first-party personal injury coverage).

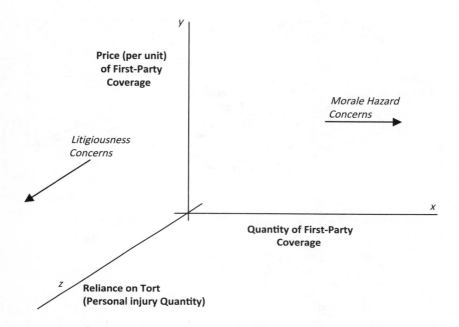

Figure 10.3
Market with Choice between Traditional Tort and Pure No-Fault [Reprinted
from page 22 of [3] with kind permission from Springer Science+Business
Media B.V.]

To depict market demand and market supply under these assumptions would require a three-dimensional coordinate system, as shown in Figure 10.3. Here, the horizontal (x-) and vertical (y-) axes are identical to those used in Figure 10.1, whereas the z-axis represents the degree to which traditional tort is relied on for personal injury recoveries.

From this figure, it can be seen that as reliance on no-fault increases, there tend to be greater problems with morale hazard in equilibrium, whereas as reliance on traditional tort increases, there tend to be greater problems with litigiousness (the underlying motivation for no-fault in the first place). Thus, morale hazard and litigiousness may be viewed as conceptually analogous behaviors: the former the pathology of excessive first-party insurance, and the latter the pathology of excessive liability insurance.

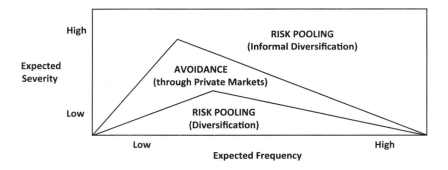

Figure 10.4
Government's Approach to Risk Finance? (Compare with Figure 7.3 for Insurance Companies.)

Government as Compensator

Previously, we considered in some detail the risk finance paradigm for insurance companies, including the proposed guidelines in Figure 7.3.[9] I now wish to turn to the case of national governments—often viewed as potential insurers of last resort—and hypothesize the paradigm in Figure 10.4 as a rough model. While partitioning the same two-dimensional (expected-frequency versus expected-severity) space into exactly the same geometric regions as those in Figure 7.3, the new diagram modifies and shuffles the labels associated with those regions as follows:

- Avoidance (through risk control) becomes risk pooling (informal diversification);
- Risk pooling (diversification) remains risk pooling (diversification); and
- Risk transfer (hedging) becomes avoidance (through private markets).

Unlike an insurance company, a national government cannot actually avoid any particular category of risk. Therefore, all exposures in the top-most region (with high expected severities, whether associated with low or high expected frequencies) must be accepted, albeit reluctantly, by the government. However, because of the political difficulty associated with setting aside sufficient financial reserves for these costliest of exposures, the government will tend to address them only as they occur, on a pay-as-you-go basis. In the bottommost region, the government can take advantage of the likely presence of many similar and uncorrelated claims with low expected severities, so this region is much like the corresponding region for insurance companies. Here, the government sets aside formal reserves for various social insurance programs (e.g., pensions, health insurance, and unemployment/disability benefits). Finally, in the middle region, the government typically tries its best to avoid these risks by encouraging firms and individuals to rely on their own private insurance products (but naturally, does not always succeed).

In the remainder of this section, I will consider the role of the national government in what is often the most controversial portion of the above regions: the catastrophe exposures in the topmost region that government must pool informally. In particular, I will address the broad question "When does government have a moral obligation to provide compensation to victims?" through a set of three compensation principles developed in joint work with my colleague Edward Lascher.[10]

Paternalism

The most paternalistic response to the above question is that government should compensate victims of all of life's uncertainties, from cradle to grave. Such an approach naturally would include the generous forms of social insurance that exist throughout much of the developed world today. For example, one would expect comprehensive social insurance programs for pensioners and the disabled, as well as national health insurance. In addition, the most paternalistic approach would provide government-financed life insurance for dependent beneficiaries in the case of untimely death, as well as various types of property-liability insurance—automobile, workers compensation, professional malpractice, etc.—presumably on a first-party/no-fault basis, but including compensation for pain and suffering as well as economic loss. Furthermore, the fully paternalistic system would not be complete without affording pain-and-suffering benefits for other untoward events not commonly insured (either privately or publicly) in today's world, such as birth defects, degenerative disease, poor upbringing, etc.

Obviously, such a paternalistic system would be prohibitively expensive even under the most ordinary, noncatastrophic conditions. In addition, the system would be subject to intolerable degrees of morale hazard, as individual citizens would have little financial incentive to take reasonable precautions against a wide variety of risks. Positing that such a paternalistic system is prima facie impracticable, let us turn to what the next most generous, but reasonably practicable compensation principle might be. In other words, having acknowledged that the moral argument for comprehensive all-risk insurance leads to a public policy vacuum, what more restrictive moral principle could one impose?

Government Liability

Essentially, one needs to introduce some further moral reason for government to be involved in compensation—that is, something beyond the simple idea that it is the responsibility of government to take care of all of its citizens' needs. One evident candidate for this criterion is the concept of liability, or culpability. That is, it seems natural to argue that government should compensate victims if government could have done more to avoid/mitigate losses, but failed to do so (or if indeed government were directly responsible for exposing individuals to risk, as in a mandatory inoculation program).

Thus, the *first compensation principle* is the following: Government should compensate victims of unpredictable events whenever it has failed to take reasonable pre-event risk control measures (and especially in the extreme case in which government intentionally exposes certain individuals to risk).

In applying this principle in practice, policymakers quickly would encounter the difficult question of whether or not certain actions of government can be construed as reasonable. For example, in the context of the September 11, 2001, attacks, it might be argued that various intelligence and security lapses of the U.S. government permitted the tragedy to occur. Would those lapses be evidence of the government's failure to take reasonable pre-event risk control steps?

In the context of terrorism or other violent criminal activity, one useful measure of government liability for failure to take preventive action is the size or extent of the criminal conspiracy involved. In other words, it seems more reasonable to expect government intelligence, defense, and law enforcement agencies to be able to prevent a criminal act perpetrated by a large, international organization (such as Al Qaeda) than one carried out by a conspiracy of two or three individuals (as in the Oklahoma City bombing of 1995).

Victim Responsibility

Let us now consider the role of individual victims. Should the failure of in-dividuals to take their own risk control and/or risk finance measures argue against government's responsibility? In other words, is there a contributory negligence clause in the social contract? Clearly, it would seem that govern-ment should, to an extent, be absolved of some of its obligation to compen-sate victims whenever: (1) government is not the direct cause of the untow-ard event; and (2) the victims made themselves more vulnerable to loss by failing to take certain obvious and easily manageable pre-event actions.

Specifically, a victim's failure to take reasonable pre-event risk control and/or risk finance measures—as in the case of an individual's construct-ing a wood-frame house in a hurricane-prone area where storm damage property coverage is not readily available—may lessen justification for government compensation. If the failure to take risk control measures is actually encouraged by the expectation of government compensation, then the problem of morale hazard must be addressed. Similarly, if the failure to take risk finance measures is encouraged by the expectation of government compensation and if this failure is limited primarily to higher-risk potential victims, then the problem of adverse selection must be addressed. Overall, it would seem that government has a stronger rea-son for compensating victims if private market insurance is either un-available (as in the case of some property-liability terrorism coverage) or unaffordable (e.g., if potential victims are simply too poor to buy even the most reasonably priced policies).

This leads to the *second compensation principle*: Government's re-sponsibility to compensate victims under the first principle is lessened if the victims failed to take reasonable pre-event risk control and/or risk fi-nance measures (and especially if the compensation program itself were to create a significant problem of morale hazard and/or adverse selection).

Utilitarianism

Putting aside questions of the comparative responsibilities of government and individuals, let us now turn to an analysis of how government's actions can affect the utility of outcomes. From a strictly utilitarian per-spective, one could ask: When is government compensation most useful in terms of maximizing social welfare?

To some extent, this question is best answered on a case-by-case basis; however, institutional experience suggests that there are two types of scenarios in which government action would be most helpful: (1) when the financial stability—and possibly even existence—of private insurance and/or reinsurance markets is threatened; and (2) when the absence of government compensation, ipso facto, is likely to cause further significant loss or other negative consequences to the economy or society as a whole.

These two scenarios are both addressed generically by the *third compensation principle*: Government should compensate victims of unpredictable events when the failure to compensate is likely to cause additional significant economic and/or social problems.

Of course, the determination of such negative consequences is apt to be difficult in the real world, where policymakers and interest groups may easily disagree as to whether or not the failure to compensate will cause significant hardships. In particular, certain parties (e.g., the airline and insurance industries after September 11, 2001) also are likely to have tactical financial reasons for exaggerating the potential untoward results of a failure to compensate.

ACT 2, SCENE 5

[Same police interrogation room. Suspect sits at table; two police officers stand.]

BAD COP: "Negligible risk"? That's the most bogus explanation I've ever heard. Those risk levels are for businesses, not individuals. And those businesses pay taxes, which are used to compensate the victims.

GOOD COP: [Quietly, to himself.] One hopes . . .

SUSPECT: But officers, I *am* a business. Specifically, I've incorporated a company under my own name and was working for the company when the killings occurred. As for taxes, I always pay what's required of me. And there's something else you've chosen to overlook: I left a $1,000 bill with each of the bodies, to compensate any dependents. How many pollution victims get that much direct compensation?

GOOD COP: But you're ignoring the most important thing: The environmental risk levels you mentioned are for deaths that occur by chance—not for premeditated murder!

SUSPECT: *Premeditation*? I think you'll have to agree that it hardly applies to me. You see, I drew the names of all twelve people at random from a list of the entire state population.

GOOD COP: So that's why the victims had so little in common. But there's still something I don't understand. You said the murders—I mean, *killings*— were intended as an experiment. That doesn't sound like much of a motive to me.

SUSPECT: Well, if you're looking for a conventional motive, I suppose you could say that I killed for the thrill of it. Not for the thrill of seeing blood or anything like that, but for the thrill of killing both *permissibly* and *paradoxically*!

BAD COP: Come again?

SUSPECT: Look, I've already explained that the letter of the law gave me permission to kill because of negligible risk and all that. I'll now explain why no killings actually took place, despite your apparent physical evidence to the contrary. We know that the letter of the law is responsible for the killings. Now, anyone familiar with words can see that if a *letter* kills, then it must do so *literally*. On the other hand, if the letter of the law is actually a *number*—like 1/1,000,000—then it must kill *figuratively* as well. You see? Finally, since the set of things that occur *literally* and the set of things that occur *figuratively* are mutually exclusive, it follows that no killings— *none whatsoever*—could have occurred!

BAD COP: [Bewildered.] Just what sort of crazy lawyer are you?

SUSPECT: Why, a Philadelphia lawyer, of course.[11]

3

Scientific Challenges

11

What Is Randomness?
Knowable and Unknowable Complexity

Eenie-meenie-miney-moe, catch a tiger by the toe.
If he hollers, let him go. Eenie-meenie-miney-moe.
—PRIMITIVE RANDOM-NUMBER GENERATOR

Few ideas in mathematics are as mysterious as the notion of randomness. As observed in Chapter 2, random variables are commonly used to model unknown quantities, including the full gamut of risks, in the physical world. However, this generally is done without either a formal definition of randomness or even a convincing demonstration that *truly* random processes actually exist. Another source of mystery—the conspicuous analogy between randomness as the uncertainty of the outside world and free will as the uncertainty of the mind—offers the alluring possibility that an understanding of randomness can offer an instructive glimpse, however metaphorical, into the fundamental principles of human behavior and ethics.

By addressing the subtleties and limitations associated with an understanding of randomness, the present chapter considers the first of several challenges to a science of risk. In subsequent chapters, I will explore the further challenges of modeling, analyzing, and drawing conclusions from various manifestations of uncertainty in our world—including those generated by the human mind itself.

God's Dice

When one looks for instances of randomness among the ordinary experiences of life, numerous examples come to mind: stock prices, coin tosses, weather patterns, industrial accidents, etc.[1] The most salient aspect of these and similar phenomena is their unpredictability; that is, they are unknown ahead of time and generally cannot be forecast with anything approaching perfect accuracy. There are, however, certain limited circumstances under which such phenomena can be predicted reasonably well: those in which the forecaster possesses what financial traders might call "insider" information.

Just as a stock trader who receives a confidential internal company report may be able to anticipate a significant upward or downward movement in the company's stock price, so may a magician who is skilled at tossing coins be able to achieve Heads with a high degree of certainty, a meteorologist with the latest satellite imagery be able to forecast the emergence of a hurricane, and a worker who recognizes his employer's poor safety practices foresee an accident "waiting to happen." This type of information is obviously available in different degrees to different observers in different contexts. Thus, whereas a privileged stock trader may know with 90 percent certainty that a yet-to-be-disclosed profit report will cause a firm's stock price to increase by at least 5 percent during the next trading day, an informed meteorologist may be only 80 percent certain that a category 5 hurricane will emerge within the next 48 hours. Moreover, whereas an experienced magician may be 99+ percent certain that his or her next coin toss will result in Heads, a novice magician may be only 75 percent certain of this outcome.

To be clear, therefore, about what is meant by "insider" information, I would say that it consists of any and all information potentially available to the most privileged, persistent, and conscientious observer, whether or not such an observer exists in practice. With regard to a given random variable, I will denote the amount of uncertainty that can be eliminated through such information as *knowable complexity* (KC). Any residual uncertainty, which cannot be dispelled by even the ideal observer, will be called *unknowable complexity* (UC).

To illustrate the difference between these two types of uncertainty—and indeed, to provide a concrete example of the latter form—consider what happens when a person tosses a coin onto a table. At the moment of releasing the coin, the individual imparts a certain velocity and rotation to it at a given distance above the table. As the coin travels through the air, it is slightly affected by friction from air molecules. When the coin strikes the surface of the table, the impact causes a succession of bounces and rolls that ultimately results in the coin's coming to rest with one of its sides exposed.

Clearly, if one could measure the exact position and velocity of every molecule, every atom, and every subatomic particle in the coin tosser's hand, the coin itself, the air, and the tabletop at the moment of the coin's release, then the outcome of the toss could be determined with complete accuracy. Under this assumption, all sources of uncertainty would constitute KC. However, such an assumption would be wrong.

No magician, no matter how skillful, can force Heads to come up on every try. This is because the coin's trajectory and final resting place are affected by events at the atomic level (for example, the minute change in momentum associated with the release of an alpha particle from a trace radioactive isotope in a sensitive nerve cell of the magician's hand), and, according to Heisenberg's uncertainty principle, an observer cannot know simultaneously both the exact position and the exact momentum of an elementary particle.[2] Consequently, there will always be some residual uncertainty, or UC, associated with the behavior of the particles involved in the coin toss.

This UC affects not only coin tosses, but also stock prices, weather patterns, industrial accidents, and all other physical phenomena. In one sense, its existence is disturbing because it is difficult to believe that every coin and other object in the universe is composed of particles that move about in unpredictable ways—making decisions on their own, so to speak.[3] Alternatively, however, one could view UC as an attractive "spice of life" and take comfort in the fact that, as technology provides ever-greater amounts of insider information, UC is the only thing preventing a bleakly deterministic future. Regardless of esthetic considerations, I would equate UC with *true randomness*.

Incompressibility

In the absence of overt insider information—in other words, when the relevant KC is actually unknown to the observer—probability theory can be used to model KC just as well as UC. This is apparent even without any knowledge of modern quantum physics and was noted by British philosopher David Hume in his famous treatise, *An Enquiry Concerning Human Understanding* (1748):[4]

It is true, when any cause fails of producing its usual effect, philoso-
phers ascribe not this to any irregularity in nature [i.e., what I am
calling UC—author's note]; but suppose, that some secret causes, in
the particular structure of parts [i.e., what I am calling KC—author's
note], have prevented the operation. Our reasonings, however, and
conclusions concerning the event are the same as if this principle had
no place.... Where different effects have been found to follow from
causes, which are to *appearance* [emphasis in original] exactly similar, all these various effects must occur to the mind in transferring
the past to the future, and enter into our consideration, when we determine the probability of the event.

Hume goes on to assert that "chance, when strictly examined, is a
mere negative word, and means not any real power which has anywhere a
being in nature."[5] In other words, the concept of chance denotes only the
absence of information about underlying causes, and does not distinguish
between UC and KC. So what, then, is the purpose of defining these two
sources of uncertainty separately? And more pointedly, what is the purpose of seeking the meaning of true randomness?

The answer is that in real life, even in the absence of overt insider information, one often possesses more than one observation of a given random variable. Although one cannot be sure whether the uncertainty associated with a single outcome involves UC or KC, it may be possible to
make this determination with a sequence of outcomes. Specifically, statistical methods can be developed to try to determine whether or not the
observations evince the systematic behavior expected of KC.

In the 1960s, three mathematicians, Russian Andrey Kolmogorov and
Americans Ray Solomonoff and Gregory Chaitin, independently proposed
a formal definition of randomness that comports well with the present
distinction between UC and KC.[6] Working with (possibly infinite) sequences of integers, these researchers suggested that a sequence of integers
of a given length is *algorithmically random* if and only if it cannot be en-
coded into another sequence of integers that is substantially shorter than
the original sequence. Such a sequence is said to be *incompressible*.

For simplicity, and without loss of generality, one can work with sequences of only 0s and 1s, viewed as binary computer code. To illustrate
their concept, consider the infinite sequence 0101010101 . . . , formed by endlessly alternating the digits 0 and 1, beginning with an initial 0. Clearly, such
a sequence is not in any sense random; but to show that it is indeed com-

pressible, one must find a means of mapping it to a shorter (finite) sequence. There are many ways to do this, and one of the most straightforward—but not necessarily most efficient—simply entails matching each letter of the English alphabet with its ordinal number expressed in base 2 (i.e., A = 00001, B = 00010, C = 00011, . . . , Z = 11010), and then assigning the remaining five-digit base-2 numbers to other useful typographical symbols (i.e., capital-letter indicator = 11011, space = 11100, apostrophe = 11101, comma = 11110, and period = 11111). Using these letters and symbols, one can write virtually any English-language phrase, and so it follows that the phrase "The infinite sequence formed by endlessly alternating the digits 0 and 1, beginning with an initial 0" can be transformed quite nicely into a finite sequence of 0s and 1s, thereby compressing the original sequence dramatically.

It is often convenient to treat (finite or infinite) sequences of 0s and 1s as base-2 decimal expansions between 0 and 1; for example, the sequence 0101010101 . . . may be interpreted as 0.0101010101 . . . in base 2, which equals

$$\frac{0}{2} + \frac{1}{4} + \frac{0}{8} + \frac{1}{16} + \frac{0}{32} + \frac{1}{64} + \frac{0}{128} + \frac{1}{256} + \frac{0}{512} + \frac{1}{1,024} + \dots$$

or 0.333 . . . in base 10. Viewing things this way, it can be shown that *almost all* of the real numbers between 0 and 1 (of which there are *C*) are incompressible. In other words, if one were to draw a real number from a continuous uniform probability distribution over the interval [0,1), then one would obtain an incompressible number with certainty. However, in the paradoxical world of the continuum, nothing is straightforward; so, although *almost every* real number in [0,1) is incompressible, Chaitin has shown that it is impossible to prove that *any particular* infinitely long decimal is incompressible![7]

Simulated Whim

There are many scientific applications in which researchers and practitioners find it useful to simulate sequences of random variables.[8] Examples range from computational methods for solving numerical problems by restating them in probabilistic terms to randomized controlled scientific studies to the testing of business and emergency management strategies under a variety of potential scenarios. Although the random variables employed in these applications could be generated by physical processes—like tossing coins and rolling dice—such processes generally are too cumbersome and time-consuming to be of practical use. Instead, researchers and practitioners typically use the chaotic behavior of certain deterministic mathematical processes to create sequences of *pseudo-random variables* (i.e., sequences that not only are characterized by KC, but also are known to the observer ahead of time).

One of the most common techniques for simulating random numbers is the *linear congruential generator* (LCG), a simple example of which is the following:

- Let the seed value of the pseudo-random sequence (that is, the 0th term, R_0) be 1.
- To get the $(i+1)$st term from the ith term, multiply R_i by 5, then add 3, and finally take the remainder after dividing by 16.

Applying this LCG yields the following values for R_1 through R_{16}:

$$8, 11, 10, 5, 12, 15, 14, 9, 0, 3, 2, 13, 4, 7, 6, 1.$$

Unfortunately, the very next integer in the above sequence is 8, which means that the simple LCG begins to repeat itself after only 16 numbers. In fact, cycling occurs with all LCGs, although the length of the cycle may be made arbitrarily long (and is typically at least $2 \times 2 \times \ldots \times 2$ [32 times] digits in practice). Other problems with LCGs—such as serial correlation—are not so easily remedied, so more sophisticated methods are often employed.

Now suppose that one would like to construct, very deliberately, an infinite sequence of numbers that is as "incompressible-looking" or "random-looking" as possible. (Keep in mind that it is known, from Chaitin's impossibility result, that one cannot generate an infinite sequence that is *actually* incompressible.) To this end, simply using an LCR or other pseudo-random number generator will not suffice; after all, those methods are designed to simulate *true* randomness, not random-*looking*ness, so it is reasonably likely that any given sequence produced by such a method would contain noticeably patterned components from time to time, just as would any truly random sequence.

A Surprising Detour

To characterize formally what is meant by a random-looking sequence, it is helpful to introduce the *surprise function*, which is a highly intuitive mathematical transformation of probability. Basically, the surprise associated with the event x, denoted by $s(x)$, is given by the negative of the base-2 logarithm of the probability $p(x)$.[9]

Without delving into a formal derivation of surprise, I will make a few observations regarding its properties. First, it can be seen that as $p(x)$ takes on values increasing from 0 to 1, $s(x)$ takes on corresponding values decreasing from positive infinity to 0. Thus, when a specific event x is very unlikely to occur, with a probability approaching 0, its surprise becomes very large, approaching infinity. Likewise, when a specific event is very likely to occur, with a probability approaching 1, its surprise becomes very small, approaching 0. Finally, if x and y are two independent events with identical probability distributions, then the surprise associated with *both x and y*'s occurring is given by the sum of the surprise associated with x and the surprise associated with y. These properties correspond fairly well to intuitive notions of how the emotion of surprise should operate.

But the real intuitive advantage of working with surprise is that, in terms of metaphorical foundations, it is a more primitive concept than probability itself. As noted previously, the basic motivation for probability is the frequency interpretation—that is, the idea of a long-run rate with which a particular event occurs among a sequence of repeated independent observations. However, surprise is an innate human emotion that requires no underlying supposition of repeated trials. When something occurs, one simply finds it surprising or unsurprising in different degrees. In this way, the concept of surprise provides an elegant unification of the frequency and subjective interpretations of probability: probability as frequency is a transformation of surprise in a context in which repeated trials take place, whereas probability as cognitive metaphor (degree of belief) is just a generic transformation of surprise.

Figure 11.1 reveals how easily surprise can be substituted for probability in a real-world application. Essentially, this plot reproduces the mortality hazard rate data from Figure 1.2, using conditional surprises of death rather than conditional probabilities of death. One particularly striking aspect of this figure is the near linearity of the surprise hazard curve, meaning that as an individual ages by one year, the surprise associated with his or her death decreases by an almost constant amount. Although

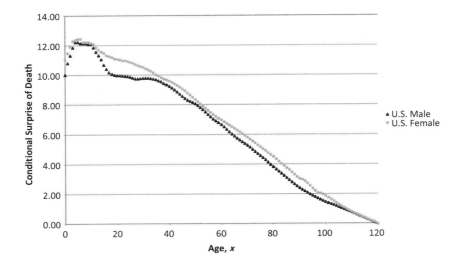

Figure 11.1
Surprise from One-Year Mortality Hazard Rate Source: Commissioners Standard
Ordinary (CSO) Mortality Table (2001).

this approximate linearity may be explained mathematically by the fact
that the logarithm of the surprise transformation roughly inverts the exponential component of the Gompertz-Makeham law,[10] it also raises an
intriguing possibility: Could the emotion of surprise be a biological mechanism calibrated specifically to recognize and assess the fragility of human
life?

Least-Surprising Sequences

Consistent with the notation in our earlier discussion of incompressibil-
ity, let us consider sequences of independent coin tosses in which one side
of the coin (Heads) is labeled with the number 1, the other side (Tails) is
labeled with the number 0, and the probability of obtaining a 1 on a given
toss is exactly 1/2. (For a real-world example, one might think of the numbers 1 and 0 as indicating whether or not individual insurance claims, as
they are closed, are settled for amounts above the claim adjustor's original
forecast—in which case a 1 is recorded, or below the claim adjustor's original forecast—in which case a 0 is recorded.) For any given sequence length,

n, I now will seek the sequence that is *least surprising* among all sequences of that length and identify that as the most random-looking sequence.

In applying the notion of surprise, one has to identify carefully the probability function from which the least-surprising random sequence is drawn. For example, setting n equal to 5 yields a sample space of 32 possible sequences of 0s and 1s of length 5 (i.e., 00000, 00001, 00010, . . . , 11111). Considering the unconditional probability that any one of these sequences occurs, one sees immediately that it must equal 1/32, so each of the 32 sequences occurs with exactly the same probability. Under this model, both the highly patterned sequence 00000 and the much less patterned sequence 10110 have the same surprise—given by the negative of the base-2 logarithm of 1/32, which equals 5—counter to the desired objective.

One way to construct a probability function that distinguishes between more highly patterned and less highly patterned sequences is to measure the statistical properties of a sequence of n independent coin tosses in terms of various sample parameters, and then to give greater weight to those sequences whose sample parameters are closer to their expected values. For example, one could consider the sample mean, which, for a sequence of 5 coin tosses may be written as

$$(X_1 + X_2 + X_3 + X_4 + X_5)/5,$$

where each X_i is a 0 or 1 that denotes the outcome of the ith coin toss. Clearly, the expected value of this sample mean is 1/2 (which is also the expected value of any one of the X_i), so it would make sense for the probability function to give more weight to those sequences such as 10110 and 00011 whose sample means are close to 1/2 (i.e., 3/5 and 2/5, respectively), than to sequences such as 00000 and 11111 whose sample means are far from 1/2 (i.e., 0 and 1, respectively).

However, using the sample mean is not enough, because one also wants to give more weight to those sequences whose 0s and 1s are more convincingly "scrambled" (i.e., have fewer instances of either long strings of identical outcomes, such as 00011 or 11100, or long strings of strictly alternating outcomes, such as 01010 or 10101). Another way of saying this is that one wishes to favor sequences manifesting less structure from one term to the next—that is, less *first-order* structure. A useful sample parameter in this regard is given by

(Number of Times Two Successive Terms Are Different)/4,

whose expected value, like that of the sample mean, is 1/2. Extending this logic further, it is easy to develop analogous sample parameters to identify sequences possessing less *second-order* structure, *third-order* structure, and *fourth-order* structure, respectively.

For any given positive integer n, the sample mean and the other sample parameters may be combined in a statistically appropriate manner to form a comprehensive summary statistic, S_n.[11] The least-surprising sequence of length n is then found recursively by choosing the value of X_n (i.e., 0 or 1) that minimizes S_n, given the least-surprising sequence of length $n - 1$. This sequence begins as follows:

$$0111010010000100001111100011111111110010111110101 \ldots .[12]$$

Converting the sequence to a base-2 decimal yields

$$0.0111010010000100001111100011111111110010111110101 \ldots ,$$

which is equivalent to the base-10 decimal 0.455142 . . . .

Heuristically, the above process admits of the following interpretation: Suppose one begins tossing a fair coin and reveals the successive coin tosses to an observer, one at a time. Assuming that there is some objective method of measuring the observer's emotional reaction to each toss—and that the observer is able to keep track of second-, third-, and higher-order structures just as well as the first-order structure and overall mean—one would find that the sequence, 0, 1, 1, 1, 0, 1, 0, 0, 1, 0, . . . would seem less surprising (and therefore more random-looking) to the observer than would any other sequence. Also, one could think of the decimal 0.455142 . . . as representing the least-surprising (and so most random) selection of a continuous uniform random variable from the interval [0,1). This number presumably balances the expectation that such a random variable should be approximately 1/2 (the true mean) with the expectation that it cannot be too close to 1/2 without appearing somewhat artificial.

Cognition and Behavior

Where do the above discussions lead with regard to the understanding of uncertainty and the ability to identify and respond to manifestations of risk? If one associates incompressible sequences with UC and compressible sequences with KC, then the preceding analyses cast a shadow of doubt over statistical hypothesis testing and, indeed, over the entire approach to human understanding known as the scientific method.

Suppose one encounters an infinite sequence of observations and wishes to evaluate whether it evinces KC or UC. Given Chaitin's impossibility result, it is illogical to state the null hypothesis as H_0: "The sequence is characterized by KC" because that assertion could never be rejected (since its rejection would imply that the sequence is incompressible, which cannot be proved). On the other hand, if one were to state the null hypothesis as H_0: "The sequence is characterized by UC," but were confronted with observations from our least-surprising sequence, then one would fail to reject the null hypothesis (i.e., commit a type-2 error) with certainty, regardless of the sample size, because the data would provide no evidence of underlying structure. Although it might be argued, quite reasonably, that the *total absence* of such structure is itself a manifestation of structure, such "no-structure" structure could never be confirmed with a finite number of observations.

In short, no systematic approach to the study of randomness can ever: (1) confirm a source of uncertainty as UC; or (2) confirm some sources of uncertainty as KC without inevitably creating type-2 errors in other contexts. These are the cognitive constraints under which we operate.

With regard to constraints on human behavior, I would begin by noting the explicit parallel between randomness in the physical world and free will in the realm of the mind. In his analysis of human liberty (of action), Hume ultimately concludes that "liberty, when opposed to necessity, ... is the same thing with chance; which is universally allowed to have no existence."[13] In other words, Hume views "liberty," like "chance," as a purely negative word; so the concept of liberty denotes only the absence of necessity in one's actions.

To explore the characteristics of this absence of necessity, let us posit a simple model of human decision making. Assume that at any point in time, t, an individual must select a vast list of decision rules, $D_1^{(t)}, D_2^{(t)}, \ldots, D_n^{(t)}$, which tell him or her what to do in any possible future situation. (For example, $D_1^{(t)}$ might indicate which foods to eat, $D_2^{(t)}$ might give directions on how hard to work, etc.) Assume further that these decision rules are chosen to maximize some overall evaluation function, $V^{(t)}(D_1^{(t)}, D_2^{(t)}, \ldots, D_n^{(t)})$. The crucial question is: Where does $V^{(t+1)}$ come from?

One possibility is that people simply are born with the evaluation function $V^{(0)}$ and that $V^{(t+1)}$ equals $V^{(0)}$ for all t. However, this type of determinism hardly satisfies the absence of necessity that is sought. Another possibility is that a purely random (e.g., quantum-based) phenomenon causes the transition from $V^{(t)}$ to $V^{(t+1)}$. But although this explanation does permit an absence of necessity, it also envisions a detached and impersonal species of free will that is quite unsatisfying. This leaves one final possibility: that $V^{(t)}$ is used to select $V^{(t+1)}$, but in a way that does not converge too quickly to a limiting value. As more than one astute observer has noted, "The purpose of an open mind is to close it."[14] Clearly, however, a mind with free will should be expected to close with a certain degree of deliberation. One way to ensure this restraint is to introduce a certain amount of KC that is unknown to the individual.

Essentially, $V^{(t)}$ has to choose $V^{(t+1)}$, but in such a way that the choice is too complex to be foreseen or analyzed easily. In other words, the individual maximizes $V^{(t)}(D_1^{(t)}, D_2^{(t)}, \ldots, D_n^{(t)})$ over $D_1^{(t)}, D_2^{(t)}, \ldots, D_n^{(t)}$, and then sets $V^{(t+1)} = D_i^{(t)}$ for some i, where identifying the optimal $D_i^{(t)}$ requires a procedure with sufficient KC that its outcome, ex ante, appears random. This may be accomplished simply by the optimization program's requiring so many steps that it cannot be computed quickly. As any puzzle enthusiast knows, solving a difficult problem often requires a large number of separate attempts, many of which turn out to be false starts. Nevertheless, throughout the challenging process, the solver never feels anything less than the complete conviction that he or she is perfectly free to find the correct solution.

To illustrate (albeit somewhat crudely) how $V^{(t)}$ may be used to select $V^{(t+1)}$, one might imagine a newborn child's entering the world with an innate philosophy of action, $V^{(0)}$, endowed by Darwinian evolution. Say, for example, that $V^{(0)}$ represents a primitive, clan-based tribalism. Then, as the child progresses through his or her first two decades, $V^{(0)}$ may be replaced by a form of religious monotheism to which the child's parents subscribe and which the child adopts out of loyalty to its family. Let us call this new philosophy $V^{(1)} = D_i^{(0)}$. Assuming that the times are peaceful and resources plentiful, the young adult may find the love and social harmony espoused by $V^{(1)}$ to be a calling to some type of intellectual estheticism, denoted by $V^{(2)} = D_i^{(1)}$. Ultimately, after many years of contemplation, the individual may employ $V^{(2)}$ to conclude that the most elegant and intellectually satisfying philosophy of all is Bayesian utilitarianism—to be called $V^{(3)} = D_i^{(2)}$—which is retained for the remainder of his or her life.

An interesting point to consider is whether or not improvements in artificial intelligence will have any impact on our perceptions of free will. Suppose that one could input all of the information relevant to $V^{(t)}(D_1^{(t)}, D_2^{(t)}, \ldots, D_n^{(t)})$ into a computer and that the problem of solving for $D_i^{(t)} = V^{(t+1)}$ could be carried out in a relatively short period of time—say, a matter of minutes. In such an eventuality, one conceivably could run through the actual sequence $V^{(t)}$, $V^{(t+1)} = D_i^{(t)}$, $V^{(t+2)} = D_i^{(t+1)}$, etc. to a point at which it became clear that the sequence either converged or diverged. In the former case, one might adopt a jaded attitude, viewing oneself as nothing more than a mechanical construction of evolution. In the latter case, one might become depressed from knowing that all decisions are essentially ephemeral in nature. At that juncture, one might welcome a discovery that UC—perhaps in the form of minute quantum effects on the human brain—actually does inject some "spice" into one's internal life.

ACT 3, SCENE 1

[Same psychiatrist's office. Doctor sits in chair; patient sits on couch.]

DOCTOR: Good day, Mrs. Morton. How are things? Is your iatrogenic asterophobia under control?

PATIENT: My what? Oh, that! Yes, actually it's fine, I mean, it *was* fine. It wasn't a problem because I had avoided thinking about it . . . until you just mentioned it.

DOCTOR: I see. These iatrogenic—or perhaps in this case I should say iatro*regenic*—disorders can be very frustrating. Have you considered stopping your visits to the doctor?

PATIENT: Yes, as a matter of fact—

DOCTOR: Of course, if you stopped your doctor visits, then you wouldn't be able to have your condition properly diagnosed as iatrogenic. So, there's a bit of a paradox there, I suppose. [Laughs.]

PATIENT: Doctor, it's funny that you should raise that issue . . . because I wanted to talk to you about switching psychiatrists.

DOCTOR: Switching? Do you mean you'd prefer to see a different doctor?

PATIENT: Yes. I'm sorry, but . . . I think it would be better for me.

DOCTOR: I see. And just what is it about my services that you find inadequate, if you don't mind my asking? It's not the business about the iatrogenic asterophobia, is it?

PATIENT: No, no. Please understand—it's nothing personal. I just think that I'd feel more comfortable ... *communicating* ... with someone else.

DOCTOR: I'm not sure that I follow you. Are you saying that you're having trouble expressing yourself to me?

PATIENT: Yes, I suppose that's it.

DOCTOR: Or is it that you think I'm having trouble understanding what you're saying?

PATIENT: Well, I'm not quite sure. But in any case, I'd like to ask you to recommend a new doctor.

DOCTOR: I'm sorry, Mrs. Morton, but I feel somewhat confused. If you're dissatisfied with my services, then why would you want to rely on my recommendation?

PATIENT: Hmm, I see your point. But what alternative do I have? I found *you* by choosing a name at random from a medical directory, and I don't want to repeat *that* procedure.

DOCTOR: No, naturally you don't. Well, then, that leaves only one solution.

PATIENT: Really? What do you suggest?

DOCTOR: It's quite obvious, isn't it? You'll just have to let *me* choose a name at random from the medical directory.

PATIENT: Doctor, you're brilliant!

DOCTOR: Yes. So are you certain you still want to switch?

12

Patterns, Real and Imagined
Observation and Theory

Let us suppose for example that some one jots down a quantity of points upon a sheet of paper helter skelter . . . ; now I say that it is possible to find a geometrical line whose concept shall be uniform and constant, that is, in accordance with a certain formula, and which line at the same time shall pass through all of those points, and in the same order in which the hand jotted them down.

—GOTTFRIED W. F. VON LEIBNIZ (*DISCOURSE ON METAPHYSICS*, 1686)[1]

When told that a particular scientific question is theoretically unanswerable, one's initial disbelief and intellectual rebellion is likely to be followed by wonder and even a certain degree of contentment. Results such as Heisenberg's uncertainty principle or Chaitin's impossibility theorem are not only intriguingly counterintuitive, but also psychologically comforting in that they tell us we have reached the end of one particular road of inquiry, and so can begin another. However, when one is told that a question is unanswerable in practice because of shortcomings with empirical methodologies, there is typically more annoyance than awe. This is because we know, or at least strongly suspect, that if we—or someone else—tried just a little harder or spent just a little more time or money, then the epistemological obstacle could be overcome.

In the previous chapter, I discussed the epistemology of randomness in theoretical terms. Given that the species of practice are generally more extensive than the genera of theory, a similar discussion of the bounds of uncertainty in practical, empirical terms will require three chapters in all. The present chapter will address fundamental problems of separating signals from noise in modeling risk-related phenomena. I then will move on to issues of data availability in Chapter 13, followed by the overall paradigm of the scientific method in Chapter 14.

Scholarly Pareidolia?

Sound empirical scientific research begins with the observation and subsequent investigation of patterns in data.[2] Fortunately, the human brain is well equipped for this task. Unfortunately, however, it is somewhat overequipped, possessing a well-known proclivity to do its best to make sense out of visual stimuli, regardless of how confusing or ambiguous they may be. This persistent tendency forms the basis for many common optical illusions (such as two-dimensional drawings of cubes that seem to switch back and forth between alternate orientations), as well as the phenomenon of *pareidolia*, in which a person believes that he or she sees systematic patterns in disordered and possibly entirely random data.

Rather ironically, the line between the overidentification and underidentification of patterns is one pattern that tends to be underidentified. In addition to dubious uses of data in pseudoscientific pursuits such as numerology and astrology, there also are various quasi-scientific methods, such as the Elliott wave principle employed by some financial analysts and neurolinguistic programming methods of business managers and communication facilitators that haunt the boundary of the scientific and the fanciful.

One context in which pareidolia is frequently cited is the field of planetary science, in which sober authorities often warn lay enthusiasts of the dangers of imagining structures from ancient alien civilizations on the surface of the Moon or Mars. Probably the most celebrated example is the "Face on Mars," an irregularly shaped plateau in the Cydonia region of the Red Planet that, in certain photographs taken from the *Viking 1* and *Viking 2* space probes, does look remarkably similar to a human face. (Unfortunately, in other photographs it looks much like a natural geological formation, which is why, in Chapter 5, I stated my personal belief that the probability this structure is the creation of an ancient civilization is less than 1 percent.)

Despite my own skepticism regarding the Martian "Face" as an alien artifact, I do think space scientists should be a bit more tolerant of those who imagine intriguing patterns where none may exist. After all, the history of astronomy owes several large debts to this phenomenon, including: (1) the naming of various (entirely imaginary) constellations by the ancients, which today provides a convenient system of locating objects in the celestial sphere; (2) the Titius-Bode law of exponentially increasing distances between the successive planets of our solar system, which spurred the search for new planetary bodies in the late eighteenth and early nineteenth centuries; and (3) the misguided claims (and detailed drawings) of "canals" on Mars, which stimulated interest and funding for the field of observational astronomy in the late nineteenth and early twentieth centuries.

The Titius-Bode law (TBL) deserves particular attention because of its remarkable similarity to the Gompertz-Makeham law (GML) of human mortality, mentioned previously. Taken together, these two principles provide a fertile basis for considering how formal models arise from empirical data and the extent to which they should be trusted.

Some Exponential Patterns

The TBL was proposed by German astronomer Johann Titius in 1766 and subsequently popularized by his compatriot, astronomer Johann Bode.[3] It asserts that the average distance from the sun to the orbit of the xth planet in our solar system is given by a linear combination of a constant term and an exponentially increasing function of x.[4],[5] Beginning several decades later, the GML was developed in two stages. First, British mathematician Benjamin Gompertz noted that the human mortality hazard rate tends to increase exponentially as a function of age (see Figure 1.2), and he therefore proposed a purely exponential hazard curve in 1825.[6] Subsequently, British actuary William Makeham generalized Gompertz's model in 1860, writing the mortality hazard rate at age x as the linear combination of a constant term and an exponentially increasing function of x (i.e., a functional form identical to that of the TBL).[7]

Figures 12.1 and 12.2 present relevant data for the TBL and GML, respectively. In the latter plot, I use the U.S. female (rather than male) population's mortality hazard rates because of their smoother behavior between the ages of 10 and 35. I also provide hazard rates only at ten equally spaced ages (10, 20, . . . , 100) to correspond visually to the ten planets of the solar system in Figure 12.1.[8],[9]

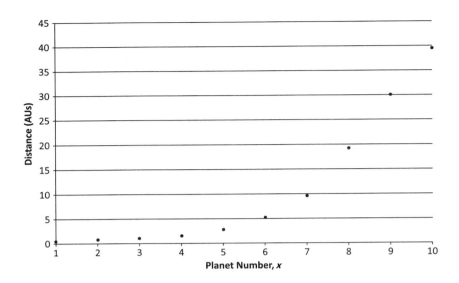

Figure 12.1
Average Planetary-Orbit Distances from Sun (Mercury = 1, . . . , Ceres = 5, . . . ,
Pluto = 10)

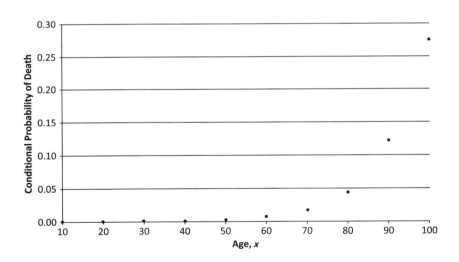

Figure 12.2
One-Year Mortality Hazard Rate (U.S. Females) Source: Commissioners Standard
Ordinary (CSO) Mortality Tables (2001).

The role of the TBL in the history of astronomy is intriguing, both for its motivation of the search for new planets and for the irony that surrounds its actual application. When first proposed, the law fit the orbits of the known planets—Mercury, Venus, Earth, Mars, Jupiter, and Saturn—quite well, and both Titius and Bode noted the conspicuous absence of a planetary body at the distance of the asteroid belt. However, the first object to be discovered after publication of the law was not one of the major asteroids, but rather the planet Uranus (by British astronomer William Herschel in 1781). Although this new planet's orbit followed the TBL fairly closely, it had not been predicted explicitly by either Titius or Bode (presumably because it fell outside, rather than within, the orbits of the known planets).

Having noted that the orbit of Uranus was approximated well by the law, Bode and others called for a cooperative effort among European astronomers to search the zodiac systematically for the "missing" planet at the distance of the asteroid belt. However, in a strange twist of fate, the first and largest of the asteroids—Ceres—was discovered by Italian astronomer Giuseppe Piazzi in 1801 independently of this effort. Thus, although the law theoretically could have guided both Herschel and Piazzi in their discoveries, it in fact did not. The law did, however, gain much credence among astronomers because of its apparent accuracy and certainly helped spur the search for additional planets. Unfortunately, the next two planets to be discovered—Neptune (in 1846) and Pluto (in 1930)—did not fit the TBL very well, so the law has fallen into general disfavor.

The successes and failures of the TBL are quite evident from Table 12.1, where its accuracy is explicitly compared with that of the GML based upon data from Figures 12.1 and 12.2. Using the error ratio

$$|(\text{Actual Value}) - (\text{Estimated Value})|/(\text{Estimated Value}),$$

it can be shown that exactly three of the mortality hazard rates—those at the end of the first, second, and fourth decades of life—and exactly three of the planetary orbits—those of Mercury, Neptune, and Pluto—deviate from their estimates by more than 10 percent.[10] Thus, according to this simple analysis, both laws fit their associated data approximately equally well.

So what is one to make of the two mathematical "laws" displayed in Table 12.1? Do they represent good science or simply good imagination? The answer, I would suggest, is not that simple or clear-cut.

Table 12.1
Comparison of Titius-Bode and Gompertz-Makeham Laws

	Titius-Bode Law		Gompertz-Makeham Law		
Planet Number, x	Average Orbit Distance (AU)	TBL Estimate	U.S. Female Age, x	Mortality Hazard Rate	GML Estimate
1 (Mercury)	0.39	0.55	10	0.00022	0.00030
2 (Venus)	0.72	0.70	20	0.00047	0.00042
3 (Earth)	1.00	1.00	30	0.00068	0.00072
4 (Mars)	1.52	1.60	40	0.00130	0.00145
5 (Ceres)	2.77	2.80	50	0.00308	0.00325
6 (Jupiter)	5.20	5.20	60	0.00801	0.00768
7 (Saturn)	9.54	10.00	70	0.01781	0.01855
8 (Uranus)	19.19	19.60	80	0.04386	0.04528
9 (Neptune)	30.06	38.80	90	0.12192	0.11099
10 (Pluto)	39.48	77.20	100	0.27573	0.27253

Exponential patterns like those in Figures 12.1 and 12.2 occur frequently in nature, often as the result of obvious underlying physical principles. (For example, it is common to find a population of bacteria growing exponentially because the rate of increase in the population is directly proportional to the population's current size.) Unfortunately, in the cases of the TBL and the GML, the observed exponential patterns are not justified by any simple underlying theory. Nevertheless, the tentative assumption of an exponential model constitutes a reasonable starting point for further investigation.

The practical question of greatest importance is how long one should retain the exponential model in the presence of contradictory evidence (e.g., the inaccurate estimates in Table 12.1). This problem—of when to switch or update hypotheses—represents a fundamental step in the scientific method. Suppose, for example, that the inaccuracies in Table 12.1 cause formal statistical hypothesis tests to reject both the TBL and the GML. In that case, the conventional decision would be to abandon those models. However, if one's prior belief in the exponential patterns were sufficiently strong—as formalized in a Bayesian framework—then an appropriate alternative might be to retain the models with certain necessary adjustments.

From Chapter 1, we recall that from ages 10 through 34, young Americans are exposed to fairly dramatic accident and homicide rates. Given how easily that age group can be distinguished from others, it would seem reasonable to believe that the GML provides an accurate reflection of human mortality hazard rates for "normal" populations, but requires one or more additional parameters to account for the accident and homicide pathologies of the U.S. population. A similar approach could be taken with the TBL, for which it might be argued that the proximity of Neptune's and Pluto's orbits, as well as the high eccentricity of Pluto's orbit, suggest that some cataclysmic event millions of years ago caused those two planets to deviate from the "natural" exponential pattern. Again, one or more additional parameters could be added to account for this anomaly.

Some Sinusoidal Patterns

For a more up-to-date example of possible scholarly pareidolia, let us turn to a characteristic of property-liability insurance markets commonly known as the "underwriting cycle." Addressed in the actuarial literature at least as early as the 1960s, this term refers to the apparently *sinusoidal* (i.e., sine-function-like) behavior of insurance company profitability data over time and is well represented by the *combined ratio* data of Figure 12.3.[11]

Cyclical behavior in insurance profitability is somewhat puzzling to insurance scholars because it belies theories of rational economic decision making, under which any sort of truly periodic behavior in financial markets should be anticipated—and thereby eliminated—by various market participants. For example, suppose that the year is 1975 and that one knows, because of the periodicity of underwriting results, that insurance companies are about to embark on an epoch of increased profitability. Then, as a rational actor, one should decide to benefit from this trend by investing heavily in insurance company stocks. If a substantial number of investors behave in this rational manner, then the insurance industry will realize a sudden influx of capital, which will permit it to expand its writings of insurance and/or to lower premiums. Lower premiums will mean, of course, higher combined ratios (and less profitability per dollar invested), which then will offset the anticipated increase in profitability. Hence, in equilibrium, there should be no cyclical behavior.

Over the past three to four decades, dozens of published research papers have attempted to explain the insurance market's failure to achieve the sort of equilibrium expected by economists. The most important classes of theories put forward to explain the cyclical pattern in underwriting results are based upon:

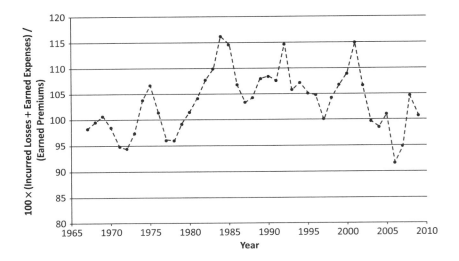

Figure 12.3
U.S. Property-Liability Combined Ratios (All Industries) Source: A. M. Best
Company (2010).

- **The influence of prevailing interest rates on markets.** For example,
an increase in interest rates will encourage insurance companies to lower premiums (per exposure unit) in order to generate more writings (and thus more
dollars in total to be invested at the higher rate of return). This will cause the
combined ratio to decrease in the short run. However, as losses from the companies' expanded business begin to come due, they will be disproportionately
large compared to premiums, so the combined ratio will increase, eventually
passing its original level. Companies then will have to raise premiums (per
exposure unit) in order to bring the combined ratio back down again.
- **The presence of significant lags between recording losses and setting
premiums.** For example, assume insurance companies set Year 2's premiums
according to the trend between Year 0's combined ratio and Year 1's combined
ratio and that a substantial increase in the frequency and/or severity of losses
occurs between Year 0 and Year 1, but there is no further change between Year
1 and Year 2. This will make Year 1's combined ratio larger than Year 0's and
cause the companies to raise premiums (per exposure unit) in Year 2. Consequently, the companies eventually will find that Year 2's combined ratio is
smaller than Year 1's, causing them to lower premiums (per exposure unit) in
Year 3. This will make Year 3's combined ratio larger than Year 2's, and the
pattern of raising and lowering premiums (per exposure unit) will continue.

- **The impact of major catastrophes or other costly events.** For example, if insurance companies must pay a large number of claims as the result of a destructive hurricane, then the combined ratio will increase substantially in the short run. To remain financially solvent, companies will have to raise premiums (per exposure unit), which will cause the combined ratio to decrease beyond its pre-hurricane level. Finally, competitive pressures will force companies to lower premiums (per exposure unit), raising the combined ratio once again.

One major difference between the statistical analyses needed to test the above theories and those needed to test the exponential patterns of the TBL and the GML is that the former require the incorporation of additional variables (such as interest rates, frequency and severity trends, and catastrophe losses) into the respective models, whereas the TBL can be tested by studying orbit distances simply as a function of planet number, and the GML can be tested by studying mortality hazard rates simply as a function of age. Both types of analyses involve observational studies, in which the researcher must rely on the data as they are collected, without the option of generating new observations according to some experimental design. However, the former are infinitely more complicated in that they open the door to arbitrarily large numbers of additional explanatory variables in attempting to assess causality, whereas the latter simply address the presence of a simple functional relationship.

In the next section, I will argue that observational studies are entirely useless for resolving matters of causal relationship, so that such studies can never select convincingly among the three major explanations for cyclical profitability listed above. For this reason, it is particularly ironic that over a period of several decades, researchers pursued causal explanations of the cyclical nature of insurance company profitability without first having carried out a formal test of this pattern. In other words, the preconception of a fundamental sinusoidal relationship was so strong among scholars that they felt it unnecessary to test the simple functional relationship between profitability and time before embarking on more extensive—and unavoidably inconclusive—investigations.

Rather remarkably, when Italian risk theorist and insurance economist Emilio Venezian proposed a formal statistical test of cyclicality in 2006, he found that, on the whole, the statistical evidence for true cyclicality was fairly weak. Specifically, for any fixed time period, at most three out of eight individual U.S. property-liability lines manifested statistically significant profitability cycles at the 5 percent level.[12] Thus, it would seem that modern-day scholars are no more immune to the temptations of pareidolia than their predecessors. However, that is not necessarily a bad thing. Although potentially misleading if retained for too long, the identification and use of simple patterns can serve as a coarse data-analytic technique to be replaced by more sophisticated alternatives later in the research process.

Confounding Variables

To explore the fundamental inferential differences between observational studies, on the one hand, and randomized controlled studies, on the other, let us consider the following research question: Are hybrid automobiles more likely than conventional automobiles to have collisions with pedestrians and bicyclists?[13] The underlying theory to support such an idea is that hybrids, with dual propulsion systems—one of which is an electric mode that is quieter than the internal combustion engine—are less likely to provide an audible warning of their approach to pedestrians and bicyclists.

A well-publicized observational study conducted by the National Highway Traffic Safety Administration (NHTSA) in 2009 suggested that the answer to this question was "Yes."[14]

Among the study's various summary statistics, the most important were the proportions of pedestrian and bicyclist collisions among total collisions experienced by hybrid automobiles (to be denoted by h_{PED} and h_{BIC}, respectively) during low-speed maneuvers, and the proportions of pedestrian and bicyclist collisions among total collisions experienced by conventional automobiles (similarly denoted by c_{PED} and c_{BIC}) during comparable maneuvers.

These proportions are shown in Table 12.2, along with the associated p-values from testing the null hypotheses: (1) H_0: $E[h_{PED}] = E[c_{PED}]$; and (2) H_0: $E[h_{BIC}] = E[c_{BIC}]$. Given the rather small p-values in the rightmost column, the NHTSA concluded that hybrid automobiles do appear to pose additional hazards to pedestrians and bicyclists.

Without rendering judgment on whether or not the NHTSA's conclusion correctly represents the true state of affairs (which I suspect it does), I would assert that the study was useless for the purposes intended. This is because it failed to recognize the presence of numerous potential confounding variables associated with driver behavior—rather than automobile propulsion systems alone—of which the following are rather conspicuous:

Table 12.2
Proportions of Pedestrian and Bicyclist Collisions for Hybrid and Conventional Automobiles During Low-Speed Maneuvers

	Hybrid Collisions	Conventional Collisions	Associated p-Values
Proportion with Pedestrians	$h_{PED}=0.012$	$c_{PED}=0.006$	$p_{PED}=0.003$
Proportion with Bicyclists	$h_{BIC}=0.008$	$c_{BIC}=0.005$	$p_{BIC}=0.030$

1. The possibility that as more environmentally conscious individuals, hybrid drivers are more likely to live in neighborhoods with high concentrations of pedestrians and bicyclists.
2. The possibility that because of the physical configurations of their automobiles (especially windows), hybrid drivers pay less attention to relatively small objects, such as pedestrians and bicyclists.
3. The possibility that because of the generally smaller sizes of their automobiles, hybrid drivers tend to avoid more dangerous roadways where collisions with other automobiles, but not pedestrians and bicyclists, are likely.

In other words, since the NHTSA's researchers did not address these behavioral possibilities, it could be argued that any one of them explains the results of the study just as well as the hypothesis that quieter motors—or any other purely physical characteristic of hybrid autmobiles—make them more dangerous to pedestrians and bicyclists.

Of course, defenders of the observational study methodology could argue that the NHTSA's researchers were simply remiss in their work and failed to carry out all necessary due diligence in eliminating various confounding variables. For example, the researchers could have controlled for the effects of items one through three by pursuing further studies to determine whether: (1) pedestrian/bicycle density is positively correlated with hybrid automobile density; (2) hybrid automobile windows are smaller and/or create more distortion than conventional automobile windows; and (3) hybrid automobiles tend to be driven less on more dangerous roads. Possibly, negative findings in each of these three additional studies would take care of items one through three. But what can be done about the potentially vast number of less-conspicuous behavioral confounding variables? For example, consider:

4. The possibility that as more cautious people, conventional drivers are more likely to drive carefully in residential neighborhoods (where concentrations of pedestrians and bicyclists are greater).
5. The possibility that as more technologically savvy people, hybrid drivers are more likely to be distracted by mobile phones and other electronic devices while driving at low speeds (i.e., in residential neighborhoods).
6. The possibility that as more self-consciously altruistic people, hybrid drivers are more likely to feel entitled to drive fast in residential neighborhoods.

One could go on and on, simply by suggesting behavioral factors that *could* be either positively correlated with both hybrid ownership and colliding with a higher proportion of pedestrians/bicyclists or negatively correlated with both hybrid ownership and colliding with pedestrians/bicyclists. To erase any doubts that this list can be made quite vast, consider that the total number of protein-encoding human genes, M, is currently estimated to be somewhere between 20,000 and 25,000. Denoting these genes by the sequence $G_1, G_2, \ldots, G_M$, one can easily introduce M potentially confounding variables of the form:

The possibility that gene G_i is responsible for traits that make an individual both more likely to purchase a hybrid vehicle and more likely to collide with pedestrians/bicyclists.

If this number is still unsatisfactorily small, then one can look at the truly infinite array of potential environmental factors: exposure to alcohol during gestation, distress at birth, birth order, use of breast- vs. bottle-feeding, parental disciplinary system, family wealth, quality of education, exposure to toxins, etc. Obviously, the NHTSA's researchers could not control for all of these effects because it is impossible to do so in any finite amount of time.

To clarify how a randomized controlled study would avoid the problem of behavioral confounding variables, consider the following experimental design:

- First, the researchers select a large number of individuals—perhaps 10,000—at random from the U.S. population and divide them randomly into two equal-sized groups, H and C.

- Next, each driver in group H is given a hybrid automobile and each driver in group C is given a conventional automobile, where the hybrid and conventional vehicles are physically identical except for their propulsion systems.
- Subsequently, all drivers are monitored for a fixed study period (say, five years) to make sure that they drive no automobiles other than those allocated.
- Finally, after keeping track of the collision experience of both groups over the study period, the researchers compute the same proportions shown in Table 12.2 and find the associated p-values to complete the relevant statistical tests.

Under this alternative study design, potential effects of most of the confounding variables proposed above—items one, four, five, and six; the 20,000-plus gene-based possibilities; and the virtually unbounded set of environmental factors—are immediately avoided through the random selection of drivers and their random assignment to hybrid and conventional automobiles. Items two and three, which are based partially upon physical differences between nonpropulsion components of hybrid and conventional vehicles, are avoided by insisting that those components be identical.[15]

Of course, carrying out such a randomized controlled study would be substantially more expensive and time-consuming than the original observational study, requiring the purchase of thousands of new automobiles (which might have to be custom-adapted to ensure that their superstructures are identical) as well as the monitoring of all participating drivers for several years. However, the presence of difficult obstacles to a sound study cannot enhance or justify the intellectual rigor of a bad study. Hence, observational studies must be recognized for their substantial scientific shortcomings.[16] As with instances of scholarly pareidolia discussed above, observational studies can provide guidance as coarse data-analytic techniques, but eventually should be replaced by more sophisticated alternatives.

Bayesian Salvation?

At this point, the perspicacious reader may raise an insightful question: Given the identified problems of observational studies, why not simply embed them in a Bayesian framework to account for the relative likelihoods of different confounding variables? After all, a close examination of the proposed confounding variables listed in the context of the NHTSA study reveals that as one moves down the list—from items one, two, and three to items four, five, and six to the vast numbers of largely hypothetical genetic and environmental factors—the subjective likelihood that the listed variable actually has an impact on the proportions of interest (i.e., h_{PED}, h_{BIC}, c_{PED}, and c_{BIC}) decreases substantially. Therefore, it would seem reasonable to place a subjective prior distribution over all possible contributions of the infinite set of all such confounding variables, and then estimate the relevant p-values by their expected values, $E[p_{PED}]$ and $E[p_{BIC}]$, taken over this prior distribution.

This type of Bayesian approach is an intriguing possibility. Despite the presumably infinite-dimensional space of all possible statistical models generated by the set of potential confounding variables, it *is* mathematically feasible to specify nontrivial prior probability distributions over such a sample space. Hence, there is no *theoretical* problem of nonmeasurability, such as that raised in the previous discussion of Knightian uncertainty. Nevertheless, the set of all possible configurations of an infinite set of explanatory variables is so vast that the task of specifying a meaningful prior probability distribution could, in many cases, take an infinite amount of time, thereby creating an insurmountable *practical* problem of nonmeasurability.

ACT 3, SCENE 2

[Offices of Trial Insurance Company. Head clerk sits at desk.]

CLERK: [Holding subpoena, gets up and walks to Other pile.] Don't think I'm not aware who's behind this, you contemptible claim! You can't intimidate me!

FORM 2: I warned you, buddy; but you wouldn't listen. You had to do things the hard way. But look, I'm a reasonable guy. Just send me to Claim Adjustment, and everything can be fixed.

CLERK: Fixed? I'll fix you, you despicable document! [Tears up subpoena.] There, look what I did to your enforcer! And remember, I can do the same to you as well!

FORM 2: Oh, you shouldn't have done that. Believe me, you *really* shouldn't have done that.

[Telephone rings. Head clerk picks up receiver.]

CLERK: Hello, this is Trial Insurance: If it isn't a Trial, it isn't a policy. Yes, Mr. Sorter works here. And you are? Detective Ferret, with the Metropolitan Police. You'd like to ask Mr. Sorter some questions? About an obstruction of justice investigation? Well, I'm sure Mr. Sorter would be very happy to speak to you, but he isn't here just at the moment. Yes, I'll certainly give him that message. Yes, I'll mention that it's very important. Thank you, Officer.

[Head clerk slams down receiver. Claim form chortles nastily.]

CLERK: [Goes over to Other pile.] Why, you pusillanimous parchment! You think you can destroy my life, do you? Well, I'll show you! [Picks up claim form.]

FORM 2: [Serenely.] Don't do anything rash, Sorter. Things can only get worse if you don't play ball with me.

CLERK: Play *ball* with you? You think this is some sort of game? I'll show you what happens to those who play games with me! [Draws cigarette lighter from trouser pocket.] I don't suppose you're fireproof, are you?

FORM 2: You wouldn't dare. Remember, I have powerful friends everywhere.

CLERK: Well, let's see your friends stop this! [Uses lighter to set fire to claim form.]

FORM 2: No! Help! I'm burning!

CLERK: [Claim form is consumed by fire, and Sorter stamps out ashes on floor.] That'll teach you, you felonious form! [Returns to desk and composes himself.] Ah, I feel much better now. And that claim form thought it could tell me what to do! Me, the head clerk! [Picks up next paper from pile.] A workers compensation death claim—now that's refreshing. [Looks at form closely.] Why, that's interesting: This poor fellow had the same birthday as I.

FORM 3: Yes, and he also worked for the same company as you and had the same street address as you. Do you see a pattern emerging?

CLERK: Well, it certainly seems like a remarkable coincidence. But Trial Insurance is a large company, and I *do* live in a large apartment building; so it may not be that remarkable after all.

FORM 3: Have you looked at the deceased worker's name?

CLERK: Why, it's the same as mine. But how can that be?

FORM 3: Perhaps you forgot what my cousin said just before you so callously torched him. He did in fact have some very powerful friends. You see, if we insurance forms say you're dead, then you certainly are dead.

CLERK: [Looking frightened, scans death claim form frantically.] Why, it can't be! It simply can't be. [Turns to second page of form and suddenly looks relieved.] Aha! I knew it couldn't be! This fellow may have the same birthday, the same employer and address, and even the same name; but look at his salary: He was paid at least 25 percent more than I am! [Speaks triumphantly.] You stupid form! You've got my salary wrong! You can't get rid of me so easily!

BOSS: [Approaches Sorter enthusiastically.] Another suspicious claim form, Mr. Sorter? That's fine work. And I must tell you, you've already made quite an impression! Because of your diligent service today—catching suspicious claims and all—I've managed to get you a generous raise!

[Death claim form laughs menacingly.]

13

False Choices and Black Boxes
The Costs of Limited Data

Floods, famines, earthquakes, volcanic action, political instability, revolutions, pillage, and plague notwithstanding, we are still here and are even insuring many phenomena. Given the potentials for disaster, why are things so good?

—MARTIN SHUBIK ("RISK, PUBLIC PERCEPTION, AND EDUCATION," 2002)[1]

In recent decades, governments, corporations, and ordinary citizens the world over have become more aware of the potential impact of *extreme-event*, or *catastrophe*, risks. Dramatic events such as the September 11 attacks (2001), the Indian Ocean tsunami (2004), Hurricane Katrina (2005), the Great Sichuan earthquake (2008), and the Tohoku earthquake and tsunami (2011) continue to raise these issues in the public mind while sending researchers from various disciplines scrambling to explain and forecast the frequencies and severities of such events.

Extreme events are, by their nature, rare. In insurance parlance, a catastrophe can be described as an event whose severity is so far out on the loss distribution that its frequency is necessarily low.[2] One inevitable result of the rarity of catastrophes is the sparseness of relevant data for estimating expected loss frequencies and severities, which leaves governments, insurance companies, and their risk-assessment experts with a difficult statistical problem: how to make reasonable forecasts of insured catastrophe losses based upon few historical observations. In the present chapter, I will consider two troublesome issues arising from the paucity of catastrophe data: (1) a tendency to oversimplify conclusions from scientific research; and (2) the use of "black-box" forecasts that are not subject to impartial scientific examination and validation.

Catastrophe Risk

To begin, let us delimit the class of exposures under discussion. By *catastrophe*, I will mean a well-defined, sudden occurrence with low expected frequency and high expected severity that falls into one of three distinct categories: (1) natural events; (2) accidental man-made events; (3) intentional man-made events. The second column in Table 13.1 provides historical examples of some of the largest and most widely publicized catastrophes for each of these categories. Given the incidents listed in this column, several questions come to mind:

- Are severe storms becoming more frequent, perhaps as a result of global climate change?
- Are man-made accidents becoming less common and/or less costly, perhaps because of improving risk management efforts?
- Are intentional man-made disasters becoming more frequent, and is there an upper bound on their severity?
- Is it meaningful—or even possible—to discern trends in such volatile events, given the limited historical database?

In *The Outline of History*, British author H. G. Wells famously stated: "Human history becomes more and more a race between education and catastrophe."[3] Although Wells was commenting on the state of humanity in the shadow of World War I, his observation certainly remains equally valid today. A brief review of the hypothetical incidents in the third column of Table 13.1 offers some idea of the possible magnitudes of such future events. It is quite sobering to recognize that even if we, as a global society, are able to find a way to avoid the use of weapons of mass destruction, we still will be confronted with the dismal inevitability of naturally occurring catastrophes: perhaps a magnitude 7+ earthquake in Los Angeles or San Francisco; or a drug-resistant plague on the scale of Europe's Black Death; or an asteroid impact on a densely populated area with a force comparable to that of the Tunguska fireball of 1908.

Table 13.1
Catastrophe Examples by Category

Category	Recent Historical Events	Speculative Future Events
Natural Catastrophes	SARS Pandemic (2002–2003) Indian Ocean Tsunami (2004) Hurricane Katrina (2005) Great Sichuan Earthquake (2008) Hurricane Ike (2008) H1N1 Pandemic (2009) Haiti Earthquake (2010) Chile Earthquake (2010) Tohoku Earthquake and Tsunami (2011)	"The Big One" (CA Earthquake) Drug-Resistant Plague Asteroid/Comet Impact Nearby Supernova
Accidental Man-Made Catastrophes	Bhopal Gas Leak (1984) Chernobyl Nuclear Accident (1986) Exxon *Valdez* Oil Spill (1989) BP Oil Spill (2010)	Liquefied Natural Gas Disaster Nuclear Plant Meltdown
Intentional Man-Made Catastrophes	Tokyo Subway Nerve-Gas Attack (1995) Oklahoma City Bombing (1995) U.S. Embassy Bombings (1998) September 11 Attacks (2001) Madrid Train Bombings (2004) Beslan School Siege (2004) Mumbai Bombings (2008)	"Dirty" Bomb Attack More Ambitious Suicide Attacks Use of Nuclear Weapons Use of Chemical Weapons Use of Biological Weapons

Given the low expected frequencies and high expected severities of catastrophe events, our paradigms of risk control and risk finance (see Figures 7.1, 7.2, and 7.3) suggest that governments, insurance companies, and other financial market makers must find ways to: (1) provide appropriate economic incentives to mitigate severities; (2) allocate sufficient capital to support meaningful levels of risk transfer for catastrophe exposures; and (3) price the relevant risk-transfer products. To understand and address these problems, practitioners need common and credible methodologies for forecasting the relevant frequencies and severities. Unfortunately, such techniques do not yet exist.

False Choices

Over the past decade, the most studied and discussed potential source of catastrophe risk undoubtedly has been global climate change (GCC). Currently, many government officials around the world believe that GCC has been (at least somewhat) responsible for recent increases in both the frequency and severity of hurricanes and that potential longer-term effects—including massive flooding of populated areas, devastating droughts, etc.—may be even more ominous. Coordinated efforts to mitigate these potential problems have focused primarily on international agreements for reducing carbon emissions, such as the Kyoto Protocol. Although the subject of GCC is much too large to be treated in any depth here, I do wish to make use of this topic to illustrate how a tendency to oversimplify conclusions from scientific research can be counterproductive.

Certainly, no political question related to GCC could be more fundamental than the economic bottom line: What is the greatest percentage, X, of your disposable income that you would be willing to sacrifice on an ongoing basis as part of a government-mandated effort to mitigate the effects of GCC? For myself, as a fundamentalist Bayesian unafraid of quantifying all of the necessary (but incredibly vague and ill-defined) probabilities underlying such a calculation, X would be about 5. That is, I would be willing to give up about 5 percent of my disposable income throughout the foreseeable future to help stabilize and reduce the record-high proportions of greenhouse gases in the planet's atmosphere.

Although I am unaware of any comprehensive surveys of the general taxpaying population, I suspect (again, with the boldness of a literalist Bayesian) that 5 percent is somewhat higher than the average value of X that U.S. citizens would offer if asked.[4] In fact, I would guess that many individuals (perhaps at least one in three) would offer an X of 0 and would be quite irritated at my suggestion that the government mandate a reduction of 5 percent of everyone's disposable income. I also would guess, however, that a small, but not insignificant proportion of Americans (say, one in twenty) would be willing to give up at least 10 percent and would look upon my meager 5 percent with a certain degree of scorn. The interesting thing is that it is quite easy to generate a prior distribution over the values of X to be offered, but incredibly difficult to anticipate the thought process underlying any individual's particular choice of X.

For example, if I were to consider a person selecting X equals 0, I might assume that he or she is skeptical of the theory of man-made GCC and therefore sees no reason to mitigate something that is not a problem. However, there are other perfectly good explanations that should be considered, including the possibility that the person is totally convinced of man-made GCC, but believes either: (1) that it is too late to stop the process; or (2) that the outcome of the process will be generally positive (either for himself/herself or the world as a whole). In a similar way, I might assume that a person selecting X equals 10 is totally convinced of man-made GCC, whereas the true explanation may be that the person is convinced of GCC, does not believe it is man-made, but nevertheless believes that some actions should be taken to mitigate it.

In short, the political discourse on GCC is far from a bilateral issue setting "believers" against "nonbelievers." Rather, it is a multilateral issue on which an individual can possess one of a variety of highly nuanced positions. To give some idea of just how many sides there can be in this debate, consider the set of all possible "Yes/No" answers a person could give to the following rather simple questions:

(A) Do you believe GCC is a real phenomenon? [If "No", then skip to question (D).]
(B) Do you believe GCC is man-made?
(C) Do you believe GCC will have a major adverse impact on the world?
(D) Do you support allocating substantial resources to mitigate potential adverse effects of GCC?

As shown in Table 13.2, there are ten distinct viewpoints that a person could have based upon nothing more than the "Yes/No" answers to the above questions. Naturally, some of these viewpoints are much more common than others. For example, it would be easy to find individuals espousing viewpoints I or VIII in the general U.S. population, whereas viewpoint II would be fairly rare. What is particularly important about the list is that there are several very reasonable viewpoints that do not fit comfortably within the common "believer/disbeliever" dichotomy of political discourse. Specifically, not everyone who answers "Yes" to question D necessarily answers "Yes" to question C, and not everyone who answers "Yes" to question B necessarily answers "Yes" to question D.

As an example, I would confess to being an adherent of viewpoint III; that is, I believe that GCC is man-made, am somewhat skeptical that it will result in a major adverse impact on the world *in the long run*, but believe that something should be done to mitigate its effects. More specifically, I suspect that on the whole there may well be more positive long-term effects of GCC (such as extended farming seasons for Canada and Russia, a permanent northwest passage from the Atlantic Ocean to the Pacific Ocean, and greater access to offshore oil drilling in the Arctic Ocean) than negative long-term effects,[5] but I am sufficiently risk averse not to want to

Table 13.2
Possible Viewpoints on Global Climate Change

Different Viewpoints	(A) GCC Real?	(B) GCC Man-Made?	(C) GCC Have Adverse Impact?	(D) Support Mitigation?
I	Yes	Yes	Yes	Yes
II	Yes	Yes	Yes	No
III	Yes	Yes	No	Yes
IV	Yes	Yes	No	No
V	Yes	No	Yes	Yes
VI	Yes	No	Yes	No
VII	Yes	No	No	Yes
VIII	Yes	No	No	No
IX	No	No	No	Yes
X	No	No	No	No

expose the world to the potential downside risk of unchecked greenhouse-gas production. Given this particular viewpoint, I find much of the political discussion of GCC to be excessively shallow.

Rather than oversimplifying the available scientific evidence to force a logical equivalence between particular beliefs (such as "GCC will have a major adverse impact") and support for particular actions (such as "allocating substantial resources to mitigate GCC"), politicians and government officials should work to build consensus based upon a clear and impartial analysis of the risks involved. Although it may be unrealistic to expect the political discourse to address detailed analyses of each of the vast number of possible long-term consequences of GCC (positive and/or negative), it does seem reasonable to expect those attempting to form a coalition in support of mitigation efforts to consider that their allies are not just those who answer "Yes" to questions A, B, and C above. Asking people to choose between support for allocating substantial resources to mitigate GCC, on the one hand, and disbelief that GCC will have a major adverse impact, on the other, is to present them with a false choice.

Black Boxes

Naturally, the problem of forecasting catastrophe frequencies and severities is even more challenging than that of analyzing their historical relationships with various factors, meteorological or otherwise.[6] For such forecasting, governments, insurance companies, and other market makers typically rely on highly specialized catastrophe risk-analysis firms.[7] These firms' predictions are based upon statistical extrapolations from complex engineering, geological, and meteorological models, as well as judgmental forecasts offered by experts in the areas of natural, accidental man-made, and intentional man-made catastrophes. Unfortunately, these forecasts are generally available only as "black-box" calculations; that is, the details of the underlying methodologies remain unpublished because of proprietary business concerns.[8]

I must admit to being somewhat skeptical of black-box forecasts. No matter how experienced or intelligent the individuals generating a prediction, they cannot escape the possibility of gross errors and oversights—some of which may have a significant impact on forecast magnitudes. Therefore, the absence of broad *outside* evaluation or oversight is necessarily troubling.

This does not mean that all black boxes are bad. I am quite comfortable relying on a vast array of high-tech gadgets—everything from CAT scanners to television sets—about whose inner workings I have little detailed understanding. However, my willingness to rely on such devices is directly related to the amount of empirical evidence supporting their efficacy. For example, I find the images of current events relayed by television useful because of the medium's long successful track record. But before purchasing a similar device purporting to provide images from the spirit world, I would require *extensive* corroboration by *impartial* sources of the seller's claims.

The problem with black-box catastrophe forecasts is the absence of both extensive validating data and impartial peer review. Fortunately, both of these issues may be addressed; the former simply by comparing the black-box forecasts with a naïve alternative, to ensure a basic reality check, and the latter by insisting that this comparison be done by an independent party.[9]

Hurricane Forecasting

To see how this approach would work, I will now consider some historical forecast data from one of the most publicly discussed (and therefore virtually transparent) black boxes in the catastrophe field: the hurricane prediction methodology of Colorado State University researchers William Gray and Philip Klotzbach.

Since 1984, Gray has employed a complex meteorological and statistical model of global weather patterns to make forecasts of the numbers of (named) tropical storms and hurricanes of various categories originating in the Atlantic Basin.[10] He was joined by Klotzbach in 2001. Prior to each year's hurricane season, the two scientists make several forecasts, typically in early December, early April, and late May/early June. For the purposes at hand, I will focus on the Gray-Klotzbach (GK) December predictions of the total number of hurricanes for the 19 years from 1992 through 2010.[11] These forecasts are presented in the second column of Table 13.3.

Using a term familiar to financial investors, the GK forecasts may be said to derive from a rigorous *fundamental* analysis of numerous prevailing meteorological conditions (comparable with the firm characteristics and market conditions considered in a fundamental analysis of stock prices). To offer a simple reality check of the value of these forecasts, I will provide a naïve *technical* analysis of the complete set of historical hurricane frequency data compiled by the National Hurricane Center (see Figures 13.1 (a), (b), and (c)), and use this technical analysis to generate a set of competing forecasts for 1992 through 2010. This latter analysis is identical to that underlying an annual hurricane forecast that I publish jointly with my wife, Imelda Powers.[12]

Although somewhat difficult to see from Figures 13.1 (a), (b), and (c), the hurricane frequency series possesses an expected value (average number of hurricanes per year) that increases slightly, but significantly, over time. A simple linear regression of the data against time yields an estimated increase of 0.01 hurricane per year.[13] Another characteristic of the time series is that it appears to show serial correlation, as the plot of the points moves up and down more smoothly than might be expected of sequentially uncorrelated observations.

To begin the competing technical analysis, I will place myself in the first half of 1984, at about the same time Gray made his first forecasts, and select a model based upon only considerations possible at that time. To that end, I will use the Atlantic-Basin hurricane data from 1851 to 1983 (i.e., all but the last twenty-seven points in the above figures).

Without descending into the gory details, I would note that a fairly straightforward and conventional analysis of autocorrelation functions suggests a first-order moving average model (MA(1)) in the first differ-

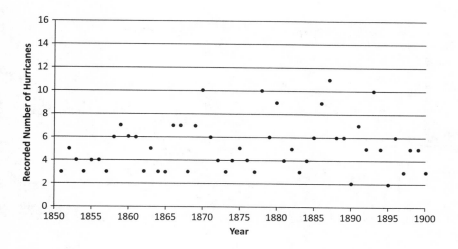

Figure 13.1 (a)
Atlantic-Basin Hurricane Frequency (1851–1900) Source: National Hurricane Center.

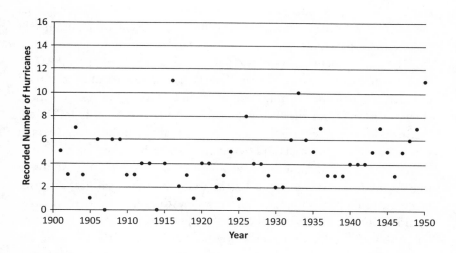

Figure 13.1 (b)
Atlantic-Basin Hurricane Frequency (1901–1950) Source: National Hurricane Center.

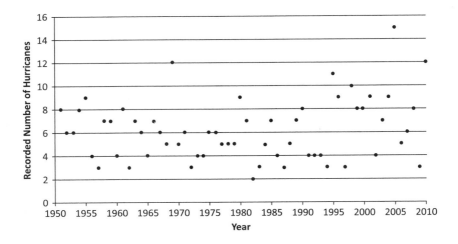

Figure 13.1 (c)
Atlantic-Basin Hurricane Frequency (1951–2010) Source: National Hurricane Center.

ences of the original hurricane series. Checking residuals further suggests including a first-order autoregressive component (AR(1)), which ultimately yields a three-parameter ARIMA(1,1,1) model.[14]

Table 13.3 presents a comparison of the GK forecasts with my ARIMA model. For each year, the forecast that is closest to the actual recorded number of hurricanes is indicated by boldface text; if both forecasts are equally distant from the true value, then neither forecast is indicated. Setting aside the latter forecasts, one can see that out of the fifteen years in which one of the forecasts did better than the other, the GK forecast is better six times and mine is better nine times. Intuitively, this seems to suggest the GK methodology is less accurate than the technical analysis; however, a simple hypothesis test fails to show that either set of forecasts is significantly better than the other (at the 5 percent level).[15]

Although unable to demonstrate the superiority of the GK forecasts over those of a simple technical model, the above exercise is clearly useful. Most importantly, it reveals that the complex GK fundamental analysis does in fact provide reasonable forecasts. As a result, I would argue that whenever confronted with black-box catastrophe forecasts, all parties of interest (insurance companies, reinsurers, rating agencies, regulators, and the public at large) should insist that such forecasts be accompanied by an impartial peer review.

Table 13.3
Atlantic-Basin Hurricane Forecasts (Made December of Prior Year)

Year	Gray-Klotzbach Forecast	Author's Forecast	Actual Number
1992	**4**	5	4
1993	6	**5**	4
1994	6	**5**	3
1995	**8**	5	11
1996	5	**6**	9
1997	7	**6**	3
1998	5	**5**	10
1999	**9**	6	8
2000	**7**	6	8
2001	5	**6**	9
2002	8	**6**	4
2003	8	**6**	7
2004	7	**6**	9
2005	6	**7**	15
2006	**9**	8	5
2007	7	**7**	6
2008	7	**7**	8
2009	7	**6**	3
2010	**6–8**	6	12
% Time Closer to Actual	32%	47%	

Note: Boldface indicates forecast closer to actual number of hurricanes.
Sources: National Hurricane Center; Dr. William M. Gray and Philip J. Klotzbach <http://typhoon.atmos.colostate.edu/forecasts/>; the author's calculations.

Terrorism Forecasting

In the aftermath of the September 11, 2001, terrorist attacks, the U.S. insurance industry confronted billions of dollars in unanticipated losses. In addition, major global reinsurers quickly announced that they no longer would provide coverage for acts of terrorism in reinsurance contracts. Recognizing that historical loss forecasts had failed to account sufficiently for terrorism events and facing an immediate shortage of reinsurance, many U.S. primary insurance companies soon declared their intention to exclude terrorism risk from future policies. This pending market disruption led the U.S. Congress to pass the Terrorism Risk Insurance Act (TRIA) of 2002 to "establish a temporary federal program that provides for a transparent system of shared public and private compensation for insured losses resulting from acts of terrorism." Subsequently, Congress passed the Terrorism Risk Insurance Extension Act (TRIEA) of 2005, which was similar (but not identical) to the TRIEA.[16]

From the U.S. Treasury Department's perspective, the TRIA was intended to provide protection for business activity from the unexpected financial losses of terrorist attacks until the U.S. insurance industry could develop a self-sustaining private terrorism insurance market. However, during the debate over the TRIEA, representatives of the U.S. property-liability insurance industry argued that the industry lacked sufficient capacity to assume terrorism risks without government support and that terrorism risks were still viewed as uninsurable in the market.

Given that the TRIEA was extended for a further seven years at the end of 2007, the debate over the need for a federal role in the terrorism insurance market is far from over. Although the federal government does not want to serve as the insurer of last resort for an indefinite period, it is clear that there are major obstacles to developing a private market for terrorism coverage.

Certainly, no category of catastrophe risk is more difficult to assess than the threat of terrorism. In addition to many of the ordinary random components associated with natural and unintentional man-made catastrophes, one must attempt to fathom: (1) the activities of the complex networks of terrorists; (2) the terrorists' socio-psychological motives and objectives; and (3) the broad range of attack methods available to the terrorists.

Despite these difficulties, it *is* possible to transfer or finance losses associated with terrorism risk. In the United States, private insurance markets for this type of risk existed before the events of September 11, 2001, and they exist today, albeit with government support under the TRIEA. Even without government support, markets for terrorism risk would exist as long as insurance companies believed that total losses could be forecast with reasonable accuracy.

Central to this requirement is that the underlying frequency and severity of terrorism losses not be perceived as fluctuating wantonly over time. To this end, the current state of risk financing has been assisted by two significant developments: (1) the lack of a substantial post–September 11 increase in the frequency of major terrorist attacks (outside of delimited war zones); and (2) the emergence of sophisticated models for forecasting terrorism losses by commercial risk analysts that, for the moment, afford market experts a degree of comfort in the statistical forecasts.

At the simplest level, the probability of a successful terrorist attack on a particular target may be expressed as the product $p_1 \times p_2 \times p_3 \times p_4$, where:

p_1 is the probability that an attack is planned;

p_2 is the conditional probability that the particular target is selected, given that an attack is planned;

p_3 is the conditional probability that the attack is undetected, given that an attack is planned *and* the particular target is selected; and

p_4 is the conditional probability that the attack is successful, given that an attack is planned *and* the particular target is selected *and* the attack is undetected.

The first of these four probabilities is essentially the underlying probability of terrorist action during a given time period. In a catastrophe risk analyst's model, this probability is generally captured by an overall outlook analysis for a particular future time period. Unfortunately, the other—and more complex—probabilities are not handled so transparently. In fact, it could reasonably be said that the methods used to calculate p_2, p_3, and p_4 are buried deeply within one or more black boxes.

Essentially, the catastrophe risk analyst develops estimates of these last three probabilities by intricate processes combining the judgmental forecasts of terrorism/security experts with the results of complex mathematical models. In some cases, the risk analyst may employ techniques from mathematical game theory (a subject to be discussed at some length in Chapter 15). Regrettably, the largest parts of these estimation techniques remain unpublished and untested, primarily because of proprietary concerns.

In a global economic culture that praises the virtue of transparency, it is rather unsettling that both rating agencies and regulators routinely countenance the use of unseen and unproved mathematical methods. Can one seriously imagine a modern patient going to the doctor for an annual checkup and accepting a diagnosis based upon a battery of secret, proprietary tests? Unless the black boxes obscuring terrorism forecasts are removed and the market's confidence justified for the long term, one thing is clear: The next major terrorist attack may not only destroy its intended target, but also seriously damage the private market for terrorism coverage.

ACT 3, SCENE 3

[Same police interrogation room. Suspect sits at table; two police officers stand.]

GOOD COP: Ms. Cutter, you can save your talk about literal and figurative killing for the judge and jury. For now, I'd like to focus on real facts—real statistics.

SUSPECT: That's certainly your prerogative, Officer.

GOOD COP: You stated that you selected the twelve victims at random from the entire population of Pennsylvania. Could you tell us more precisely how you did that?

SUSPECT: Well, as I already mentioned, a death rate of less than 1/1,000,000 is considered negligible. So I began by dividing the state population—about 12.5 million—by 1 million and that yielded a number close to 12.5. I then rounded down to the nearest integer, because—as you know, Officers—people are best counted in integers. The next step was to select exactly twelve individuals from the most recent census list, which I did with the help of my computer. Of course, those individuals had to be selected randomly; so I first assigned each individual his or her own number—from 1 to about 12.5 million—and then asked my computer to select exactly twelve numbers, one after the other, from the complete list.

BAD COP: Aha! But what did you do if your computer selected the same number twice?

SUSPECT: Well, fortunately, that didn't happen. But if it had, I was prepared for it. I simply would have thrown out the duplicate number and selected a thirteenth to replace it. That's a common statistical practice.

GOOD COP: So then, to summarize, your selection process was constructed to choose exactly twelve—no more and no fewer—individuals.

SUSPECT: That's correct.

GOOD COP: But don't you realize that your selection process, albeit somewhat random, is entirely different from the random processes covered by the concept of negligible risk? When a business releases toxins into the environment with a death rate of 1/1,000,000, that doesn't mean that *exactly* one person out of every million will die. What it means is that *on the average*, one person out of every million will die. In fact, it may happen that no one dies, or that everyone dies, depending on chance.

SUSPECT: I see where you're going with that, Officer, and I commend you for your insight. However, I'm afraid that you're wasting your time. You see, the people who make and implement the laws and regulations regarding negligible risk have no appreciation for the subtlety you're describing.

GOOD COP: And just how do you know that?

SUSPECT: Well, I don't think it would be bragging to say that I've done substantial research in the area. A close reading of the guidelines for environmental impact statements, for example, makes my point abundantly clear.

GOOD COP: [Suddenly smiles.] Oh, that reminds me of something that's been nagging me all along, Ms. Cutter.

SUSPECT: Yes, Officer?

GOOD COP: With what federal or state agencies did you say you *filed* your environmental impact statements? That is, after you determined that your so-called business would cause a death rate somewhat below the 1/1,000,000 threshold, to which agencies did you report your assessment?

[Cutter rubs forehead and looks worried, but says nothing.]

BAD COP: Go ahead, Cutter, answer the question.

SUSPECT: I'm afraid you've got me on that one, gentlemen.

GOOD COP: Yes, apparently.

SUSPECT: And do you find it satisfying, Officer, to defeat a woman on the absence of some trivial paperwork? To prevail on a mere legal technicality?

GOOD COP: That depends, Ms. Cutter. Are you speaking literally or figuratively?

14

Nullifying the Dull Hypothesis
Conventional Versus Personalized Science

There are two objectionable types of believers: those who believe the incredible and those who believe that "belief" must be discarded and replaced by "the scientific method."

—MAX BORN (*NATURAL PHILOSOPHY OF CAUSE AND CHANCE*, 1949)[1]

Chapters 12 and 13 addressed two significant issues frequently encountered in empirical analysis: model selection and data availability, respectively. I now will turn to an even more fundamental issue: the soundness of the scientific method (SM) itself. Although widely touted as the most effective available guide to human understanding, the SM is imprecisely defined and inconsistently implemented. Not only is there no universally accepted method for all scientific disciplines, but also statements of such methods, where they exist, are usually only idealized descriptions of the actual practice of science. This state of affairs is rather disquieting given that the SM is often proffered as the soul of modern science—the sine qua non of enlightened empirical reasoning, effectively poised to dispel the confusion and darkness of "inferior" modes of understanding (intuition, superstition, prejudice, mythology, religion, etc.).

In the present chapter, I will examine the SM as it is commonly practiced. First, I will address a number of inconsistencies in the way the SM is applied, observing how these inconsistencies may lead researchers to ignore important phenomena, especially when the phenomena are of a subtle and/or transient nature. Subsequently, I will consider issues related to the SM's philosophical foundations—specifically, the inefficiency and inertia caused by the SM's collectivist, frequentist orientation—and argue that these problems may be avoided by a more individualist, Bayesian approach.

Conventional Formulation

Formal statements of the SM usually envision scientific progress as occurring over time through a succession of replicable experimental tests of well-specified hypotheses describing relationships between observable quantities.[2] This process may be divided into a number of distinct steps, whose characteristics are somewhat sensitive to the particular needs/eccentricities of a given scientific field. A conventional outline of these steps is as follows:

1. **The development of a null hypothesis (H_0)** summarizing the relationship to be tested. This hypothesis may be based upon either derivations from theory or judgmental inferences from previously recorded observations. It may be as simple as stating the range for a parameter of interest (e.g., H_0: "The length of the underwriting cycle for U.S. workers compensation insurance is greater than six years") or it may involve the specification of a cause-and-effect relationship (e.g., H_0: "Hybrid automobiles are more likely than conventional automobiles to have collisions with pedestrians and bicyclists").

2. **The identification of an observable phenomenon that is predicted by the underlying hypothesis and not otherwise explicable.** For example, to test H_0: "The length of the underwriting cycle for U.S. workers compensation insurance is greater than six years," a researcher may identify the estimated cycle length for U.S. insurance company i (based upon profitability data from the past twenty years and denoted by ℓ_i) as the observable phenomenon and take the assumption that ℓ_i is a random variable with expected value greater than 6 as equivalent to H_0.

3. **The design of an experiment comprising a reasonably large number of individual observations, each of which reflects the presence/absence of the identified phenomenon.** This includes such critical issues as identifying the statistical properties of the observations (e.g., whether or not they represent independent and identically distributed outcomes), how many observations will be made, and at what level of significance (α) the null hypothesis will be rejected. In testing the H_0 from step 2 above, the researcher may de-

cide, based upon previous work, that the ℓ_i are approximately multivariate-normal random variables, positively correlated and with potentially different standard deviations. Furthermore, given that twenty years' data are needed for each insurance company, the study must be restricted to only those companies that have existed for at least that time period. Finally, the researcher may decide, based upon common practice in the insurance economic literature, to set α equal to 0.05.

4. **The replication of the experiment by several independent researchers.** The primary purpose of experimental replication is to reduce the possibility of systematic error (such as fraud, prejudice, and simple incompetence) associated with individual researchers. A secondary purpose is to enhance the statistical significance of the results by adding more observations. Thus, regardless of the particular outcome of the test of H_0, the researcher should encourage the replication of his or her analysis by others, ideally with additional data, and welcome the publication of such studies.

This outline reveals that the SM borrows heavily from the framework of frequentist hypothesis testing. In short, steps 1 through 3 are primarily an application of hypothesis testing to a specific scientific problem, accomplished by writing the scientific principle under investigation in the formal mathematical terms of a null hypothesis. As mentioned before, there are clear disparities in the way the SM is employed in different natural and social scientific disciplines. These occur most conspicuously in steps 3 and 4.

To my mind, the disparity of greatest substance is that researchers in certain disciplines, such as physics and psychology, generally are able to make arbitrarily large numbers of the desired observations in step 3, whereas researchers in other disciplines, such as climatology and insurance economics, often have to work with a limited number of observations (e.g., an insurance economist can no more create additional insurance companies than a climatologist can precipitate additional hurricanes). This distinction is essentially the difference between those fields that rely primarily on randomized controlled studies and those that rely primarily on observational studies. Given that observational studies can never be used to settle matters of causality, it is clear that the type of "science" practiced in the latter fields is of a qualitatively different, and inferior, nature. In Chapter 15, I will discuss ways in which researchers in these latter disciplines may employ techniques of mathematical modeling and statistical simulation—

and in particular, game theory (where applicable)—to elevate the rigor of their conclusions.

Other discipline-based variations involve the selection of α in step 3 and the number of independent researchers in step 4. For example, in biomedical research, scientists and government regulators may choose small values of α to protect patients from exposure to inadequately tested drugs. In certain manufacturing processes, however, in which the speed of innovation outweighs the need for statistical accuracy, larger values of α may be acceptable.

I hasten to point out that the above disparities do not constitute the pejorative inconsistencies mentioned at the beginning of the chapter. However, I do believe that it is critical to insist that discipline-based variations in the SM be emphasized more frequently so that people clearly understand that the standard of proof for the laws of quantum physics (for example) is quite different from that for the theory of evolution.

Inconsistencies in Application

Where consistency *is* essential is in the SM's manner of application over time within a given field. Unfortunately, in virtually every scientific discipline, the SM is degraded by one or more of the following problems: apples-to-oranges replications, censorship of results, double standards in setting levels of significance, and moving targets in selecting hypotheses. Unlike outright fraud, which is universally condemned by the research community, these other problems are routinely tolerated—sometimes even encouraged—by various institutional structures and incentives. Let us now consider each of them in turn.

- **Apples-to-oranges replications.** From step 4 of the SM outline, it can be seen that the replication of experimental results after their initial publication is crucial to the SM. However, this step is rarely carried out conscientiously because researchers know that scientific funding, whether from government agencies or private grants, tends not to be given to support projects that simply repeat previous work and that scholarly journals will not publish results considered "old hat." Consequently, what often passes for a replication in the sciences is actually a different experiment from the original—that is, one that is sufficiently distinct to make it "interesting."

• **Censorship of results.** In a sense, the apples-to-oranges problem is a problem of a priori censorship, since many corroborative experiments that should be done are not done. Another major form of censorship is the failure of researchers to publish so-called negative results. For example, suppose that a researcher has derived the hypothesis H_0: "The length of the underwriting cycle for U.S. workers compensation insurance is greater than six years" from the mathematical theory of risk, and then proceeds to test it as described above. Suppose further that the observed data support rejecting this hypothesis in favor of the alternative H_1: "The length of the underwriting cycle for U.S. workers compensation insurance is less than or equal to six years," but the researcher is unable to develop any theoretical explanation for H_1. Under such circumstances, it is fairly likely that the researcher would either engage in self-censorship by not submitting his or her results for publication or would submit the work for publication, but find it deemed unacceptable by scholarly journals.

• **Double standards in setting levels of significance.** Although levels of significance may differ by field of research, it is crucial that α remain constant over time within a given area of investigation; otherwise, certain hypotheses may be favored over others based upon prejudice and other subjective considerations. An extreme example of this problem arises in the field of parapsychology, where research is subjected to much smaller levels of α than in other subfields of psychology.[3] Although some would justify such double standards by stating that extraordinary claims require extraordinary evidence, I would argue that that is an unreasonable interpretation of the SM outlined above. Clearly, an experimental outcome that contradicts a previously demonstrated result (i.e., a result that already has satisfied step 4) should be met with a healthy dose of skepticism—after all, the prior result has passed the test of the SM and therefore is entitled to a certain degree of deference. However, if an experimental outcome is simply novel—albeit unsupported by theory—then it bears no burden other than the requirement of replication (step 4). Harking back to the problem of finding empirical support for H_1: "The length of the underwriting cycle for U.S. workers compensation insurance is less than or equal to six years" without any accompanying theory, I would argue that H_1 should be considered a perfectly legitimate and publishable result worthy of replication efforts.

• **Moving targets in selecting hypotheses.** To maintain the integrity of the SM, it is imperative that researchers select the statement of the null hypothesis, as well as the level of significance, prior to collecting and analyzing observations. Otherwise, they are simply fishing for significance by calling attention to a hypothesis only after finding it to be supported by data. Although this practice is perfectly acceptable as an exploratory statistical technique, it can never satisfy step 3 of the SM. Unfortunately, this type of fishing is quite common in those disciplines that rely primarily on observational studies and is easily illustrated by a slight reorientation of our underwriting cycle example. Suppose that instead of studying workers compensation insurance in just the United States, a researcher is interested in whether or not workers compensation insurance possesses a cycle length greater than six years in all markets throughout the world. Thus, the researcher computes estimated cycle lengths from the past twenty years' data for companies in each of 100 different nations (one of which happens to be the United States). Suppose further that, after carrying out statistical tests for each of the 100 different nations with an α of 0.05, it is found that the United States is the only nation for which the data support a cycle length greater than six years. If the researcher publishes the U.S. result alone, then he or she is abusing the SM because the hypothesis has been identified a posteriori. In other words, the conclusion would be meaningless because "significant" test results would arise by chance alone from approximately 5 percent of all nations tested.

Although the above inconsistencies are rather serious, my purpose is not to discredit the SM's basic structure, but rather to encourage researchers to conduct their investigations in a manner designed to avoid the stated flaws. Otherwise, it is quite likely—and perhaps even inevitable—that important scientific phenomena will be ignored, especially if they are subtle (i.e., numerically small) and/or transient (i.e., temporally variable). Researchers in the fields of insurance and finance should be particularly concerned about the latter possibility because many properties of insurance and other financial markets are sensitive to structural variations over time.

Philosophical Foundations

Circular Reasoning?

Turning to the SM's philosophical underpinnings, one quickly encounters what appears to be a problem of circular logic.[4] This is because the SM, as a process of human understanding, is entirely empirical in nature, and at the same time, its intellectual justification seems to arise exclusively from its empirically observed successes. In other words, to place credence in the SM, one must already accept the SM as a means of generating belief.

This apparent shortcoming is a fundamental problem of *British empiricism*, the philosophy that the SM formalizes. Developed by the late-Renaissance thinkers John Locke, George Berkeley, and David Hume, empiricism argues that human knowledge derives from the observation of objects in the external world through the body's senses (induction) and that internal reflection is useful primarily for identifying logical relationships among these observables. In his famous treatise, *An Enquiry Concerning Human Understanding*, Hume acknowledges the issue of circularity as follows:[5]

> We have said that all arguments concerning existence are founded on the relation of cause and effect; that our knowledge of that relation is derived entirely from experience; and that all our experimental conclusions proceed upon the supposition that the future will be conformable to the past. To endeavor, therefore, the proof of this last supposition by probable arguments, or arguments regarding existence, must be evidently going in a circle, and taking that for granted, which is the very point in question.

Hume ultimately sidesteps this problem by arguing that the intellectual justification for relying on observations is simply human "custom" or "habit." "All inferences from experience, therefore, are effects of custom, not of reasoning," he writes; and subsequently: "All belief of matter of fact or real existence is derived merely from some object, present to the memory or senses, and a customary conjunction between that and some other object."[6]

The issue of circularity is mentioned not because I believe it to be a fatal shortcoming of the SM, but rather because it shows how easily many of today's science devotees accept the SM based upon an uncritical enthusiasm akin to religious zeal. Surely, basing a belief in the SM solely upon its successful track record is no more "scientific" than basing a belief in creationism solely upon the Book of Genesis. Tautology is tautology.

So how does one escape the SM's circularity problem? Chronologically, humanity had to wait only slightly more than thirty years from the publication of Hume's cited work for an insightful approach provided by the German philosopher Immanuel Kant. Famously stating that he was roused from his "dogmatic slumber" by reading Hume's work, Kant spent ten years of his life trying to reconcile the arguments of empiricism with those of *rationalism*, a philosophy developed by René Descartes, Benedict de Spinoza, and Gottfried von Leibniz. In contrast to empiricism, rationalism argues that human knowledge can be derived from internal reflection (deduction) and that the experience of the external world is useful primarily for providing practical examples of internal ideas.

The principal fruit of Kant's ten-year labor was *The Critique of Pure Reason*, in which he proposed the philosophy of *transcendental idealism*.[7] This philosophy argues that certain types of knowledge, such as mathematical reasoning and the understanding of time and space, are built into the human mind. Subject to these a priori conditions, human beings learn about the world through observations as they are processed by, and conform to, the a priori conditions. Using this type of approach, it is a simple matter to remove the circularity of the SM by arguing that acceptance of the SM is just part of the mind's intrinsic construction—specifically, that human beings innately believe that a principle that holds true at one particular point in time and space also should hold true at neighboring points (i.e., during later repetitions of the same experiment).[8] One then is free to employ the SM to one's heart's content.

Although the substitution of "a priori conditions" for "custom" and "habit" may sound like little more than a semantic means of begging the question, it actually provides a logically rigorous foundation for the SM. Essentially, human decision makers *have no choice* but to accept the a priori conditions built into their brains, whereas customs and habits are discretionary and subject to change. For anyone interested in preserving the type of human free will described in Chapter 11, the only thing that remains is to explain how the SM is formed in the brain. In theory, this could be accomplished by arguing that the SM is implied by an evaluation function, $V^{(t)}$, that "selects itself" by following a procedure with sufficient knowable complexity that its outcome, ex ante, appears random. But what if some individuals (like myself) simply fail to select a $V^{(t)}$ that implies the SM?

Feckless Frequentism Vs. Bespoke Bayesianism

My primary concern with the SM's philosophical framework is its conventional formulation in terms of frequentist hypothesis testing. The decision to employ frequentism over Bayesianism is generally made implicitly, and for the unstated reason that, since the SM is supposed to represent a collective decision-making process for all of humanity, it would be impermissible for different individuals to impose their own prior distributions over any unknown parameters. This idea was expressed clearly by British statistician Ronald Fisher in his 1956 book, *Statistical Methods and Scientific Inference*:[9]

> As workers in Science we aim, in fact, at methods of inference which shall be equally convincing to all freely reasoning minds, entirely independently of any intentions that might be furthered by utilizing the knowledge inferred.

Although this approach seems quite reasonable in certain situations—for example, the measurement of particle masses in physics and melting points in chemistry—there are other contexts—such as financial planning—in which such a process is both slow and inefficient.

Consider, for example, the two hurricane prediction models discussed in the previous chapter, and suppose that the sophisticated fundamental analysis of Gray and Klotzbach represents the current state of human knowledge, whereas the simple technical model proposed by the author represents a brand-new and purportedly superior alternative. Then, under the SM, the null hypothesis would be given by H_0: "The fundamental model is better for predicting the number of Atlantic-Basin hurricanes in a given year," and the alternative hypothesis would be H_1: "The technical model is better for predicting the number of Atlantic-Basin hurricanes in a given year."

From the perspective of an academic meteorologist who has just embarked on the study of hurricane frequency, it is fairly clear how to proceed. Having learned of the technical model and how it was shown to be a somewhat better predictor of the number of Atlantic-Basin hurricanes using a given collection of historical data, the meteorologist would look for ways to replicate the technical analysis using different sets of data. Perhaps the scientist would seek alternative measurements of the same input values used by the author for the Atlantic Basin, or perhaps he or she would compare the two models in a more limited geographical context (e.g., among hurricanes making landfall in the United States). In either case, after conducting the new study, the meteorologist would publish the results, thereby providing more or less support for the technical approach and helping to move forward the cause of good science.

Now, however, suppose that one is not an academic researcher, but rather the director of a risk management and emergency planning agency for a state or municipality along the U.S. Gulf Coast. Suppose also that the agency director has been in this job for a number of years and has witnessed firsthand the relative inaccuracy of the fundamental forecasts as they were published year after year. Given the agency's serious responsibilities, the director might be torn between wanting to embrace wholeheartedly the technical model (because of its apparently greater accuracy) and sticking with the fundamental model (because it represents the status quo, and as a public official, he or she cannot be too capricious in making decisions). As a consequence, the director may decide to continue using the fundamental forecasts in planning, but to incorporate some information from the technical forecasts as well (e.g., by using a weighted average of the two forecasts, or employing the fundamental forecast only if it provides a more conservative—i.e., larger—predicted frequency).

In a third scenario, consider the case of a hedge fund manager contemplating the purchase of weather derivatives for Atlanta, Georgia, that are traded by the Chicago Mercantile Exchange. To understand these instruments better, the manager does a little research into weather prediction and soon comes across both the fundamental and technical hurricane forecasts. Because of the investor's relative lack of expertise in the area, he or she contacts a number of reputable meteorologists, who (not surprisingly) offer comments such as: "Gray and Klotzbach are the real experts in this area; the technical model was developed by some insurance guy who doesn't know anything about weather systems," and "Frankly, I don't understand why anyone would trust the technical model." As a result of this additional information and given that the manager's motive is solely to seek the very best outcomes on behalf of the fund's investors, he or she decides to ignore the technical model entirely.

From the above examples, it can be seen that Fisher's ideal of an SM that is "equally convincing to all freely reasoning minds, entirely independently of any intentions" is largely an impossible dream. Although it may work reasonably well for academic researchers who are able to proceed at a leisurely pace and who are uncomfortable relying on personal judgment, it becomes more problematic for those in need of prompt answers to address important time-sensitive issues, as well as for those with personal beliefs who do not see any need to be constrained by published results.

The question arises, therefore, whether or not it is reasonable to embrace, explicitly, an alternative SM—let us call it a "personalized scientific method" (PSM)—in which one is free to: (1) advance the current state of knowledge at one's own pace (i.e., to select levels of significance with which one is most comfortable, possibly higher than those used by most academic researchers); and (2) incorporate personal beliefs through a Bayesian framework.

Clearly, such a program of acquiring knowledge would generate a tremendous amount of chaos if it were to replace the SM. With every researcher "on a different page" from his or her colleagues, there would be no general standard for distinguishing facts from illusion and truth from wishful thinking. Recalling the inconsistency problems with the SM, listed above, it is easy to see that both the apples-to-oranges and the moving targets problems would be greatly aggravated by a PSM, as researchers abandoned any pretense of consensus in the selection of experiments to conduct and allowed their personal beliefs to be unduly influenced by fishing for statistical significance.

Nevertheless, there would be some benefits of a PSM. For one thing, it likely would counteract the inconsistencies of censorship and double standards mentioned previously, as researchers would be free to incorporate negative results into their personal beliefs and to offset bias in the selection of alphas with their own discretion in that regard. And perhaps the best argument for a PSM already has been intimated: Since large numbers of researchers—like our agency director and hedge fund manager—already use one, why not simply acknowledge it?

Explicitly embracing a PSM does not have to mean abandoning the conventional SM. Researchers could continue to follow the SM as before, but simply inject more opinion, speculation, and subjective judgment into their analyses and conclusions. In fact, this is exactly what professional actuaries do in the field of insurance, where limited data often necessitate intellectual compromise via the averaging of estimates and forecasts from different sources.[10] As mentioned previously, insurance actuaries often employ Bayesian methods in their work, and it is undoubtedly this Bayesian influence that has allowed them to recognize formally the usefulness of personal judgment. In a world with an accepted PSM, researchers who found the new approach offensive naturally would be free to express their opinions and to organize scholarly journals adhering to the strictest standards of the SM (which, as we know, is no mean feat).

One of the supreme ironies of modern intellectual life is the great chasm that exists between rigorous science, on the one hand, and established faith, on the other. In today's world, the two opposing camps have reached an uneasy truce under which they officially profess to respect each other's domains and even allow safe passage for some of their respective adherents to travel back and forth across the bridge that separates them. However, anyone who tarries on the bridge too long or—God (?) forbid!—jumps off is immediately branded a quack or crackpot. A PSM would permit people to explore this middle ground without fear of ridicule; and it is this appealing characteristic that, I suspect, has led to my own choice of a $V^{(t)}$ that implies a PSM.

ACT 3, SCENE 4

[The gates of Heaven. Deceased stands in front of magistrate-style desk; St. Peter sits behind desk.]

ST. PETER: Hello, Mr. Powers. Welcome to the gates of Heaven.

DECEASED: Why, thank you. May I enter?

ST. PETER: Well, that's the big question, isn't it? Unfortunately, it seems there are a few matters that need attending.

DECEASED: I see.

ST. PETER: To begin with, there appears to be an unresolved issue about your parking under a tree, with the expectation that a large branch would fall on your car and destroy it.

DECEASED: Oh, *that* again? I thought I had explained elsewhere—

ST. PETER: Excuse, me, Mr. Powers—this is Heaven. We already know what you've explained elsewhere.

DECEASED: Well, then, you must know that my action didn't constitute insurance fraud. It couldn't, because there was no moral hazard involved.

ST. PETER: Again, Mr. Powers—this is Heaven. We'll be the judges of what is and what isn't *moral* hazard.

DECEASED: Certainly. But you must recognize that the falling branch was clearly an act of God!

ST. PETER: Yes, of course; and that's precisely the problem. You see, God doesn't like being a party to insurance fraud.

DECEASED: But it wasn't fraud! Even though I believed the branch would fall, no one else would have believed it.

ST. PETER: I see. So you thought the probability of the branch's falling was very large—above 90 percent, perhaps?

DECEASED: Yes.

ST. PETER: And everyone else, the tree experts included, thought the probability was very small—below 1 percent, perhaps?

DECEASED: Yes, exactly.

ST. PETER: But why should it matter what others believed, if you yourself believed the branch would fall?

DECEASED: Well, on Earth, that's how we evaluate—I won't presume to say *judge*—the decisions of our fellow human beings. Since we all can't agree on the same subjective probability of an event's occurring, we just use the observed long-run frequency of the event. And in this case, a tree like the one in my yard would break with a probability of less than 1 percent.

ST. PETER: So you believed that the probability of the branch's falling was greater than 90 percent, but you were willing to go along with a frequentist analysis when it suited your purposes?

DECEASED: Yes, I suppose that's true . . .

ST. PETER: Well, then, we have a problem.

DECEASED: We do?

ST. PETER: Yes. You see, in Heaven we're all *fundamentalist* Bayesians.

15

Games and the Mind
Modeling Human Behavior

If it was a matter of catching a stag, everyone well understood that he must keep his position faithfully; but if a
hare came to pass within reach of one of them, undoubtedly he went after it without scruple, and having caught
his prey did not worry much about having made his
companions lose theirs.

—JEAN-JACQUES ROUSSEAU
(*A DISCOURSE ON INEQUALITY*, 1755)[1]

If the preceding three chapters have created the impression that serious
deficiencies exist in some empirical scientific research, especially in fields
relying primarily on observational studies, then they have succeeded to
that limited extent. And that leads to the question: What can scientists do
to improve the credibility of their research if randomized controlled studies are not feasible? As mentioned briefly in Chapter 14, my principal
recommendation is that researchers embrace a much broader use of mathematical modeling and statistical simulation to replicate the complex processes under study. This is because such modeling essentially permits one
to conduct randomized controlled studies as either purely analytical or
computer-assisted thought experiments.

In physical sciences such as climatology and cosmology, computer-
based mathematical and statistical models already are employed to a great
extent, although we have not yet reached a stage where complex simula-
tions can predict weather accurately for more than a few days into the future. In social sciences such as insurance and financial economics, there is

an additional component—human behavior—that must be incorporated into any successful model. In this final chapter, I will address the somewhat perplexing problem of modeling human behavior and suggest that, until we have figured out a way to create truly lifelike models of human beings, the most practicable alternative is to use the powerful techniques of mathematical game theory.

Game Theory

In a way, the mathematical theory of games is as good as mind reading as long as the preferences of all relevant decision makers are known. Using the methods of game theory, one can often predict, with great reliability, the outcomes of economic, social, and political encounters among two or more individuals. Some of my own research involves the application of market games—a branch of game theory developed by Martin Shubik and Pradeep Dubey for purposes of describing the behavior of buyers and sellers in economic markets—to problems in insurance.[2],[3] By employing game-theoretic models, one is able to study such things as insurance market efficiency for arbitrary market configurations—that is, through mathematically facilitated thought experiments—without having to limit study to the particular market configurations available to observational studies.

The simplest type of mathematical game is the *two-by-two* (2 × 2) *matrix game*, which involves two players (Player A and Player B), each of whom has two possible strategies (Strategies A1 and A2 for Player A, Strategies B1 and B2 for Player B). As shown in Table 15.1, this type of game may be represented by the 2 × 2 matrix formed by four possible strategy pairs (A1 and B1, A1 and B2, A2 and B1, and A2 and B2), where the four cells of the matrix contain the resulting payoffs to Player A and Player B, respectively.

Table 15.1
Generic 2 × 2 Game

		Player B	
		Strategy B1	Strategy B2
Player A	Strategy A1	$A_{1,1}, B_{1,1}$	$A_{1,2}, B_{1,2}$
	Strategy A2	$A_{2,1}, B_{2,1}$	$A_{2,2}, B_{2,2}$

Cold War (Nuclear Arms Race)

One of the best-known applications of 2×2 games is an abstract model of the nuclear arms race between the United States and the Soviet Union during the Cold War, depicted in Table 15.2 (a). In this game, each superpower has only the two alternative strategies: Disarm (i.e., unilaterally eliminate its stockpile of nuclear weapons) or Arm (i.e., maintain and upgrade its nuclear weaponry). As presented in Table 15.2 (a), the game is characterized by *ordinal* payoffs (i.e., each player possesses a simple ranking of the four possible outcomes, with 1 indicating the least desirable outcome and 4 indicating the most desirable outcome), although some authors may use hypothetical *cardinal* payoffs to indicate the relative magnitudes of different outcomes. In all of the subsequent discussion of 2×2 games, I will work with payoffs that are nominally ordinal (i.e., that consist of only the integers 1, 2, 3, and 4), but will interpret the payoffs as cardinal numbers in certain cases to be noted.

Obviously, the nuclear arms race game is *symmetric* because the row and column players can be interchanged without affecting the nature of the conflict. To clarify the entries in the matrix, each nation ranks the four outcomes, from best to worst, as follows:

We arm, but they disarm (best = 4).
We disarm, and they disarm (second best = 3).
We arm, and they arm (third best = 2).
We disarm, but they arm (worst = 1).

This game is particularly easy to solve because the Arm strategy is dominant for both players; that is, regardless of what Player B does, Player A obtains its better payoff by arming and vice versa. To the credit of game theory, such a persistent tendency to arm was a hallmark of relations between the United States and the Soviet Union from the end of World War II up to the disintegration of the latter.

Of course, 2×2 game analyses can be extended to consider alternate histories. Whereas Table 15.2 (a) treats the two superpowers as equally hawk-like in terms of their resolve to stand up to each other, Tables 15.2 (b) and 15.2 (c) consider the cases of a dove-like superpower against a hawk-like superpower and two dove-like superpowers, respectively. The preferences of a dove-like nation are captured by rearranging the above ranking of outcomes as follows:

Table 15.2 (a)
Nuclear Arms Race: Hawk-Like Nation vs. Hawk-Like Nation

		Nation B (Hawk)	
		Disarm	Arm*
Nation A (Hawk)	Disarm	3, 3	1, 4
	Arm*	4, 1	[2, 2]

Table 15.2 (b)
Nuclear Arms Race: Dove-Like Nation vs. Hawk-Like Nation

		Nation B (Hawk)	
		Disarm	Arm*
Nation A (Dove)	Disarm*	4, 3	[2, 4]
	Arm	3, 1	1, 2

Table 15.2 (c)
Nuclear Arms Race: Dove-Like Nation vs. Dove-Like Nation

		Nation B (Dove)	
		Disarm*	Arm
Nation A (Dove)	Disarm*	[4, 4]	2, 3
	Arm	3, 2	1, 1

Notes: Asterisks indicate dominant strategies. Square brackets indicate dominant strategy solutions.

We disarm, and they disarm (best = 4).
We arm, but they disarm (second best = 3).
We disarm, but they arm (third best = 2).
We arm, and they arm (worst = 1).

Interestingly, the games in both Tables 15.2 (b) and 15.2 (c) remain easy to solve because each player still possesses a dominant strategy. In the Dove versus Hawk game (which is naturally asymmetric), the Dove ends up disarming, whereas the Hawk continues to arm. In the Dove versus

Dove game (which, like the original formulation, is symmetric), both players choose to disarm. These results are not particularly surprising and suggest that the greatest geo-political imbalance results from one side accepting the idea of unilateral disarmament while the other does not.

War on Terror (Attack on Civilian Target)

Shifting to a more contemporary form of conflict arising from the struggle between Western governments and Islamic terrorism, one can readily apply the 2×2 game paradigm to the problem of attacks on civilian targets, as shown in Table 15.3. This game, which represents a particular form of the Colonel Blotto game,[4] is intrinsically asymmetrical because of the imbalance between the interests and resources of the two sides.

To model the problem of how governments must allocate defensive resources in the face of potential terrorist attacks, let us assume that there are only two possible civilian targets in a given city: (1) a big structure (possibly a landmark skyscraper or sports stadium) with a great potential for loss of life; and (2) a small building (possibly a government office or train station) with fewer lives exposed.[5] I will further assume that the government has only sufficient resources to defend one of the locations and that the terrorist has only enough resources to attack one of the locations. Thus, the government's possible strategies are Defend Big Target and Defend Small Target, whereas the terrorist's possible strategies are Attack Big Target and Attack Small Target.

To recognize the differences in target values, the government ranks the four possible outcomes as follows:

Table 15.3
Attack on Civilian Target

		Terrorist	
		Attack Big Target (.5)	Attack Small Target (.5)
Government	Defend Big Target (.75)	3, 2	2, 3
	Defend Small Target (.25)	1, 4	4, 1

Note: Decimals in parentheses indicate probability weights applied in mixed strategy Cournot-Nash equilibrium.

We defend the small target, and they attack the small target (best = 4).
We defend the big target, and they attack the big target (second best = 3).
We defend the big target, but they attack the small target (third best = 2).
We defend the small target, but they attack the big target (worst = 1).

Similarly, the terrorist ranks the four possible outcomes as:

We attack the big target, but they defend the small target (best = 4).
We attack the small target, but they defend the big target (second best = 3).
We attack the big target, and they defend the big target (third best = 2).
We attack the small target, and they defend the small target (worst = 1).

Looking at the two players' payoffs for each possible outcome, one can see that—if taken to be cardinal numbers—they always sum to 5, so this particular game is what is known as a *constant-sum* (or sometimes *zero-sum*) game. In other words, the game happens to be structured so that the government's loss is the terrorist's gain and vice versa.[6] Unfortunately, the game is not nearly as easy to solve as those in Tables 15.2 (a), (b), and (c) because there is no dominant strategy for either player. Consequently, one must turn to the Cournot-Nash (CN) equilibrium concept and look for a pair of strategies with the property that if Player A selects its equilibrium strategy, then Player B cannot benefit from deviating from its own equilibrium strategy and vice versa.

This equilibrium concept, in which each player's equilibrium strategy is the best response to its opponent's, was first proposed by French economist Antoine Cournot in 1838 to model the behavior of duopolies making competitive quantity offers.[7] It was developed formally and generalized by American mathematician and economist John Nash in 1951.[8] An important part of Nash's work was the extension of Cournot's concept to *mixed strategies* in the case of cardinal games, in which players select randomly from their *pure strategies* (e.g., Strategies A1 and A2 for Player A, and B1 and B2 for Player B in the 2×2 case), and evaluate strategies by their resultant *expected* payoffs. This becomes directly relevant to our terrorism game by assuming that the payoffs are cardinal numbers and noting that the only CN equilibrium consists of mixed strategies in which the government defends the big target with probability 0.75 and the small target with probability 0.25, whereas the terrorist attacks the big target with probability 0.5 and the small target with probability 0.5.

By applying this type of model to all potential targets within a city (or an entire nation, for that matter), it is possible to solve the resource allocation problem for both the government and the terrorist in such a way that inferences can be drawn about the expected frequencies with which structures of certain types will be attacked. This type of analysis could be used to provide an estimate of the conditional probability that a particular target is selected, given that an attack is planned (i.e., p_2) in the terrorism forecasting process described in Chapter 13.[9]

Modeling Virtue

Naturally, game theory need not be restricted to problems of warfare.[10] In fact, one of the earliest examples of game-theoretic analysis is Swiss philosopher Jean-Jacques Rousseau's illustration of the role of cooperation in the *social contract*. In a famous passage, reproduced at the beginning of this chapter, Rousseau describes how the social contract may have developed among our human ancestors through the necessities of hunting.[11] His argument is formalized in a 2×2 game known today as the Stag Hunt (see Table 15.4).

Essentially, Rousseau's observation is that human beings can achieve better results by cooperating than by working alone. In the case at hand, if two hunters work together, then they can kill a stag—an objective that cannot be realized by either hunter working alone. This outcome is best for both hunters because each maximizes the amount of meat he takes home

Table 15.4
Stag Hunt

		Hunter B	
		Hunt Stag (Cooperate)	Hunt Hare (Defect)
Hunter A	Hunt Stag (Cooperate)	{4, 4}	1, 3
	Hunt Hare (Defect)	3, 1	2, 2

Notes: Curly brackets indicate Pareto-dominant pure strategy Cournot-Nash equilibrium.

(and thus obtains the best possible ordinal payoff, 4). If both hunters choose not to cooperate, then each relinquishes the possibility of killing a stag and has to compete for a hare (with an ordinal payoff of 2). Finally, if one hunter agrees to cooperate, but the other is faithless, then the former hunter comes up empty-handed (obtaining the worst payoff of 1), whereas the defector is able to find a hare faster than he could if the two hunters were competing against each other (obtaining a payoff of 3).

The Stag Hunt possesses two pure strategy CN equilibrium solutions: one in which both hunters choose to cooperate (to be denoted by (C, C)) and the other in which both hunters choose to defect (to be denoted by (D, D)). By definition, each of these solutions is stable in the sense that one player cannot gain by a unilateral deviation in strategy. However, since solution (C, C) yields a better payoff than (D, D) for both players—a property called Pareto dominance—it is reasonable for the players to try to coordinate on the former outcome. This mutual understanding of the optimal solution provides a simple model of the social contract.

The problem with the social contract thus formulated is that it is sensitive to small changes in the payoff structure of the game. Consider, for example, what happens to the Stag Hunt if the payoff level for cooperation (i.e., 4) switches places with the payoff level for defection (i.e., 3) when the other hunter has chosen to cooperate. Suddenly, the original game is transformed into the Prisoner's Dilemma, an even more celebrated 2×2 game (see Table 15.5).

The story behind the Prisoner's Dilemma is that two individuals have been arrested for their participation in a major crime, and are interrogated separately by police. Each prisoner knows that if neither prisoner con-

Table 15.5
Prisoner's Dilemma

		Prisoner B	
		Not Confess (Cooperate)	Confess (Defect)*
Prisoner A	Not Confess (Cooperate)	3, 3	1, 4
	Confess (Defect)*	4, 1	[2, 2]

Notes: Asterisks indicate dominant strategies. Square brackets indicate dominant strategy solution.

fesses to the crime, then each will be charged with a lesser offense, involving less jail time. However, if both prisoners confess, then both will serve normal jail sentences for the major crime. If one prisoner refuses to confess, but the other prisoner does confess, then the former will serve an extra-long jail sentence for the major crime, whereas the latter will serve no jail time. A careful inspection of this game shows that it is identical to the nuclear arms race game of Table 15.2 (a), and therefore amenable to the same analysis; in other words, it possesses a dominant strategy equilibrium formed by both players' choosing to defect, (D, D).

One thing that is particularly interesting about the Stag Hunt and the Prisoner's Dilemma is that they can be generalized to a complete class of eight 2×2 games that possess two important properties: (1) the payoffs are symmetric; and (2) the sum of the payoffs (taken as cardinal numbers) from a given outcome never decrease as more players cooperate. In joint work, my former student Zhan Shen and I have found that these properties are useful for studying the benefits of cooperation between pairs of individual, homogeneous members of society.[12]

For convenience, I will employ the following conventional terminology for symmetric 2×2 games:

- The payoff to either player in outcome (C, C) will be called the Reward (R) result for joint cooperation;
- The payoff to player A in (C, D) or to player B in (D, C) will be called the Sucker (S) result for cooperating when one's opponent defects;
- The payoff to player A in (D, C) or to player B in (C, D) will be called the Temptation (T) result for defecting when one's opponent cooperates; and
- The payoff to either player in (D, D) will be called the Punishment (P) result for joint defection.

This terminology is summarized in Table 15.6.

From property two above, it is known that if exactly one player cooperates, then the aggregate outcome is typically greater than (or at least no less than) the aggregate outcome if neither player cooperates and that if both players cooperate, then the aggregate outcome is typically greater than (or at least no less than) the aggregate outcome if exactly one player cooperates. Table 15.7 provides a complete list of the eight symmetric 2×2 games possessing this property, where the games are identified by their unique quadruples, (R, S, T, P).

Table 15.6
Generic Symmetric 2 × 2 Game

		Player B	
		Cooperate	Defect
Player A	Cooperate	*R, R*	*S, T*
	Defect	*T, S*	*P, P*

Table 15.7
Games of Interest

Game I: (3, 4, 1, 2)			
		Player B	
		Cooperate*	Defect
Player A	Cooperate*	[3, 3]	4, 1
	Defect	1, 4	2, 2

Game II: (4, 3, 1, 2)			
		Player B	
		Cooperate*	Defect
Player A	Cooperate*	[4, 4]	3, 1
	Defect	1, 3	2, 2

Game III: (3, 4, 2, 1)			
		Player B	
		Cooperate*	Defect
Player A	Cooperate*	[3, 3]	4, 2
	Defect	2, 4	1, 1

Table 15.7
(*Continued*)

Game IV: (4, 3, 2, 1)

		Player B	
		Cooperate*	Defect
Player A	Cooperate*	[4, 4]	3, 2
	Defect	2, 3	1, 1

Game V: (4, 2, 3, 1)

		Player B	
		Cooperate*	Defect
Player A	Cooperate*	[4, 4]	2, 3
	Defect	3, 2	1, 1

Game VI: (4, 1, 3, 2), Stag Hunt

		Player B	
		Cooperate	Defect
Player A	Cooperate	{4, 4}	1, 3
	Defect	3, 1	2, 2

Game VII: (3, 2, 4, 1)

		Player B	
		Cooperate (.5)	Defect (.5)
Player A	Cooperate (.5)	3, 3	2, 4
	Defect (.5)	4, 2	1, 1

Table 15.7
(*Continued*)

Game VIII: (3, 1, 4, 2), Prisoner's Dilemma

		Player B	
		Cooperate	Defect*
Player A	Cooperate	3, 3	1, 4
	Defect*	4, 1	[2, 2]

Notes: Asterisks indicate dominant strategies. Square brackets indicate dominant strategy solutions. Curly brackets indicate Pareto-dominant pure strategy Cournot-Nash equilibrium. Decimals in parentheses indicate probability weights applied in mixed strategy Cournot-Nash equilibrium.

Table 15.8
Social Virtues

Social Virtue	Definition	Explanation (from Player B's Perspective)
Empathy (E)	$R > T$	If A chooses Cooperate, then B prefers Cooperate.
Forgiveness (F)	$S > P$	If A chooses Defect, then B prefers Cooperate.
Justice (J)	$S > T$	If A chooses Defect and B chooses Cooperate, then B's payoff is greater than A's.
Contrition (C)	$P > T$	If B chooses Defect, then B hopes that A chooses Defect.
Abnegation (A)	$S > R$	If B chooses Cooperate, then B hopes that A chooses Defect.

To explain why some of the games in this list yield fully cooperative (C, C) solutions, whereas others do not, it is instructive to define five "social virtues" (SVs)—empathy, forgiveness, justice, contrition, and abnegation—as shown in Table 15.8.

In Table 15.9, the numbers of SVs possessed by each game are compared with the degree of cooperation in its solution. From this table, it can be seen that there is a positive relationship between the SVs and cooperation. In

Table 15.9
Social Virtues and Cooperation

Game	E	F	J	C	A	# SVs	Solution
I	Yes	Yes	Yes	Yes	Yes	5	(C, C)*
II	Yes	Yes	Yes	Yes	No	4	(C, C)*
III	Yes	Yes	Yes	No	Yes	4	(C, C)*
IV	Yes	Yes	Yes	No	No	3	(C, C)*
V	Yes	Yes	No	No	No	2	(C, C)*
VI	Yes	No	No	No	No	1	(C, C)**
VII	No	Yes	No	No	No	1	Mixed (0.5, 0.5)***
VIII	No	No	No	No	No	0	(D, D)*

* Indicates dominant strategy solution.
** Indicates Pareto-dominant pure strategy Cournot-Nash equilibrium.
*** Indicates mixed strategy Cournot-Nash equilibrium with probability weight of 0.5 applied to each strategy.

other words, the more SVs a society can impose on its citizens (through economic and legal incentives), the greater the likelihood that individuals will cooperate with each other. Of course, these SVs may be expensive for governments to impose (such as a comprehensive judicial system to ensure justice). Thus, it is particularly interesting that cooperation can be obtained so "cheaply" through the Stag Hunt payoff system (Table 15.7, Game VI), thereby highlighting the profound usefulness of empathy among human beings.

Is Game Theory Parapsychology?

Earlier in this chapter, I stated somewhat cavalierly that "the mathematical theory of games was as good as mind reading" under certain circumstances. Now I would like to return to that particular idea and ask quite seriously: Is game theory a form of parapsychology, in the sense that it permits observers to predict the actions of others both before they occur (i.e., precognitively) and/or without communication with the individuals involved (i.e., telepathically)?

Although certain types of game-theoretic solutions—in particular, those dictated by the presence of dominant strategies—are clearly no more precognitive or telepathic than predicting that a hungry child will devour a cookie, the success of the CN equilibrium solution, in the absence of dominant strategies, does seem a bit preternatural. For example, in a single play of the Stag Hunt, there is no compelling reason for the players to coordinate on (C, C). After all, even if I, as Player A, decide to cooperate, there is no guarantee that Player B will do the same thing. Although I may reason that my opponent would do worse by defecting than by cooperating (given that I have decided to cooperate), I also have to keep in mind that: (1) I will have to pay a heavy price if I misjudge my opponent's decision; and (2) my opponent is no more certain that I will cooperate than I am that he or she will. So what is the true psychological (or parapsychological) process under which my decision is made?

As a fundamentalist Bayesian, I would argue that one's strategic decision ultimately involves no more than a simple optimization problem. Viewing the game probabilistically, I would note that by cooperating, I am eligible for possible payoffs of 4 and 1 (depending on what my opponent does), whereas by defecting, I am eligible for corresponding payoffs of 3 and 2, respectively. Therefore, if I possess a Bayesian prior probability, p_{Coop}, that my opponent will cooperate, then the expected value of my (cardinal) payoff will be $3p_{\text{Coop}} + 1$ by cooperating and $p_{\text{Coop}} + 2$ by defecting, so I will do better on the average by cooperating if and only if p_{Coop} is greater than 1/2.

The origin of the prior probability, p_{Coop}, naturally would take into account all of the standard notions of game theory, but only as filtered through my own perceptions of what my opponent is likely to think and do. Thus, if I believe my opponent is firmly committed to the CN equilibrium concept, then I will place greater probability on the choice of cooperation. However, if I have no idea of my opponent's views of game-theoretic concepts, but understand him or her to be a generally uncooperative person, then I will place greater probability on defection.

To answer the question posed at the beginning of this section, I thus would say two things. For a Bayesian, game theory is clearly *not* a form of parapsychology. However, for a non-Bayesian, who must rely entirely on second-guessing both players' decisions, I would argue that it *is*.

What About the Real (or Surreal) Thing?

Having considered a variety of matters, both theoretical and empirical, related to the epistemology of randomness, I would like to complete this last chapter by addressing an issue at the margin of science that nevertheless is of importance in the overall understanding of risk: the possible connection between human consciousness and the physical events of our world. Unlike some science writers who have probed a possible role for human consciousness at the foundations of theoretical physics, I simply will present my thoughts by way of a single empirical anecdote.

As noted previously, I acknowledge a special relationship with trees—one that is both unusual and difficult to describe. I certainly am not overly fond of my woody neighbors and in no respect a "tree hugger" or other manner of dendrophile. In fact, I must admit to having as much animosity as kindliness toward trees (which are, after all, the autumnal enemies of the sedentary as well as a perennial peril to houses, automobiles, and other property). So suffice it to say that my relationship with trees is rather mixed and complex.

The remarkable event that first illuminated this relationship occurred during my senior year of high school. At that time, I lived in a quiet residential town about fifteen miles southwest of Boston. Although the incident in question took place in October, it was preceded by another remarkable occurrence five months earlier: a freak snow-and-ice storm in May that caused severe damage to the new growth of trees in the region. In my neighborhood several trees were toppled, and many others suffered broken and twisted limbs. There was one tree in particular that was left with a large upper branch dangling by a thin piece of wood, seemingly little more than a strip of bark.

Intrigued by the strange angle and tenuous connection formed by the broken branch, I found myself drawn to look at it from time to time. This occurred throughout the remainder of the spring and the ensuing summer and early fall. Then, one day in October, as I was unlocking the front door of my house, I happened to turn in the direction of the tree, and pausing for a moment to look at the broken branch, I was stunned to see it separate in the perfectly still noontime air, accompanied by only the gentlest of cracks. Of all the opportunities the branch could have taken—from rainy days when I stayed indoors to long dark nights when the winds howled—it chose this particular moment to consummate its secession. Was it just coincidence (i.e., chance) that I was there to witness this event, or was there an element of the paranormal to it?

To answer that question, of course, requires a working definition of the term *paranormal*. To that end, I would propose that an event be deemed paranormal if it involves a relation of cause and effect that cannot be explained by the current state of scientific knowledge. This is, of course, a very broad definition, simply requiring ignorance or incompetence on the part of science, rather than the presence of any particular type of phenomenon: clairvoyance, precognition, telepathy, psychokinesis, etc. But in the absence of any convincing theories outside current physics that could explain the relationship between my observation of the tree branch and its final breaking, such a definition will suffice.

Now let us do a little calculation. Suppose that the tree originally splintered on May 15, and then broke completely on October 15. That would give five months, or approximately 150 days, in which the branch could have come apart. Now suppose that I had looked at the tree five times per day during that period (a gross overestimate, since the actual frequency would have been no more than five times on the most active of days) and that each time I looked, my eyes beheld the tree for ten seconds (again, a gross overestimate, since the actual time elapsed would have been no more than ten seconds on the most obsessive of occasions). Then the total number of seconds during which I viewed the tree would have been at most $150 \times 5 \times 10$, or 750 seconds, out of a total of $150 \times 24 \times 60 \times 60$, or 12,960,000 seconds. In other words, assuming that the final break was equally likely to have occurred at any instant during the five-month period, the chances of my having witnessed that particular event would have been no more than 750/12,960,000, or approximately 0.00005787.

Expressing this analysis in the language of hypothesis testing, one could say that the null hypothesis is given by H_0: "The final tree break occurred independently of my observation," and the p-value is 0.00005787, so for any value of α greater than 0.00005787 (including the commonly used standards of 0.05 and 0.01), the null hypothesis would be rejected. In short, it would seem that there is at least prima facie evidence of a paranormal event's having taken place!

Before getting too excited about this discovery, however, let us consider what the skeptics would have to say about such anecdotal observations (i.e., observations not made under controlled scientific conditions).

First, skeptics would argue (quite reasonably) that anecdotal observations are not dependable for testing natural phenomena because of the likelihood of misspecifying the null hypothesis by defining the category of "unusual" outcomes too narrowly. In the case at hand, I used H_0: "The final tree break occurred independently of my observation." However, this null hypothesis presumably was identified *after* observing the tree's final break, an event I considered unusual. Had some other unusual event occurred—for example, had I happened to be looking at the sky the moment a bright fireball appeared—then I simply would have specified the null hypothesis differently (i.e., H_0: "The fireball's appearance occurred independently of my observation"). Essentially, I seem to be guilty of the moving targets problem described in Chapter 14—that is, fishing for statistical significance.

Skeptics also would argue (again, quite reasonably) that anecdotal observations are not dependable because of the likely selective adduction of evidence caused by remembering only statistically significant outcomes and ignoring the more mundane, negative outcomes. Specifically, in focusing only on witnessing the tree break, I presumably am neglecting all of the perfectly ordinary things that I saw at times when I actually expected to see something unusual. In other words, I seem to be guilty of the censorship problem (also described in Chapter 14).

So what do I have to say in my defense?

Interestingly, I believe that both concerns can be addressed satisfactorily. While acknowledging that anecdotal observations certainly are susceptible to the aforementioned shortcomings, I would argue that my observation was not as casual as might be supposed.

At the time of the events described, I had taken a limited interest in the paranormal—and in psychokinesis in particular. As a result of this interest, I occasionally tested my own psychokinetic abilities in either of two ways: by trying to bend metal keys—which I failed miserably to accomplish on at most ten occasions—and by trying to break the filaments in glowing incandescent light bulbs—which I thought would be easier than bending keys, but which yielded no better results on at most twenty occasions. The tenuously attached tree branch in my yard provided a fortuitous additional—and I should say, the *only* additional—context for such trials.

Thus, although I most assuredly would not claim that my efforts with keys, filaments, and the tree branch constituted scientifically controlled experiments, I do believe that they did not suffer that greatly from either the moving targets problem or the censorship problem. There was no moving target because the informal tests were carried out intentionally with the purpose of determining whether or not I possessed any psychokinetic ability, rather than simply as reactions to randomly appearing unusual events. And there was no censorship problem because I certainly did not neglect to remember my failures with the keys and filaments. Naturally, one might inquire why I did not continue my psychokinetic experiments with tree branches after this singular success. But the answer is rather obvious: tenuously dangling branches are simply too few and far between to permit a serious effort.

The point I wish to make here is not that there is sufficient evidence of a paranormal event to publish a research article according to the standards of the scientific method, or even to convince a fellow human being that such an event occurred. I would argue, however, that there is more than ample evidence for me, under my own personalized scientific method, to reject a null hypothesis that paranormal events do not occur. In fact, I would go somewhat further and say that to ignore this personal evidence by trying to pretend that it can be discredited by moving targets, censorship, or some other facile explanation would be intellectually dishonest. Thus, it is really not a question of *choosing* to believe in something viewed as dubious by practitioners of science and established religion alike. Rather, I am stuck with this particular outcome because of my a priori selection of an evaluation function, $V^{(t)}$, that implies my personalized scientific method, whether I like the outcome or not.

As a final, somewhat bemusing point, I would like to address one further possible criticism of the above analysis: If, as has been argued, observational studies constitute only a very crude and inferior type of science, then how could I possibly rely on an *observational* test of significance to support a conclusion of paranormal activity?

Strangely, the answer is quite simple: A conclusion of paranormal causality is the only one that is logically valid based upon an observational study! Recall that the null hypothesis was H_0: "The final tree break occurred independently of my observation." Thus, when I rejected the null hypothesis, it left me with the alternative that there *was* some connection between the tree break and my observation. However, since I could not identify that connection, I had to refer to it as paranormal. Now, recognizing that my observational test of significance may have failed to account for some unknown confounding variable that is either positively correlated with both the breaking branch and my observation or negatively correlated with both events, I must further acknowledge there could have been some unknown connection between the two events, mediated by this confounding variable. However, since such a confounding variable is unknown, it must be paranormal (according to the above definition) as well.

ACT 3, SCENE 5

[A hospital room. Old man lies awake in bed; Grim Reaper approaches quietly.]

REAPER: Good evening, Mr. Wiley. It's me again, the Grim Reaper.
MAN: A good evening to you, my friend.

REAPER: It's been another thirty-three years. Time to call in my debt. But this time, no tricks. I'm quite aware that you're a much better statistician than I.

MAN: Oh, Reaper, it's kind of you to say so. But I can still sense a bit of regret in your voice. You've gotten in some trouble with your boss for this long delay, haven't you?

REAPER: Yes.

MAN: And He instructed you not to accept any more probabilistic challenges from me, didn't He?

REAPER: Yes.

MAN: But He didn't say anything about other sorts of challenges, did He?

REAPER: [Opens eyes suspiciously.] No. But what do you have in mind?

MAN: Well, I suppose poker or other chance-based card games would be out of the question. So how about checkers . . . or racquetball?

REAPER: Somehow, those choices seem a bit too lowbrow for a mortality challenge.

MAN: Well, what about chess . . . or squash?

REAPER: Despite all the rumors to the contrary, I never liked chess much; and I'm afraid that you're in no condition for squash right now.

MAN: Then how about Simon Says?

REAPER: [Eyes brighten.] Well, that certainly would be an interesting choice, although a bit juvenile for a man of your age. I suppose you'd want to be Simon?

MAN: Yes, of course.

REAPER: But how would we determine when the game is over? You see, I don't anticipate being tricked again.

MAN: Oh, I'll be able to beat you quickly enough. Just give me half an hour.

REAPER: *Half an hour*? With all the time I've already wasted on your case, that simply isn't possible. Do you know how many wars and famines are behind schedule because of you? [Pauses.] Look, I can give you at most ten minutes.

MAN: OK, I guess that'll have to do.

REAPER: Good. So let's begin!

MAN: Yes, let's! Simon says, "Touch your nose with your right index finger."

REAPER: Easy. [Touches right index finger to nose.]

MAN: Simon says, "Put your right thumb in your mouth."

REAPER: Rather infantile, but a simple matter. [Inserts right thumb into mouth.]

MAN: "Take your thumb out of your mouth."

[Reaper makes incoherent sound with thumb remaining in mouth.]

MAN: OK. Simon says, "Twirl your scythe with your left hand."

[Reaper makes incoherent sound, twirls scythe.]

MAN: Simon says, "Keep twirling your scythe, but put your right thumb in your right ear."

REAPER: No problem. [Twirls scythe while inserting right thumb in ear.]

MAN: Very good. Now Simon says, "Go away and never come back."

REAPER: [Stops twirling scythe and removes thumb from ear, face red with anger.] Damn, damn, triple damn! I'm going to catch hell for this. [Face suddenly relaxes into cunning expression.] You're good, you know; very good. But you also must know that a delay is one thing, but giving you immortality is quite another. If I can't take you, then I have to take somebody else. [Pauses.] There's a young girl sleeping in the next room. She was going to make a full recovery from surgery. But I suppose *your* win is *her* loss. [Pauses.] Alas, she's such a small and innocent child: only 5 years old! Are you sure you don't want to reconsider?

MAN: "Just take the girl and go."

REAPER: As you wish, then. [Moves toward door.]

MAN: [Smiles.] Where are you going, Reaper? I didn't say "Simon says."

NOTES

1. The Alpha and the Omega of Risk

1. See Freud (1915).

2. Portions of this and subsequent sections are based upon [6].

3. Insurance terminology makes a formal distinction between *perils*, which are specific causes of loss, and *hazards*, which are additional factors that can aggravate an underlying peril.

4. Portions of this section are based upon [13].

5. See Halley (1693).

6. This figure differs slightly from the supposed theoretical histogram because the 2001 CSO tables are intended to offer a "snapshot" of the insured U.S. population at a single point in time. This means that individuals with greater ages (x) were born further in the past and so tend to have shorter life expectancies than those with lesser ages (and in particular, a baby born today). In addition, insured individuals have passed through an underwriting selection process and so are expected to have longer life expectancies than people chosen at random from the U.S. population.

7. It should be emphasized that the mortality hazard rate specified here is *discrete* in the sense that it describes the probability of death within a fixed interval of time of positive length—in this case, one year. In practice, the term *force of mortality* is used to describe the limiting probability of death within a *continuous* interval as the interval's length shrinks to 0.

8. In other words, the mortality hazard rate at age x is given by $h(x) = a + be^{cx}$, where $e \approx 2.71828$ denotes the base of the natural logarithm, and the constants a, b, and c must be estimated statistically from empirical data. (See Gompertz, 1825; Makeham, 1860.)

9. See Martinez (1998).

10. This is reminiscent of the condemned prisoner's plight in the "unexpected hanging" paradox. The prisoner is told by the authorities that: (1) he will be executed on one of the following seven days (Sunday through Saturday); but (2) he never will be able to deduce ahead of time on which day his death will occur. Since there is an endpoint to the week—that is, Saturday—the prisoner concludes that Saturday is impossible (because it would violate the second condition). Once Saturday is ruled out, the prisoner similarly knows that he cannot be hanged on Friday; once Friday is ruled out, he knows he cannot be hanged on Thursday, etc. Thus, by backward induction, the prisoner decides that conditions (1) and (2) are logically inconsistent and that therefore he cannot be hanged. However, on Wednesday morning he finds himself walking to the gallows with no violation of either (1) or (2). (See, e.g., Erickson and Fossa, 1998.)

11. See Clarke (1962).

12. Interestingly, Clarke revised his predictions in an updated version of the same book (see Clarke, 1984). The later table suggests a closer date of 2015 for suspended animation, but a more distant time—"beyond 2100"—for immortality.

13. See Lem (1987:90).

2. Into the Unknown

1. See Hume (1748).

2. Although the examples used in this chapter all involve sets of real numbers, there is no requirement that x be a number. For example, in tossing a standard coin, the two possible outcomes are actually the nonnumerical categories $x =$ Heads and $x =$ Tails (although statisticians often convert these categories to numbers using the convention that Heads = 1 and Tails = 0).

3. The words *sum* and *add up* are placed in quotation marks because those terms must be extended using concepts from the calculus to apply to a certain class of random variables (i.e., *continuous* random variables).

4. The latter probability distribution is a geometric distribution with parameter 0.0002, but is shifted to the left so that its sample space comprises the nonnegative integers, $\{0, 1, 2, 3, \ldots\}$.

5. Mathematically, this may be shown by contradiction: Assume there is a uniform probability function, $p(x) = k$, where k is some positive constant. Then, summing up the probability function over all x yields $p(1) + p(2) + p(3) + \ldots = k + k + k + \ldots$, which equals infinity, rather than 1. Hence, no such uniform probability function can exist.

6. A googol is the fancifully large number 10^{100}. Although of little practical use, it is often cited by mathematicians as an example of a "very large number" to which other large numbers may be compared. Those who find the googol too mundane may ponder the googolplex, which equals 10^{googol}.

7. See Cantor (1915).

8. To unify these disparate approaches requires methods of *measure theory*, a branch of mathematical analysis that provides the technical foundations for probability theory.

9. Interestingly, it is *not* possible to select a point at random, with uniform probability, from an *unbounded* interval such as the set of positive real numbers. This is because making the interval unbounded introduces problems analogous to those encountered in attempting to select an element at random, with uniform probability, from the set of positive integers.

10. The circumflex, carat, or "hat" symbol ($\wedge$) is commonly used by statisticians to denote an estimate or forecast of a specified quantity.

11. This model, although purely hypothetical, was inspired by a game-theoretic model for the frequency of terrorism-related losses developed in [26].

12. Named after British mathematician Thomas Bayes (c. 1702–1761), whose work will be discussed in Chapter 5.

13. Portions of this section are based upon [17].

14. Possibility theory was formulated by Iranian American mathematician Lotfi Zadeh (b. 1921), the inventor of *fuzzy logic*, as an explicit alternative to probability theory. See Zadeh (1978).

15. See, for example, Derrig and Ostaszewski (1995).

16. See Lindley (1987:24).

3. The Shapes of Things to Come

1. See Fisher (1956).

2. Named after Italian economist Vilfredo Pareto (1848–1923).

3. This particular family is often called the *Pareto II* family to distinguish it from the similar, but not identical, two-parameter *Pareto I* family. The latter family is less useful for illustrative purposes because its sample space varies with one of its parameter values (and never consists of the entire set of positive real numbers).

4. Named after German mathematician Carl Friedrich Gauss (1777–1855).

5. See Mandelbrot (1963).

6. Named after French mathematician Paul Lévy (1886–1971).

7. In other words, if X is recorded in dollars, then $Var[X]$ is recorded in dollars-squared (which is not easily interpretable), whereas $SD[X]$ is recorded in dollars.

8. Sometimes the ratio of the standard deviation to the expected value, known as the *coefficient of variation*, provides a convenient risk measure that modifies the stan-

dard deviation to account for the *scale*, or likely size, of the underlying random variable.

9. The general rule for this distribution is that the *k*th moment is finite if and only if *a* is greater than *k*.

10. Portions of this section are based upon [24] and [28].

11. By independent, I mean that the failure (or survival) of one component has no impact on the failure (or survival) of any of the other components. The concept of statistical independence will be addressed in greater detail in Chapter 4.

12. See, for example, Nešlehová, Embrechts, and Chavez-Demoulin (2006) and [28].

13. The insurance industry's "crisis" of insufficient asbestos and pollution liability reserves was and is a multidecade phenomenon that traces its roots to policies written in the mid-twentieth century and persists as a financial drain on certain segments of the industry today.

14. This is a simplified version of a model proposed in [8], in which traders also may hold short positions for single or multiple time periods.

15. See [24].

16. See, for example, Bidarkota and McCulloch (2004).

17. The inappropriate use of the Gaussian assumption in modern financial theory is discussed at some length by Taleb (2007).

18. For example, if these parameters were themselves drawn from an underlying gamma distribution, then the tails would follow a power law over time.

19. See [12].

20. See [25].

21. The symmetric Lévy-stable distribution with $a = 1$ is called the *two-parameter Cauchy distribution* (named after French mathematician Augustin-Louis Cauchy, 1789–1857).

4. The Value of Experience

1. As a member of the symmetric three-parameter Lévy-stable family, the Gaussian distribution is a member of the four-parameter Lévy-stable family a fortiori.

2. Portions of this section are based upon [23].

3. Denoting the value of the negative correlation by *c*, this is true because $Var[(X_1 + X_2 + \ldots + X_n)/n] = (1/n)^2[nVar[X] + 2(n-1)cVar[X]] = (Var[X]/n)[1 + 2(n-1)c/n] < Var[X]/n$, where the last term is the variance of the sample mean of a random sample of size *n*.

4. Somewhat coincidentally, I will return to this type of primitive hunting scenario when discussing Jean-Jacques Rousseau's "stag hunt" in Chapter 15.

5. See Rubin (2003) for a discussion of the prominent role of constant-sum (or equivalently, zero-sum) economics in hunter-gatherer societies.

6. See Williams et al. (1987).

5. It's All in Your Head

1. See Bayes (1764).
2. See Jaynes (2003) for a discussion of different approaches to Bayesianism.
3. Portions of this section are based upon [4].
4. See Bernoulli (1738).
5. See Menger (1934).
6. See Kahneman and Tversky (1979).
7. See Knight (1921:19–20).
8. Portions of this section are based upon [27].
9. Other commonly cited causes of uninsurability include: (1) unavoidable problems of adverse selection; (2) unavoidable problems of moral and/or morale hazard; and (3) an insurance company's inability to hedge or diversify the risks under consideration.
10. In conventional expected-utility analysis, boundedness is frequently required of utility functions, as in Menger's (1934) resolution of the St. Petersburg Paradox.
11. See, for example, [16] and [21].
12. See Allais (1953).
13. See Savage (1954:102–103).

6. Aloofness and Quasi-Aloofness

1. Portions of this and the following section are based upon [18].
2. See Nelli (1972).
3. Reinsurance is the insurance purchased by a primary (i.e., ordinary) insurance company to cover some portion of the company's total losses.
4. In insurance terminology, the word *policyholder* refers specifically to the owner of an insurance policy, whether an individual or a firm. For simplicity, however, I will use this word to include both (1) the actual policy owner and (2) any other individual or firm afforded coverage by the relevant policy (i.e., any other insured).
5. The precise distinction between these two hazards will be explained in Chapter 8.
6. Portions of this and subsequent sections are based upon [11].
7. A catastrophe bond is a custom-made debt instrument whose interest and principal payments are subject to restructuring in the event of a specifically defined catastrophe.
8. Recall that these two concepts were introduced in Chapter 1.
9. See Shubik (2006:12).
10. Shubik's (2006) reference is to Schumpeter's work on the problem of how innovations are financed within an economy.
11. A random (or *stochastic*) process formed by a sequence of random variables propagating through time is usually written as a random variable with a time index,

t (e.g., $X(t)$ or X_t). In the present discussion, this index is suppressed because the various random processes are always evaluated at (or just prior to) the same generic instant t.

7. Trustworthy Transfer; Probable Pooling

1. See Parker (1928).

2. Portions of this section are based upon [18].

3. This four-step ERM paradigm is generally applicable to all organizations, not just insurance companies.

4. See, for example, Baranoff, Brockett and Kahane (2009).

5. This process also may be called *risk retention*.

6. See [32].

7. Portions of this section are based upon [30].

8. Most likely, the principal reason that pacification tends to be ignored is the (mistaken) intuition that no individual or firm can benefit by offering X_{In} in exchange for X_{Out} if $SD[X_{In}]$ is less than $SD[X_{Out}]$ *and* the overall expected value of the portfolio remains unchanged (i.e., $E[X_{In}]$ equals $E[X_{Out}]$). However, it is quite possible for an individual or firm to benefit from such an exchange if X_{Out} possesses statistical properties that the individual or firm finds useful in hedging.

9. Diversification and hedging take place simultaneously if $Corr[X_{Keep}, X_{Out}]$ is positive and $Corr[X_{Keep}, X_{In}]$ is negative. Unfortunately, this can be a source of confusion. For example, if an insurance company with an investment portfolio consisting exclusively of stock in a company that makes raincoats sells a portion of those shares and uses the proceeds to purchase stock in a company that makes suntan lotion (whose profits presumably are negatively correlated with the raincoat maker's), then some may think of this transaction as diversification, whereas others may consider it hedging. In fact, the transaction rightfully should be identified as both.

10. Portions of this section are based upon [2].

11. See *Sears v. Commissioner*, 96 T.C. 61 (1991), aff'd in part and rev'd in part, 972 F.2d 858 (7th Cir. 1992).

12. See *Helvering v. LeGierse*, 312 U.S. 531 (1941).

13. The case of *Helvering v. LeGierse* involved the application of real estate tax law to benefits from a life insurance policy in a case in which the policyholder had purchased the life insurance policy in conjunction with a life annuity that effectively offset the risk of death from both the insurance company's and the policyholder's perspectives.

14. See *AMERCO v. Commissioner*, 96 T.C. 18 (1991) Aff'd 979 F.2d 162 (9th Cir. 1992), *The Harper Group v. Commissioner*, 96 T.C. 45 (1991) Aff'd 979 F.2d 1341 (9th Cir. 1992), the *Sears* case, and *ODECO v. U.S.*, 24 Cl. Ct. 714 (1991), 92-1 U.S.T.C. 50,018.

15. See *Humana v. Commissioner*, 88 T.C. 197 (1987), aff'd in part and rev'd in part, 881 F.2d 247 (6th Cir. 1989).

16. See [2].

17. This is explicitly mentioned in the discussion of diversification in the prior section of the present chapter.

8. God-Awful Guessing and Bad Behavior

1. Portions of this section are based upon [18].

2. In the European Union, Pillar 1 of the Solvency II program performs functions similar to those of the U.S. RBC system.

3. Portions of this and the following section are based upon [9].

4. Naturally, this expectation is based upon an assumption that insurance-company losses are sufficiently light-tailed to permit benefits from diversification. Although this assumption is too broad to be universally true, it will be accepted as reasonable for the purposes of the present and following sections.

5. For purposes of studying the financial leverages of insurers, it is more appropriate to aggregate individual companies into their corporate groups, which have some ability to share financial resources internally. However, apart from the immediate description of the data presented in Figures 8.1 and 8.2, I will continue to frame the discussion in terms of insurance companies, rather than insurance groups.

6. The data shown in the scatter plot represent all U.S. property-liability groups (formed of both primary insurers and reinsurers) operating in calendar year 2009 for which A. M. Best recorded—on a consolidated basis—both a positive net written premium and a positive surplus.

7. This type of error can be subdivided into two separate components—*model-selection error* and *parameter-estimation error*—based upon two technical steps in the actuarial analysis used to set prices.

8. The Peter Principle is "any of several satirical 'laws' concerning organizational structure, especially one that holds that people tend to be promoted until they reach their level of incompetence." (Named after Canadian educator Laurence J. Peter, 1919–1990. See the Random House Dictionary, 2011.)

9. At times (e.g., during the late 1980s), Philadelphia policyholders have had to pay some of the highest automobile insurance premiums in the United States.

9. The Good, the Bad, . . .

1. See Phelps (1895).

2. Portions of this section are based upon [18].

3. Portions of this section are based upon [29].

4. One possible substitute is a schedule of varying contract benefits/prices that permits different types of policyholders to "classify" themselves (i.e., reveal their individual risk characteristics) by selecting different contract terms in market equilib-

rium (e.g., low-risk policyholders might purchase higher deductibles than high-risk policyholders; see Rothschild and Stiglitz, 1976).

5. This is a simplification. In common practice, premium loadings for profits and expenses may be subdivided into a number of separate components, some of which are not directly proportional to expected losses (but rather are fixed on a per-policy basis or proportional to the final premium itself).

6. The new law's requirement that all individuals purchase health insurance is scheduled to become effective in 2014. However, numerous weaknesses of this provision, including the availability of certain exemptions (e.g., for religious beliefs), the relatively small fines for noncompliance, and even the provision's possible unconstitutionality, may undermine the economic logic of the entire health care law.

7. Note that the specific positions assigned to the various insurance lines in Figure 9.1 are based entirely upon the author's subjective appraisals.

8. Portions of this and subsequent sections are based upon [31].

9. See [31].

10. . . . And the Lawyerly

1. See Breyer (1993).

2. Portions of this section are based upon [14].

3. See Shapley (1953).

4. 105 is the total number of ways the seven bottles can be permuted without distinguishing among the various bottles of any given color (i.e., $7!/(4!2!1!) = 105$).

5. See Aumann and Shapley (1974).

6. Note that this formulation assumes that the box tips at exactly five bottles, rather than at some arbitrary point between five and six bottles. However, the exact tipping point is immaterial to the argument in the continuous case.

7. Portions of this section are based upon [3].

8. See Keeton and O'Connell (1965).

9. Portions of this section are based upon [5].

10. In [5], the three compensation principles actually were subdivided into four principles.

11. A Philadelphia lawyer is "a lawyer of outstanding ability at exploiting legal fine points and technicalities." (See the Random House Dictionary, 2011.)

11. What Is Randomness?

1. Portions of this and the following section are based upon [19].

2. See Heisenberg (1956).

3. German physicist Albert Einstein famously expressed his aversion to this fundamental randomness by declaring, "I am convinced that He [God] does not play dice." (See letter to Max Born, December 4, 1926, in Einstein, Born, and Born, 1969:130.)

4. See Hume (1748), Section VI.

5. See Hume (1748), Section VIII, Part I.

6. See Solomonoff (1964a, 1964b); Kolmogorov (1965); Chaitin (1969).

7. See Chaitin (1974). Perhaps Chaitin's result should not be viewed as too surprising. After all, to show that an infinitely long sequence is incompressible seems to presuppose the ability to describe, or at least apprehend, the sequence in intimate detail; but it also seems reasonable to believe that such familiarity is possible only if the sequence is compressible.

8. Portions of this section are based upon [20].

9. In Claude Shannon's information theory, the expected value of the surprise function denotes the *entropy* of the associated random variable and may be interpreted as the expected number of *bits of information* available in one random observation. (See Shannon, 1948.)

10. For more on the Gompertz-Makeham law, see Chapters 1 and 12.

11. See [20] for the mathematical details.

12. There is actually a second, mirror-image sequence that is just as unsurprising, which is formed by exchanging the 0s for 1s and vice versa in the specified sequence (i.e., 100010110 . . .).

13. See Hume (1748), Section VIII, Part I.

14. This quote is frequently attributed, without precise citation, to either British writer G. K. Chesterton or American writer William F. Buckley, Jr.

12. Patterns, Real and Imagined

1. See von Leibniz (1686).

2. Portions of this section are based upon [13].

3. See Bode (1772).

4. This distance is expressed in astronomical units (AU), where 1 AU equals the average distance of Earth from the sun.

5. Specifically, the distance from the sun to planet x is given by $d(x) = 0.4 + 0.3 \times 2^{x-2}$. Letting $a = 0.4$, $b = 0.15$, and $c = \ln(2) \approx 0.69315$, the TBL can be rewritten as $a + be^{cx}$, which is mathematically identical to the GML.

6. See Gompertz (1825).

7. See Makeham (1860).

8. These ten planets include Ceres and Pluto, now formally designated dwarf planets.

9. The GML estimates are based upon the equation $h(x) = a + be^{cx}$, with parameter values chosen to mimic the approach of the TBL. First, I selected $a = 0.00022$ judgmentally to match the mortality hazard rate at age $x = 10$ (comparable to the choice of

$a = 0.4$ for Mercury's orbit in the TBL), and then solved for the other two parameters, $b = 0.000034$ and $c = 0.09$, by statistical estimation (using semi-loglinear regression for simplicity).

10. Note that the estimate for Mercury's orbit (0.55) is actually different from that originally proposed by Titius and Bode (0.40) because the original estimate was obtained by effectively defining $2^{x-2} = 2^{-1} = 0$ in the case of Mercury, for which $x = 1$. However, this step is essentially numerology. To fit Mercury's orbit exactly within the framework of the TBL, one must introduce a fourth parameter (i.e., an additional parameter beyond a, b, and c).

11. In insurance, the *combined ratio* is an inverse measure of profitability (i.e., a higher [lower] value indicates less [more] profitability). It is computed by dividing the sum of incurred losses and earned expenses by earned premiums.

12. See Venezian (2006); Venezian and Leng (2006:Tables I and II).

13. The term *hybrid* refers to the automobile's propulsion system rather than its fuel source.

14. See National Highway Traffic Safety Administration (2009).

15. The insightful reader may note that the proposed randomized controlled study fails to address one confounding variable introduced by the study's design itself: The possibility that a driver's knowledge of which type of automobile he or she has been assigned will affect his or her driving behavior (e.g., that a hybrid driver will make a special effort to drive carefully to improve the hybrid vehicles' overall collision statistics). This is, undeniably, a valid source of concern, and one that cannot be addressed by imposing a *double-blind* configuration—in which drivers do not know which type of automobile they have been assigned—because it is not possible to disguise a vehicle's propulsion system. However, it does seem rather unlikely that a driver's behavior over the long (five-year) course of the research study would be more heavily influenced by the abstract motivations of the study than by the routine incentives imposed by law enforcement penalties, insurance policy surcharges, and possible civil litigation.

16. To some extent, the authors of the NHTSA's hybrid study did acknowledge the limitations of their analysis, writing: "This study is exploratory in nature and aims to guide researchers when designing pedestrian and bicyclist crash prevention research." However, the authors appeared to be concerned primarily with problems of small sample sizes, rather than the presence of potential confounding variables.

13. False Choices and Black Boxes

1. See Shubik (2002).

2. In fact, Property Claim Services—a division of ISO (the Insurance Services Office)—currently defines a *catastrophe* in the United States as a single event generating at least $25 million in insured property losses.

3. See Wells (1920).

4. There is a growing economic literature on the "willingness to pay" for mitigative efforts in the context of GCC. However, as shown by Johnson and Nemet (2010), the heterogeneity of approaches taken by researchers in this area—in terms of populations sampled, timings of surveys, stated effects of mitigation, etc.—has led to an extremely wide range of average annual dollar amounts that subjects would be willing to sacrifice (specifically, $22 to $3,623 per household). This empirical work thus affords little evidence either to confirm or to contradict my assertions regarding the random variable X.

5. I recognize that these views are at odds with the general tenor of the Intergovernmental Panel on Climate Change's (2007) report on the likely impacts of GCC and thus may indicate a certain degree of thermophilia on my part.

6. Portions of this section are based upon [7], [10], and [26].

7. The largest commercial risk-analysis firms are Risk Management Solutions, Applied Insurance Research, and Eqecat.

8. One notable exception is the Florida Public Hurricane Loss Model, funded by the Florida Office of Insurance Regulation, whose technical transparency serves as a model to be emulated.

9. Again, the state of Florida provides an example worthy of emulation. Currently, the Florida Commission on Hurricane Loss Projection Methodology—an independent entity created by the state legislature—must review and approve all hurricane models used in computing relevant property insurance premiums in the state.

10. See http://typhoon.atmos.colostate.edu/forecasts/.

11. The 1992 hurricane season was the earliest for which Gray made a December forecast.

12. See <http://astro.temple.edu/~powersmr/#forecasts>.

13. This is true whether or not the 2005 spike is included. The small estimated increase is clearly relevant in assessing whether or not GCC is responsible for increases in hurricane frequency, especially when it is observed that the number of recorded hurricanes in earlier years (i.e., prior to the weather satellite era) may have been underreported.

14. See [10] for the modeling details.

15. The simplest such test is the nonparametric sign test using only the fifteen years for which one forecast is better than the other. Under the null hypothesis, H_0: "The two forecast methodologies are equally good," each year's pair of forecasts yields an independent "0-1" trial, with probability $1/2$ that the GK forecast is better (or worse) than the author's. For this test, the two-tailed p-value is approximately 0.30.

16. The principal changes were that in the TRIEA: (1) several lines of business, such as commercial automobile and surety, were deleted from the covered list; (2) the insurance company deductible rate was raised from 15 percent in 2005 to 20 percent in 2007; and (3) the federal share of insured losses exceeding the deductible was decreased.

14. Nullifying the Dull Hypothesis

1. See Born (1949).

2. Portions of this and the following section are based upon [15].

3. See Radin (1997) for discussions of the restrictive standards—in terms of experimental conditions as well as choices of α—required of parapsychology studies.

4. Portions of this section are based upon [16].

5. See Hume (1748), Section IV, Part II.

6. See Hume (1748), Section V, Part I.

7. See Kant (1781).

8. To my knowledge, this particular argument was not made explicitly by Kant, but rather is a presumptive interpretation of my own.

9. See Fisher (1956:107).

10. These techniques are often called *credibility methods* because weights are assigned to the different sources of information based upon their relative credibilities, or intrinsic levels of believability to the decision maker. This terminology reflects a Bayesian orientation.

15. Games and the Mind

1. See Rousseau (1755).

2. See Dubey and Shubik (1978, 1980).

3. See, for example, [1].

4. Regarding the Colonel Blotto game, see, for example, [26].

5. Naturally, a more realistic model would account for all venues within the city, but the principles would be the same as in the simpler analysis.

6. Note that this structure is not necessarily appropriate for every such game; for example, the terrorist might well reverse the order of the third-best and worst outcomes if he or she is more interested in conserving resources through a smaller engagement than in gaining publicity through a larger engagement.

7. See Cournot (1838).

8. See Nash (1951).

9. See, for example, [26].

10. Portions of this section are based upon [22].

11. See Jervis (1978). Powers and Shubik (1991) provide an alternative motivation for this game in which a young man and a young woman whose romance is new and tentative have to decide whether or not to send each other a Valentine's Day card. In this formulation, both young people would prefer the outcome in which each sends a card to the other, but each would be embarrassed if he or she were to send an unreciprocated card.

12. See [22].

AUTHOR'S EDITORIALS AND OTHER WRITINGS

[1] Powers, M. R., and Shubik, M., 1998, "On the Tradeoff Between the Law of Large Numbers and Oligopoly in Insurance," *Insurance: Mathematics and Economics*, 23, 2, 141–156.

[2] Porat, M. M., and Powers, M. R., 1999, "What Is Insurance? Lessons from the Captive Insurance Tax Controversy," *Risk Management and Insurance Review*, 2, 2, 72–80.

[3] Lascher, E. L., Jr., and Powers, M. R., 2001, "Choice No-Fault Insurance: Efficiency and Equity," in *The Economics and Politics of Choice No-Fault Insurance* (Edward L. Lascher, Jr., and Michael R. Powers, eds.), Boston: Kluwer Academic Publishers, 17–28.

[4] Powers, M. R., 2003, "'Leapfrogging' the Variance: The Financial Management of Extreme-Event Risk," *Journal of Risk Finance*, 4, 4, 26–39.

[5] Lascher, E. L., Jr., and Powers, M. R., 2004, "September 11 Victims, Random Events, and the Ethics of Compensation," *American Behavioral Scientist*, 48, 3, 281–294.

[6] Powers, M. R., 2005, "Mortality: The Alpha and the Omega of Risk," *Journal of Risk Finance*, 6, 3, 189–191.

[7] Powers, M. R., 2005, "The Terror of the 'Black Box,'" *Journal of Risk Finance*, 6, 4, 289–291.

[8] Powers, M. R., Schizer, D. M., and Shubik, M., 2005, "How Taxes Affect Market Price: The 'Longs and Shorts' of Discounting and Information," *Journal of Derivatives Accounting*, 2, 2, 155–164.

[9] Powers, M. R., 2006, "An Insurance Paradox," *Journal of Risk Finance*, 7, 2, 113–116.

[10] Powers, M. R., 2006, "Catastrophe Forecasting: Seeing 'Gray' among the 'Black Boxes,'" *Journal of Risk Finance*, 7, 5, 458–462.

[11] Drennan, R. B., Jr., and Powers, M. R., 2007, "What Is Insurance? Toward a Theory of 'Aloof' and 'Quasi-Aloof' Financial Risks," *Journal of Insurance and Risk Management*, 5, 10, 1–11.

[12] Powers, M. R., 2007, "Using Aumann-Shapley Values to Allocate Insurance Risk: The Case of Inhomogeneous Losses," *North American Actuarial Journal*, 11, 3, 113–127.

[13] Powers, M. R., 2007, "Human Mortality: Written in the Stars?" *Journal of Risk Finance*, 8, 1, 5–10.

[14] Powers, M. R., 2007, "Sharing Responsibility: What They Didn't Teach You in Kindergarten," *Journal of Risk Finance*, 8, 2, 93–96.

[15] Powers, M. R., 2007, "Thoughts on the 'Scientific Method': Part 1—Ignorance through Inconsistency," *Journal of Risk Finance*, 8, 3, 209–213.

[16] Powers, M. R., 2007, "Thoughts on the 'Scientific Method': Part 2—Frequentist Fecklessness," *Journal of Risk Finance*, 8, 4, 325–329.

[17] Powers, M. R., 2007, "Intuition and Surprise," *Journal of Risk Finance*, 8, 5, 429–433.

[18] Powers, M. R., and Khovidhunkit, P., 2007, "Insurance," in *Encyclopedia of Electrical and Electronics Engineering*, Volume 10 (John G. Webster, ed.), New York: John Wiley and Sons.

[19] Powers, M. R., 2008, "The Nature of Randomness: Part 1—Knowable or Unknowable?" *Journal of Risk Finance*, 9, 1, 5–8.

[20] Powers, M. R., 2008, "The Nature of Randomness: Part 2—Cognitive Constraints," *Journal of Risk Finance*, 9, 2, 101–105.

[21] Powers, M. R., 2008, "Combining Information About . . . Combining Information," *Journal of Risk Finance*, 9, 5, 417–421.

[22] Powers, M. R., and Shen, Z., 2008, "Social Stability and Catastrophe Risk: Lessons from the *Stag Hunt*," *Journal of Theoretical Politics*, 20, 4, 477–497.

[23] Powers, M. R., 2009, "Constant-Sum Sampling: An Apology for Statistics' 'Original Sin,'" *Journal of Risk Finance*, 10, 4, 317–320.

[24] Powers, M. R., 2009, "How Money Got Its Tail (Not Too Heavy; Not Too Light; but 'Just So')," *Journal of Risk Finance*, 10, 5, 425–429.

[25] Powers, M. R., and Powers, T. Y., 2009, "Risk and Return Measures for a Non-Gaussian World," *Journal of Financial Transformation*, 25, 51–54.

[26] Powers, M. R., and Shen, Z., 2009, "*Colonel Blotto* in the War on Terror: Implications for Event Frequency," *Journal of Homeland Security and Emergency Management*, 6, 1, 18, 1–16.

[27] Powers, M. R., 2010, "Presbyter Takes Knight," *Journal of Risk Finance*, 11, 1, 5–8.

[28] Powers, M. R., 2010, "Infinite-Mean Losses: Insurance's 'Dread Disease,'" *Journal of Risk Finance*, 11, 2, 125–128.

[29] Powers, M. R., 2010, "Where Ignorance Is Bliss: The 'Dark Corner' of Risk Classification," *Journal of Risk Finance*, 11, 4, 353–357.

[30] Powers, M. R., 2010, "Diversification, Hedging, and 'Pacification,'" *Journal of Risk Finance*, 11, 5, 441–445.

[31] Chapman, Z. A., and Powers, M. R., 2011, "On the Use of Controversial Risk Classifications in Personal Insurance," Discussion Paper, Philadelphia: Temple University.

[32] Powers, M. R., and Powers, T. Y., 2011, "Risk Finance for Catastrophe Losses with Pareto-Calibrated Lévy-Stable Severities," Discussion Paper, Philadelphia: Temple University.

BIBLIOGRAPHY

Allais, M., 1953, "Le Comportement de l'Homme Rationnel devant le Risque: Critique des Postulats et Axiomes de l'École Américaine," *Econometrica*, 21, 503–546.

Aumann, R. J., and Shapley, L. S., 1974, *Values of Non-Atomic Games*, Princeton University Press, Princeton, NJ.

Baranoff, E., Brockett, P. L., and Kahane, Y., 2009, *Risk Management for Enterprises and Individuals*, Flat World Knowledge, http://www.flatworldknowledge.com/node/29698#web-0.

Bayes, T., 1764, "An Essay Towards Solving a Problem in the Doctrine of Chances," *Philosophical Transactions of the Royal Society of London*, 53, 370–418.

Bernoulli, D., 1738, *Specimen Theoriae Novae de Mensura Sortis*.

Bidarkota, P. V., and McCulloch, J. H., 2004, "Testing for Persistence in Stock Returns with GARCH-Stable Shocks," *Quantitative Finance*, 4, 256–265.

Bode, J. E., 1772, *Anleitung zur Kentniss des Gestirnten Himmels*.

Born, M., 1949, *Natural Philosophy of Cause and Chance*, Oxford University Press, Oxford, UK.

Breyer, S. G., 1993, *Breaking the Vicious Circle: Toward Effective Risk Regulation*, Harvard University Press, Cambridge, MA.

Cantor, G., 1915, *Contributions to the Founding of the Theory of Transfinite Numbers*, Open Court Publishing Company, Chicago.

Cass, D., and Shell, K., 1983, "Do Sunspots Matter?" *Journal of Political Economy*, 91, 193–227.

Chaitin, G. J., 1969, "On the Simplicity and Speed of Programs for Computing Infinite Sets of Natural Numbers," *Journal of the ACM*, 16, 407–422.

Chaitin, G. J., 1974, "Information-Theoretic Limitations of Formal Systems," *Journal of the ACM*, 21, 403–424.

Clarke, A. C., 1962, *Profiles of the Future: An Inquiry Into the Limits of the Possible*, Harper and Row, New York.

Clarke, A. C., 1984, *Profiles of the Future: An Inquiry Into the Limits of the Possible*, Holt, Rinehart, and Winston, New York.

Cournot, A. A., 1838, *Recherches sur les Principes Mathématiques de la Théorie des Richesses*.

Derrig, R. A., and Ostaszewski, K. M., 1995, "Fuzzy Techniques of Pattern Recognition in Risk and Claim Classification," *Journal of Risk and Insurance*, 62, 3, 447–482.

Dubey, P., and Shubik, M., 1978, "A Theory of Money and Financial Institutions. 28. The Non-Cooperative Equilibria of a Closed Trading Economy with Market Supply and Bidding Strategies," *Journal of Economic Theory*, 17, 1–20.

Dubey, P., and Shubik, M., 1980, "A Strategic Market Game with Price and Quantity Strategies," *Zeitschrift für Nationalökonomie*, 40, 25–34.

Einstein, A., Born, H., and Born, M., 1969, *Albert Einstein, Hedwig und Max Born, Briefwechsel: 1916–1955*, Nymphenburger Verlagshandlung, Munich.

Erickson, G. W., and Fossa, J. A., 1998, *Dictionary of Paradox*, University Press of America, Lanham, MD.

Fisher, R. A., 1956, *Statistical Methods and Scientific Inference*, Oliver and Boyd, Edinburgh.

Fitzgerald, F. S., 1925, *The Great Gatsby*, Charles Scribner's Sons, New York.

Freud, S., 1915, *Zeitgemässes über Krieg und Tod*, Imago, 4, 1, 1–21.

Gompertz, B., 1825, "On the Nature of the Function Expressive of the Law of Human Mortality, and on a New Mode of Determining the Value of Life Contingencies," *Philosophical Transactions of the Royal Society of London*, 115, 513–585.

Halley, E., 1693, "An Estimate of the Degrees of the Mortality of Mankind, Drawn from Curious Tables of the Births and Funerals at the City of Breslaw; with an Attempt to Ascertain the Price of Annuities upon Lives," *Philosophical Transactions of the Royal Society of London*, 17, 596–610 and 654–656.

Harvey, C. R., and Siddique, A., 2000, "Conditional Skewness in Asset Pricing Tests," *Journal of Finance*, 55, 3, 1263–1295.

Heisenberg, W., 1956, "The Uncertainty Principle," in Newman, J. R. (Ed.), *The World of Mathematics*, Volume II, Simon and Schuster, New York.

Hume, D., 1748, *An Enquiry Concerning Human Understanding*.

Intergovernmental Panel on Climate Change, 2007, *Climate Change 2007—Impacts, Adaptation and Vulnerability: Working Group II Contribution to the Fourth Assessment Report of the IPCC*, Cambridge University Press, Cambridge, UK.

Jaynes, E. T., 2003, *Probability Theory: The Logic of Science*, Cambridge University Press, Cambridge, UK.

Jervis, R., 1978, "Cooperation Under the Security Dilemma," *World Politics*, 30, 2, 167–214.

Johnson, E., and Nemet, G. F., 2010, "Willingness to Pay for Climate Policy: A Review of Estimates," *La Follette School Working Paper*, No. 2010-011, University of Wisconsin–Madison.

Kahneman, D., and Tversky, A., 1979, "Prospect Theory: An Analysis of Decision Under Risk," *Econometrica*, 47, 2, 263–291.

Kant, I., 1781, *Kritik der Reinen Vernunft*.

Keeton, R. E., and O'Connell, J., 1965, *Basic Protection for the Traffic Victim*, Little, Brown and Company, Boston.

Knight, F. N., 1921, *Risk, Uncertainty, and Profit*, Hart, Schaffner, and Marx/ Houghton Mifflin Company, Boston.

Kolmogorov, A. N., 1965, "Three Approaches to the Quantitative Definition of Information," *Problems of Information Transmission*, 1, 1, 1–7.

Lem, S., 1987, *Fiasco*, Harcourt Brace Jovanovich, San Diego, CA.

Lindley, D. V., 1987, "The Probability Approach to the Treatment of Uncertainty in Artificial Intelligence and Expert Systems," *Statistical Science*, 2, 1, 17–24.

Makeham, W. M., 1860, "On the Law of Mortality and the Construction of Annuity Tables," *Journal of the Institute of Actuaries and Assurance Magazine*, 8, 301–310.

Mandelbrot, B., 1963, "The Variation of Certain Speculative Prices," *Journal of Business*, 36, 394–419.

Martinez, D. E., 1998, "Mortality Patterns Suggest Lack of Senescence in Hydra," *Experimental Gerontology*, 33, 3, 217–225.

Menger, K., 1934, "The Role of Uncertainty in Economics," *Zeitschrift für Nationalökonomie*, Vol. 5, in Shubik, M. (Ed.), 1967, *Essays in Mathematical Economics*, Princeton University Press, Princeton, NJ.

Minsky, H., 1986, *Stabilizing an Unstable Economy*, Yale University Press, New Haven, CT.

Nash, J. F., Jr., 1951, "Noncooperative Games," *Annals of Mathematics*, 54, 286–295.

National Highway Traffic Safety Administration, 2009, *Incidence of Pedestrian and Bicyclist Crashes by Hybrid Electric Passenger Vehicles*, U.S. Department of Transportation, http://www-nrd.nhtsa.dot.gov/Pubs/811204.PDF.

Nelli, H. O., 1972, "The Earliest Insurance Contract—A New Discovery," *Journal of Risk and Insurance*, 39, 2, 215–220.

Nešlehová, J., Embrechts, P., and Chavez-Demoulin, V., 2006, "Infinite-Mean Models and the LDA for Operational Risk," *Journal of Operational Risk*, 1, 1, 3–25.

Parker, D., 1928, *Sunset Gun—Poems*, Boni and Liveright, New York.

Phelps, J. T., 1895, *Life Insurance Sayings*, Riverside Press, Cambridge, MA.

Powers, I. Y., and Shubik, M., 1991, "The Names of the Games," *International Security and Arms Control Discussion Paper*, No. 7, Yale University, New Haven, CT.

Radin, D. I., 1997, *The Conscious Universe: The Scientific Truth of Psychic Phenomena*, HarperEdge, New York.

Rothschild, M., and Stiglitz, J., 1976, "Equilibrium in Competitive Insurance Markets: An Essay on the Economics of Imperfect Information," *Quarterly Journal of Economics*, 90, 4, 629–649.

Rousseau, J.-J., 1755, *Discours sur l'Origine et les Fondements de l'Inégalité parmi les Hommes*.

Rubin, P. H., 2003, "Folk Economics," *Southern Economic Journal*, 70, 1, 157–171.

Savage, L. J., 1954, *The Foundations of Statistics*, Chapman and Hall, London.

Schumpeter, J. A., 1961, *The Theory of Economic Development*, Harvard University Press, Cambridge, MA (republication of 1911 original).

Shannon, C. E., 1948, "A Mathematical Theory of Communication," *Bell System Technical Journal*, 27, 379–423 and 623–656.

Shapley, L. S., 1953, "A Value for *n*-Person Games," *Contributions to the Theory of Games*, Vol. II, Princeton University Press, Princeton, NJ.

Shubik, M., 2002, "Risk, Public Perception, and Education: Quantitative and Qualitative Risk," in Choi, J., and Powers, M. R. (Eds.), *Global Risk Management: Financial, Operational, and Insurance Strategies*, JAI/Elsevier Science, Amsterdam.

Shubik, M., 2006, "Theory of Money and Financial Institutions: A Summary of a Game-Theoretic Approach," *Cowles Foundation Discussion Paper*, No. 1572, Yale University, New Haven, CT.

Solomonoff, R., 1964a, "A Formal Theory of Inductive Inference, Part I," *Information and Control*, 7, 1, 1–22.

Solomonoff, R., 1964b, "A Formal Theory of Inductive Inference, Part II," *Information and Control*, 7, 2, 224–254.

Taleb, N. N., 2007, *The Black Swan: The Impact of the Highly Improbable*, Random House, New York.

Tucker, A. W., 1950, "A Two-Person Dilemma," Discussion Paper, Stanford University, Stanford, CA.

Venezian, E. C., 2006, "The Use of Spectral Analysis in Insurance Cycle Research," *Journal of Risk Finance*, 7, 2, 177–188.

Venezian, E. C., and Leng, C.-C., 2006, "Application of Spectral and ARIMA Analysis to Combined-Ratio Patterns," *Journal of Risk Finance*, 7, 2, 189–214.

von Leibniz, G. W. F., 1686, *Discours de Métaphysique*.

Wells, H. G., 1920, *The Outline of History—Being a Plain History of Life and Mankind*, Macmillan Company, New York.

Williams, S. D., Birch, R., Einhorn, L. H., Irwin, L., Greco, F. A., and Loehrer, P. J., 1987, "Treatment of Disseminated Germ-Cell Tumors with Cisplatin, Bleomycin, and Either Vinblastine or Etoposide," *New England Journal of Medicine*, 316, 23, 1435–1440.

Zadeh, L., 1978, "Fuzzy Sets as the Basis for a Theory of Possibility," *Fuzzy Sets and Systems*, 1, 3–28.

INDEX